ARCHITECTS
OF THE NEW

MILLENNIUM

Published in Australia in 2000 by
The Images Publishing Group Pty Ltd
ACN 059 734 431
6 Bastow Place, Mulgrave, Victoria 3170, Australia
Telephone +(61 3) 9561 5544
Facsimile +(61 3) 9561 4860
E-mail: books@images.com.au

ISBN: 1 86470 079 3

Designed by The Graphic Image Studio Pty Ltd,
Mulgrave, Australia
Printed in Hong Kong

ARCHITECTS
OF THE NEW

NIUM

Introduction

The new millennium holds many fears and just as much potential. The latter is particularly evident in the world of architecture where we may see many of the buildings and constructions currently on the computer and in the architect's imagination become a reality as we progress with technology and are able to produce construction materials thought impossible by previous generations.

This book celebrates architects who have been involved in The Images Publishing Group's 'International Architecture Yearbook' over the last six issues. It is a comprehensive guide to who's who in architecture. While it does not pretend to include all of the great names involved in the profession, those who are portrayed here are certainly at the pinnacle of design.

The Images Publishing Group is in its 18th year of publishing architecture and is proud to have been involved with recording significant projects around the world. Alessina Brooks and Paul Latham would like to take this opportunity to thank and congratulate all the many friends, acquaintances and collaborators who have been involved in establishing The Images Publishing Group as one of the leading architectural publishers.

Without the cooperation of the international architects and designers, our publishing house could not exist. On the birth of the new century, we hope that architecture and design by people will never be replaced by machines.

Featured Architects

Adrian Maserow Architects
Architects and Interior Designers

South Africa
12th Avenue
Rivonia, Johannesburg
Tel: +(27 11) 807 7505
Fax: +(27 11) 807 7509
E-mail: webaba.co.za

Directors
Adrian Maserow and Connor Kinsella

Associates
Jenny Aspoas
Martin Patey

Persons to Contact
Adrian Maserow, Director
Connor Kinsella, Director

Number of Employees
12

Date of Establishment
1993

Project Types
Civic Council Chambers
Computer Training Campuses
Headquarters Buildings
Housing Projects and Estates
Leisure Schemes
Office Parks
Warehousing
Showrooms
Refurbishments
Residential Schemes and Apartments
Interior Design
Gymnasiums

Disciplines
Architecture
Interior Design
Project Management
Development Facilitation

Current and Recent Projects
New Headquarters for Microsoft, Sandton,
  South Africa
Board of Executors Private Bank, Sandton, South
  Africa
11 Avenue Headquarters, Houghton, South
  Africa
Alpha Cement Interiors, Constantial Park, South
  Africa
Sherwoods Advertising Headquarters, Sandton,
  South Africa
Macsteel International Headquarters, Sandton,
  South Africa
New Headquarters for Drager, Sandton, South
  Africa

Selected Clients
Grinaker Projects
Microsoft S.A.
5th Avenue Developments
Sage Properties
Board of Executors
Macsteel International

Design Philosophy and History
The philosophy of each member of this design
team seeks to display the unique fusion of
cultures in South Africa through a vision of an
exuberant architecture.

Often the firm's designs express the
expectations, aspirations, illusions and the
collective memory of contemporary Africa
through the opportunities revealed in
contrasting form, texture, symbol and geometry.

Adrian Maserow Architects continually reinvents
'AMA Architecture', an architecture dedicated to
the art of design which aims to make each
commission an enduring work of value to its
users.

The firm is influenced by local and international
architects, crafts, materials and technologies
and participates at the highest level with the
leaders of business and state.

1

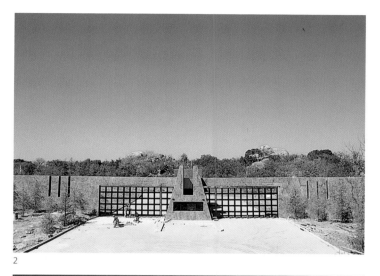

2

3

4

5

6

1&5 Board of Executors, Sandton
  2 Highveld Housing Estate
  3 Nandos Headquarters, Johannesburg
  4 Sherwoods Advertising, Sandton
  6 Fourways Health and Raquet Club

Alfred Wong Partnership Pte Ltd
AWP Chartered Architects

Singapore
111 North Bridge Road
#12-02/04 Peninsula Plaza
Singapore 179098
Tel: +(65) 337 6777
Fax: +(65) 339 6956
E-mail: awplc@singnet.com.sg
Website: http://awp.com.sg

Directors
Alfred H.K. Wong
Edward H.Y. Wong
Goh Peng Thong
Ang Choon Kiat

Associate Directors
Wong Meng Ling
Tan Tee Hong
Peter S.S. Thomas

Date of Establishment
1957

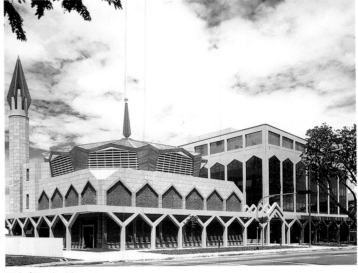

Wakaf Kassim Mosque
Photo credit: Al Studio Pte Ltd

Robinson Point
Photo credit: Al Studio Pte Ltd

Main Lobby of Sofitel Hotel Plaza, Ho Chin Minh City, Vietnam
Photo credit: courtesy Alfred Wong Partnership Pte Ltd

JTC Headquarters
Photo credit: courtesy Alfred Wong Partnership Pte Ltd

Disciplines
Master Plans
Urban Designs
Feasibility Studies
Schematic Designs
Full Architectural Services
Interior Architecture
Landscape Designs
Retrofit

Current and Recent Projects
Gleneagles Hospital Redevelopment, Singapore
  280-bed hospital and 10-storey medical centre block
UOB Building, Xiamen, China
  Comprehensive developments comprising commercial offices,
  banks and service apartments
Keppel Distripark, Singapore
  137,338 square metres covered container freight station
  Design Consultant to the PSA, Design & Planning Department,
  Engineering Division
Raffles Marina, Singapore
  42,374 square metres, the first marina in Singapore

Pasir Ris Central Community Club
Photo credit: AI Studio Pte Ltd

Singapore Chinese Chamber of Commerce & Industry
Photo credit: courtesy Alfred Wong Partnership Pte Ltd

Alfredo De Vido Architects

Alfredo De Vido
Photo credit:
Norman McGrath

USA
412 East 85th Street
New York, New York 10028
Tel: +(1 212) 517 6100
Fax: +(1 212) 517 6103

Director
Alfredo De Vido

Number of Employees
4

Date of Establishment
1968

Project Types
Commercial   Residential
Educational   Theatre

Disciplines
Architecture
Landscape Architecture

Current and Recent Projects
School, Bridgehampton, New York
Stores, New York, New York
Residential, New York, Connecticut,
 Pennsylvania
Theatres, New York, Virginia, Pennsylvania

Selected Clients
Private clients, City of New York
National Park Service, Philadelphia
Fairmont Park Commission
Private Institutions, primarily schools

Garraty House, Sag Harbor, New York
Photo credit: courtesy Alfredo De Vido Architects

Mann Music Centre, Philadelphia, Pennsylvania
Photo credit: courtesy Alfredo De Vido Architects

Moore House, Sharon, Connecticut
Photo credit: Norman McGrath

Community Church, Astoria, Queens, New York
Photo credit: courtesy Alfredo De Vido Architects

Sheehy House, East Hampton, New York
Photo credit: courtesy Alfredo De Vido Architects

Word of Mouth, New York, New York
Photo credit: courtesy Alfredo De Vido Architects

Wertheimer House, Delaware
Photo credit: courtesy Alfredo De Vido Architects

Sametz House, Garrison, New York
Photo credit: courtesy Alfredo De Vido Architects

Wirth House, Waccabuc, New York
Photo credit: courtesy Alfredo De Vido Architects

Walf Trap Farm Park, Vienna, Virginia
Photo credit: Bill Maris

222 Columbia Heights, Brooklyn, New York
Photo credit: O Baitz, Inc. Photography of Architecture

Design Philosophy and History

Alfredo De Vido received a Bachelor of Architecture degree from Carnegie Mellon University in 1954. He was awarded the American Institute of Architects Prize and the Pennsylvania Society of Architects Award for his school work. He went on to receive a Master of Fine Arts in Architecture degree from Princeton University in 1956.

Mr De Vido served for three years in Japan in the US Navy Civil Engineers Corp. ('Seabees'). His work for the Navy included the design and construction of government facilities and buildings, and the design of seven houses at US Naval Air Station Atsugi. For this work he was commended by the regional Japanese government.

Following naval service, Mr De Vido attended the Royal Academy of Fine Arts in Copenhagen, where he received a Diploma in Town Planning. During this time he worked in various town planning offices, including that of Professor Peter Bredsdorff.

After Denmark and subsequent travel, Mr De Vido worked in Italy in the office of The Architects Collaborative (Gropius) and Luigi Moretti.

Upon his return to the USA, Mr De Vido worked with Marcel Breuer and Ernest J. Kump, and as the associate and partner of John H. MacFadyen and Edward F. Knowles, before founding the firm of Alfredo De Vido Architects in 1968.

Mr De Vido's career has continued with the design and construction of houses and housing developments, and also of theatres, which have become an increasingly important part of the firm's work. Other architectural projects have included retail shops, offices, historic renovations, and parks. Working on a steady flow of single-family houses has led him to develop modular systems as an aid to design innovation and construction.

Design awards have been received from national, state, local and city AIA groups, the Architectural Record, the US Department of Housing and Urban Development, the City Club of New York, and other professional and trade organizations.

Mr De Vido is the author of three books: *Designing Your Client's House – An Architect's Guide to Meeting Design Goals and Budgets*, *Innovative Management Techniques for Architectural Design and Construction,* published in 1983 and 1984 by the Whitney Library of Design, and *The Design and Building of Houses*, published in 1995 by John Wiley & Sons, Inc.

In addition, there are two monographs on the firm's work, *Ten Houses*, published by Rockport in 1998, and *Master Architect Series III, Alfredo De Vido – Selected and Current Works*, The Images Publishing Group, 1998.

Matthews House, East Hampton, New York
Photo credit: courtesy Alfredo De Vido Architects

Alsop and Störmer (Atlantic) Ltd
Architects

Professor William Alsop OBE
Photo credit: Roderick Coyne

UK
Parkgate Studio, 41 Parkgate Road
London, SW11 4NP
Tel: +(44) 20 7978 7878
Fax: +(44) 20 7978 7879
E-mail: info@alsopandstormer.co.uk

Germany
Fleetinsel, Michaelisbrücke 1
Hamburg 20459
Tel: +(49 40) 369 7370
Fax: +(49 40) 369 73737
E-mail: alsop.stoermer@okay.net

Russia
Studio 7, 57 Sadovinicheskaya
Moscow 113035
Tel: +(70 95) 792 5900
Fax: +(70 95) 792 5901
E-mail: alsops@cityline.ru

Directors
Professor William Alsop OBE (Chairman)
James Allen
Peter Angrave
Christophe Egret
Stephen Pimbley
Jan Störmer

Associate Directors
Woon Juen Yee
Jonathan Leah
Duncan Macaulay

Persons to Contact
James Allen, London
Jan Störmer, Hamburg
James McAdam, Moscow

Number of Employees
48, London
101, worldwide

Date of Establishment
1979

Project Types
Cultural and Educational
Infrastructure and Transport
Leisure
Office
Public Buildings
Residential

Disciplines
Architecture
Interior Design
Landscaping
Quantity Surveying
Urban Planning

Current and Recent Projects
Hotel du Departement des Bouches du Rhone, Marseille, France
Peckham Library, London
C/Plex Arts Regeneration Project, West Bromwich
Jersey Cafe, St Helier, Jersey
Hannover Expo 2000, Hannover, Germany
North Greenwich Underground Station, London
Southpoint, London

Selected Clients
Blackfriars Investments (pd) Ltd
British Broadcasting Corporation
C/Plex
London Underground Ltd
Railtrack Plc
Conseil General des Bouches-du-Rhone
London Docklands Development Corporation

Design Philosophy and History
The office has a completely open mind about what architecture is. This is not a closed question as far as the firm is concerned. There is a continuing exploration of form, colour, functional, social and behavioural issues. These investigations resolve themselves in buildings and structures that offer a richer experience to both the user and the visitor; the client is considered as an integral part of the design team. This is necessary in order to establish a base which will allow the project to step beyond the expectations of all involved in the design process.

1

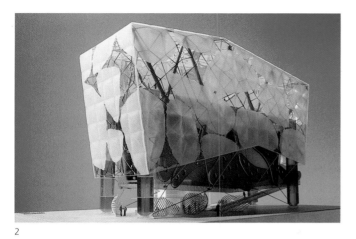

2

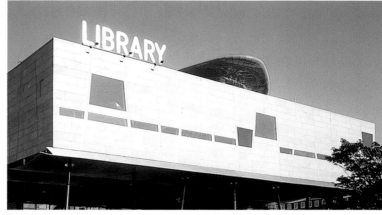

3

4

5

1 Hotel du Departement des Bouches du Rhone, Marseille, France
Photo credit: Paul Raftery

2 Hannover Expo 2000, Hannover, Germany
Photo credit: Roderick Coyne

3 Peckham Library, Peckham, London
Photo credit: Roderick Coyne

4 North Greenwich Underground Station, London
Photo credit: Roderick Coyne

5 C/Plex Arts Regeneration Project, West Bromwich, UK
Photo credit: Roderick Coyne

Ancher Mortlock Woolley
Architects

Australia
Level 5, 790 George Street
Sydney, NSW 2000
Tel: +(61 2) 9211 4466
Fax: +(61 2) 9211 9733
E-mail: amw@s054.aone.net.au

Directors
Ken Woolley, AM B Arch LFRAIA
Steve Thomas, B Arch FRAIA
Dale Swan, B Arch MSc FRAIA
Phil Baigent, B Arch RAIA

Disciplines
Architecture
Planning
Urban Design
Interiors

Current and Recent Projects
Park Hyatt Hotel Restaurant extension, Sydney
  Cove, Sydney, Australia
Burswood Convention, Resort & Casino
  Expansion Project, Perth, Australia
State Library of Victoria, Melbourne, Australia
Control Tower, Sydney Airport, Australia
Sydney Convention & Exhibition Centre South,
  Darling Harbour, Sydney, Australia
Royal Agricultural Showground, Dome &
  Exhibition Halls, Homebush Bay, Sydney,
  Australia
Sydney Olympic Hockey Stadium, Homebush
  Bay, Sydney, Australia
Red Cross Blood Bank, Parramatta, Sydney,
  Australia

Design Philosophy and History
Founded in 1946 by Sydney Ancher, the practice
has had several manifestations and always been
at the leading edge of architectural design and
quality. It is expected that the tradition will
continue into the next millennium with the
emergence of new, young participating
architects, nurtured in a design studio
environment in which standards and experience
are of the highest. The complement varies
between 25 and 50.

A wide variety of building types and sizes has
always been part of the work profile. Innovation
and the ability to solve problems are special
features and achievements, with new projects
continually setting standards for other clients to
follow. The practice is accredited for Quality
Assurance to ISO 9001.

Other notable projects are the Children's
Medical Research Institute, apartments at Rose
Bay, and at Darling Point, and the Atrium for the
TAB Offices. Important earlier projects include
the Australian Embassy, Bangkok; Town Hall
House & Sydney Square; housing in New
Caledonia and Fiji; Radio Stations in Honiara and
Vanuatu and the ABC Centre at Ultimo.

The practice has received all the major RAIA
architectural awards including the Sulman
Award, Zelman Cowan National Award, Robin
Boyd house award, four Wilkinson awards, three
Blackett awards and numerous Merit, Civic and
Project House awards, as well as industry awards
for steel, timber, metal and construction
technique.

1

1 Royal Agricultural Showground Dome, Homebush Bay, Australia
Photo credit: Patrick Bingham-Hall
2 Royal Agricultural Showground Exhibition Halls, Homebush Bay, Australia
Photo credit: Patrick Bingham-Hall

3 State Library of Victoria, Melbourne, Australia
Photo credit: Patrick Bingham-Hall
4 Courtyard, State Library of Victoria, Melbourne, Australia
Photo credit: John Gollings

5 Garvan Institute of Medical Research, Darlinghurst, Australia
Photo credit: Eric Sierins
6 Garvan Institute of Medical Research, Darlinghurst, Australia
Photo credit: Eric Sierins

2

3

4

5

6

7

8

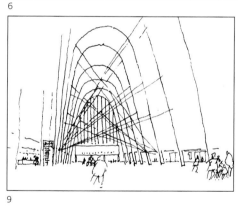

9

10

11

12

13

7 Sydney Convention & Exhibition Centre, Sydney South, Australia
Photo credit: Eric Sierins
8 Olympic Hockey Stadium, Homebush Bay, Australia
Photo credit: Patrick Bingham-Hall

9 Burswood Convention Centre, Perth, Australia
Sketch: Ken Woolley
10 Blood Bank, Parramatta, Australia
Photo credit: Eric Sierins
11 Park Hyatt Hotel, Sydney Cove, Australia
Photo credit: John Gollings

12 ABC Radio and Orchestra Centre, Ultimo, Australia
Photo credit: Eric Sierins
13 Sydney Airport Control Tower, Australia
Photo credit: Ken Woolley

Ann Beha Associates, Inc.

USA
33 Kingston Street
Boston, Massachusetts 02111
Tel: +(1 617) 338 3000
Fax: +(1 617) 482 9097
E-mail: preiter@annbeha.com

Directors
Ann M. Beha, FAIA
Pamela W. Hawkes, AIA
Thomas M. Hotaling, AIA

Associates
Kenneth R. Guditz, AIA
Richard Panciera, AIA
Peter C. Sugar, AIA

Person to Contact
Patricia Reiter AIA, Director of Business
Operations, Boston

Number of Employees
33

Date of Establishment
1977

Project Types
Academic Buildings
Historic Preservation
Libraries
Museums
Performing Arts Centres
Religious Facilities

Disciplines
Architecture
Historic Preservation and Restoration
Master Planning

Current and Recent Projects
The First Church of Christ, Scientist, Boston,
  Massachusetts
Symphony Hall, Boston, Massachusetts
Portland Art Museum, Portland, Oregon
The Taft Museum, Cincinnati, Ohio
Ca'd'Zan, Ringling Museum, Sarasota, Florida
Hensel Concert Hall, Franklin & Marshall
  College, Lancaster, Pennsylvania
Hawthorne-Longfellow Library, Bowdoin
  College, Brunswick, Maine
Sotterley Manor House and Plantation,
  Hollywood, Maryland
The Adirondack Museum, Blue Mountain Lake,
  New York
Worcester Academy Master Plan, Worcester,
  Massachusetts

Selected Clients
Harvard University
Dartmouth College
Boston Symphony Orchestra
Isabella Stewart Gardner Museum
Brown University
National Park Service
New England Conservatory of Music
Metropolitan Museum of Art
Wadsworth Atheneum
The Taft Museum
Massachusetts Historical Society
Worcester Art Museum
National Trust for Historic Preservation
General Services Administration

1

2

Design Philosophy and History

Founded in 1977, Ann Beha Associates is a Boston-based architectural firm which provides planning, design, and historic preservation services to cultural, community, and academic clients throughout the United States. The firm is led by three principals and a staff of 30, including outstanding architects with specialized experience in museum, library, religious and educational facilities, as well as building technology, interior design, and materials conservation. Ann Beha Associates is dedicated to architecture as a means to support, expand, and enrich community life.

Ann Beha Associates is a national leader in historic preservation, skilled in both the careful research leading to accurate restoration of significant landmarks, and the technology of seamlessly integrating modern systems into older buildings. The firm's work has increasingly focused on the challenges of updating twentieth century buildings to accommodate changing needs, and creating new architectural forms that speak to the spirit of special places.

Ann Beha Associates' work has been widely recognized for its integrated use of craft and traditional materials with modern design. Awards include honours from the National Trust for Historic Preservation; the American Wood Council; the International Masonry Institute; and the Interfaith Forum on Religion, Art, and Architecture; the 25th Anniversary Award from the Massachusetts Historical Commission; the Lifetime Achievement Award from the Victorian Society in America; *Architectural Record's* 'In the Public Interest' Award; and honours from the Boston Society of Architects.

1 Lobby interior, Kalamazoo Institute of Arts, Kalamazoo, Michigan, USA
Photo credit: Hewitt/Garrison Architectural Photography

2 Exterior and new main entrance, Kalamazoo Institute of Arts, Kalamazoo, Michigan, USA
Photo credit: Hewitt/Garrison Architectural Photography

3 Original building and new addition, Nantucket Atheneum, Nantucket, Massachusetts, USA
Photo credit: Hewitt/Garrison Architectural Photography

4 Children's library interior, Nantucket Atheneum, Nantucket, Massachusetts, USA
Photo credit: Hewitt/Garrison Architectural Photography

5 Gallery interior, Kalamazoo Institute of Arts, Kalamazoo, Michigan, USA
Photo credit: Hewitt/Garrison Architectural Photography

3

4

5

Antoine Predock Architect

USA
300 12th Street, NW
Albuquerque, New Mexico 87102
Tel: +(1 505) 843 7390
Fax: +(1 505) 243 6254
E-mail: studio@predock.com

529 Victoria Avenue
Venice, California 90291
Tel: +(1 310) 577 4656
Fax: +(1 310) 577 4676

Directors
Antoine Predock FAIA, Principal

Number of Employees
21

Date of Establishment
1967

Project Types
Administrative/Office
Auditoria/Theatres
Classrooms
Educational Facilities
Galleries
Hotels
Laboratories/Research Facilities
Libraries
Museums
Nature Centres
Omnimax Theatres
Planetaria
Residential Housing
Stadia

Disciplines
Architecture

Current and Recent Projects
Nelson Fine Arts Center, Arizona State
  University, Tempe, Arizona
Turtle Creek Residence, Dallas, Texas
Ventana Vista Elementary School, Tucson,
  Arizona
Spencer Theater for the Performing Arts, Alto,
  New Mexico
Civic Arts Plaza, Thousand Oaks, California
Dance Studio, University of California, San
  Diego
Tang Teaching Museum and Art Gallery,
  Skidmore College, Saratoga Springs, New York
Gateway Center, University of Minnesota,
  Minneapolis, Minnesota

Design Philosophy and History

The elemental power of New Mexico is inescapable. New Mexico has formed Antoine Predock's experience in an all pervasive sense. In New Mexico, one is aimed toward the sky and at the same time remains rooted in the earth with a geological and cultural past. The lessons Antoine learned here about responding to the forces of a place are implemented in his buildings sited in many distinct contexts. He doesn't have to invent a new methodology for new contexts. New Mexico has already prepared him.

Antoine is influenced enormously by the fundamental connection between the earth and sky through the mute, blank adobe walls found in the Southwest. In adobe architecture, the wall acts as a bridge between earth and sky. Adobe is an extension of the earth aspiring toward the sky.

In Antoine's work, the connection to the sky is always there. He explores, at times quite literally, going into the sky and into the earth simultaneously. The Turtle Creek House has a ramp that aims toward the sky, establishing a trajectory that one follows on ascent. His buildings in the desert are dug into the site, right into the ground.

While he was a student at Columbia University, Antoine became involved in dance and with the body in space. This influenced his work profoundly. His buildings are processional events, choreographic events; they are an accumulation of vantage points both perceptual and experiential. At Mandell Weiss Forum one comes through a eucalyptus grove and there, in a clearing, out of the blue, stands a two-hundred-and-seventy-foot-long mirror. One is suddenly part of the procession of arrival. It is a ritual—the encounter with this giant mirror, the collective straightening of the tie, and the passage through the looking glass to what lies beyond. His buildings, on many levels, are about dissolving boundaries and expectations.

Antoine's aspiration toward the making of a timeless architecture also contains an aspiration toward social responsibility. La Luz Community, from 1967, demonstrates a reaffirmation of the large-scale use of adobe brick in the context of a project whose five-hundred acre site plan was based on sustainability and protection of the ecosystem. The social and programmatic value of his projects is reinforced by an underlying, less tangible, intention.

When working on projects with his team, it is important to underscore the collaborative component in Antoine's work—they are constantly reminded by him that they are involved in a timeless encounter with another place, not just a piece of land. Everything influences Antoine's work. Anything that comes along is potentially of great interest to him; it can be something theoretically based or it can be the most ephemeral topical information.

The choices Antoine makes come from the spirit and from an understanding of the actual world around him, both in terms of the present and the past. Rather than being a highly rational methodology, Antoine's process remains connected to spirit through the body and to the personal space that the body defines. Antoine's built work expresses the initial physical and spiritual impulse, amongst the original content.

1

2

3

4

5

1&4 American Heritage Center/Art Museum, University of Wyoming, Laramie, Wyoming
Photo credit: Timothy Hursley

2&3 Nelson Fine Arts Center, Arizona State University, Tempe, Arizona
Photo credit: Timothy Hursley

5&6 Turtle Creek Residence, Dallas, Texas
Photo credit: Timothy Hursley

6

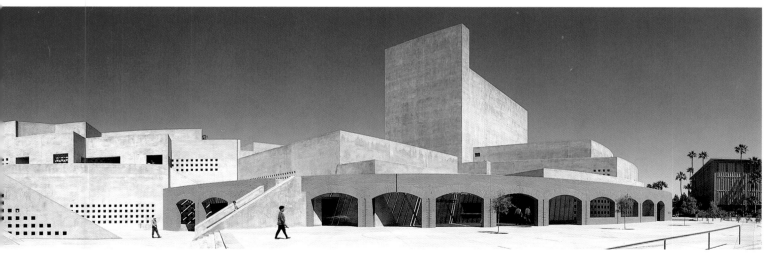

Architects 49 Limited

Directors
Nithi Sthapitanonda,
Surasing Prompoj, Prabhakorn Vadanyakul,
Anusorn Paksukcharern, Suwat Vasapinyokul,
Pichai Wongwaisayawan

Thailand
81 Sukhumvit 26
Bangkok 10110
Tel: +(66 2) 260 4370/259 3533
Fax: +(66 2) 259 3872
E-mail: a49@a49.com
Website: A49.com

Directors
Nithi Sthapitanonda
Surasingh Prompoj
Prabhakorn Vadanyakul
Anusorn Paksukcharern
Suwat Vasapinyokul
Pichai Wongwaisayawan

Associates
Supanit Chookhae
Prasert Yangthara
Pinthip Chaleewan
Adul Leesawat
Anuchit Sukontasub
Patikorn Na Songkhla
Kiattisak Veteewootacharn
Unnop Veeravutthiphol
Krisada Teerapongprachya
Chatchai Assawasukee

Person to Contact
Nithi Sthapitanonda

Number of Employees
80

Date of Establishment
1983

Project Types
Corporate Headquarters
Commercial Buildings
Convention Halls
Clubhouse and Sports Facilities
Embassies
Healthcare Facilities
Hotels and Resorts
Industrial Buildings
Institution/Education
Religious Buildings
Residential Buildings
Training Centres

Disciplines
Architecture
Construction Management
Engineering
Feasibility Studies
Master Planning

Current and Recent Projects
Holiday Inn Green Hills Hotel, Chiang Mai, Thailand
Holiday Inn Saigon, Ho Chi Minh City, The Socialist Republic of Vietnam
Shangri-La Hotel, Chaopraya Wing, Bangkok, Thailand
State Bank of Hanoi, The Socialist Republic of Vietnam
Ministry of Foreign Affairs, Bangkok, Thailand
Tipco Headquarters, Bangkok, Thailand
Thammasat University Academic and Conference Center, Bangkok, Thailand
Mass Communication Organization of Thailand, Bangkok, Thailand
Department of Export Promotion Trademart, Bangkok, Thailand
Mae Fah Luang University, Chaing Rai, Thailand
Esso Refinery Administration Building, Cholburi, Thailand

Selected Clients
Shangri-La Hotel, Bangkok
Tipco Group of Companies
Esso Thailand
The Shell Company of Thailand Ltd
Ministry of Foreign Affairs
Mass Communication Organization of Thailand
Telephone Organization of Thailand
Department of Export Promotion
Petroleum Authority of Thailand
State Bank of Hanoi, The Socialist Republic of Vietnam
Schering Chemical Limited
Bukit Cahaya Country Resorts Sdn. Bhd.
Auchan Chiangmai
Goldman Sachs (Asia) L.L.C.

Design Philosophy and History
The design concept of Architects 49 Limited is to create buildings along clean simple elegant lines. While the overall appearance should be welcoming and inviting, the internal layout must be functional and practical, allowing for smooth circulation and maximizing useable space. Maintenance requirement should be uncomplicated and economical. At the same time, each design should be aesthetically pleasing to both daily users and occasional visitors alike.

All of the firm's projects, from large commercial buildings to private residences, reflect the firm's careful attention to detail in all aspects of design, even in the selection of materials. Thoughtful consideration is given to short-term and long-term effects on the residents, the community and the environment. The firm's structures should assimilate gracefully, becoming an integral part of their surroundings, yet maintaining their distinct artistic appeal.

Motivated by this philosophy, Architects 49 Limited are determined to maintain their internationally-accepted standards of design and production. The firm regards their work as a labour of love which it hopes to continue to forge ties between the designer on one hand and the user and community on the other.

1 Muang Thai-Phatra Complex (phase II), Rajadapisek Road, Bangkok, Thailand
Photo credit: Skyline Studio

2 Oriflame, Asoke Road, Bangkok, Thailand
Photo credit: Skyline Studio

3 Holiday Inn Saigon, Ho Chi Minh City, The Socialist Republic of Vietnam
Photo credit: Skyline Studio

4 Tipco Headquarters, Rama VI Road, Bangkok, Thailand
Photo credit: Skyline Studio

5 Ministry of Foreign Affairs, Sri Ayutthaya Road, Bangkok, Thailand
Photo credit: Skyline Studio

6 Genco Rayong Hazardous Waste Facility, Mabtapub, Industrial Estate, Rayong, Thailand
Photo credit: Skyline Studio

1

2

3

4

5

6

Architectural Resources Cambridge, Inc. (ARC)

USA
140 Mount Auburn Street
Cambridge, Massachusetts 02138
Tel: +(1 617) 547 2200
Fax: +(1 617) 547 7222
E-mail: ARCmail@arcusa.com

Person to Contact
James F. Davies, President

Number of Employees
55

Date of Establishment
1969

Project Types
Academic
Athletic
Corporate
Historic Reuse
Laboratory
Library
Manufacturing
Master Planning
Residence Halls

Disciplines
Architecture
Interiors
Planning

Current and Recent Projects
Boston College, Alumni Stadium, Boston,
  Massachusetts, USA
Case Western University, Dively Executive
  Education Center, Cleveland, Ohio, USA
Genzyme Corporation, Biopharmaceutical Plant,
  Boston, Massachusetts, USA
Harvard University, Kennedy School of
  Government, Cambridge, Massachusetts, USA
Polaroid Corporation, New Offices, Norwood,
  Massachusetts, USA
Tufts University, Biomedical Research Complex,
  Boston, Massachusetts, USA
University of Iowa, Papajohn School of Business
  Administration, Iowa City, Iowa, USA

Selected Clients
Arthur D. Little
Bayer Diagnostics
Compaq
Genzyme Corporation
GTE Laboratories
Polaroid Corporation
Boston College
Boston University
Duke University
Harvard University
New York University
University of Iowa

Design Philosophy and History
ARC's design philosophy is based on three
fundamental objectives:

A building designed to reflect the historical,
geographical, and architectural context in
which it is to be sited;

An image which reflects the designated and
perceived purpose of the building; and

A building that meets the needs of the user
in a functional and efficient manner.

Founded in 1969, Architectural Resources
Cambridge, Inc. (ARC), provides professional
services in the fields of architecture, planning,
and interior design. As the new millennium
approaches, ARC is celebrating 30 years of
design excellence.

The firm employs a professional design staff
with a wide range of architectural experience.
With this broad knowledge, ARC contributes
to technological advances in both the corporate
and academic worlds.

As a service-oriented design firm, ARC is highly
responsive to the needs and concerns of its
clients. ARC strives to develop strong working
relationships with its clients and encourages
close interaction among the project team and
client from the initial planning stage through
design and project completion.

Thirty years of experience has shown that
continuous personal service is the most effective
formula for a successful project.

Genzyme Corporation Biopharmaceutical Plant
ARC created a master plan for Genzyme Corporation's
facilities on a prominent site along the Charles River in
Boston. Phase I of the plan was the construction of a
130,000 square foot biopharmaceutical plant. The next
two phases on the 9.4 acre site include a corporate
office building of 280,000 square feet and a parking
garage, with Phase III reserved for expansion of the
manufacturing facility.

The plant is a state-of-the-art facility incorporating
bioreactors for mammalian cell culture, protein
purification suites, sterile filling operations, and
laboratory space. It is used for the production of
Cerezyme, a treatment for Gaucher's disease. The
building has been designed to fit comfortably between
its Harvard University neighbour to the west and MIT
to the east.
Photo credit: Nick Wheeler

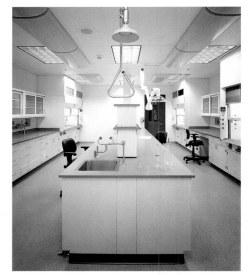

Bayer Diagnostics
Photo credit: John Horner

Harvard University Kennedy School of Government

ARC has provided professional services to the School since the initiation of planning and design in 1976, for the first building on the site, the Littauer Center of Public Administration.

Since that time, the Kennedy School campus has expanded with the addition of three buildings following the original master plan.

The Belfer Center of Public Management was completed in 1986. The firm's most recent KSG project, completed in 1998, is a state-of-the-art classroom renovation.
Photo credit: Nick Wheeler

GTE Laboratories

ARC designed campus-wide renovation and additions to GTE Laboratories' Waltham, Massachusetts facilities. Following the completion of a Master Plan, design and construction proceeded on a fast-track, multi-phased schedule. Renovated areas include executive and staff offices, electronics laboratories, as well as specialized environments.
Photo credit: Nick Wheeler

University of Iowa Pappajohn School of Business Administration

'What excites me most about the Pappajohn Building is that it has dramatically changed the way we teach. The new technology, with which every classroom is equipped, allows our faculty to combine traditional course materials and electronic media to create a whole new curriculum—one that is expressly designed to meet the technological demands and international dimensions of business in the next century. At the same time, the building brings students and faculty closer together; both in and out of class, so that the human touch isn't lost in the midst of technology. The Pappajohn Building has truly created the best of both worlds.'
Gary Fethke, Dean
College of Business Administration
Photo credit: Nick Wheeler

Architecture Studio

1

France
10 rue Lacuée
Paris 75012
Tel: +(33 1) 4345 1800
Fax: +(33 1) 4343 8143
E-mail: as@architecture-studio.fr
Website: www.architecture-studio.fr

Associates
Martin Robain
Rodo Tisnado
Jean-François Bonne
Alain Bretagnolle
René-Henri Arnaud
Laurent-Marc Fischer
Marc Lehmann

Number of Employees
80

Date of Establishment
1973

Project Types
Athletic Facilities
Commercial
Cultural/Educational
Healthcare
Housing
Industrial
Infrastructure and Transportation
Office Buildings
Town Planning

Selected Clients
European Parliament
Silesian Academy of Medicine
Politecnico of Milan
Town of Paris
Ministry of Justice
Ministry of Foreign Affairs

Current and Recent Projects
European Parliament, Strasbourg, France
Academic Centre of Medicine, Zabrze, Poland
Bovisa District, Politecnico University and AEM
  Head Office, Milan, Italy
Extension of the Exhibition Ground, Paris-Nord
  Villepinte, France
Our Lady of the Ark of the Covenant Church,
  Paris, France
Urban Amenagement of the Ringroad,
  Bordeaux, France
National Institute of Judo, Paris, France
Apartment Buildings, Paris, France

Law Courts, Caen, France
Retirement Residence, Paris, France
University Residence, Paris, France
Ecole des Mines, Albi-Carmaux, France
La City Business Centre, Besançon, France
Citadel University, Dunkerque, France
Arab World Institute, Paris, France (with J.
  Nouvel, G. Lezenes and P. Soria)
High School of the Future, Jaunay-Clan, France
French Embassy in Muscat, Sultanate of Oman

Design Philosophy and History
Architecture Studio, created in 1973 in Paris,
is a structure based on an original intellectual
project which assumes a collective philosophy
for a collective architecture.

Through a collaborative process of conception
and an approach of the built project conditioned
to the specifics of its context, the architectural
practice is constantly evolving in its mode of
expression.

Architecture Studio consists of seven associates,
city planners, architects and interior designers
of various nationalities. The firm undertakes all
types of programs, supported by a world-wide
network of technical partners, financial
resources and specialized consultants.

3

2

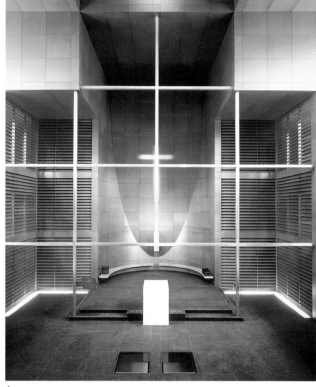

4

1 Architecture Studio's Associates
  Photo credit: Gaston

2 European Parliament, Strasbourg, France
  Photo credit: G. Fessy

3 Arab World Institute, Paris, France
  Architects: Architecture Studio With J. Nouvel, G. Lezenes, P. Soria
  Photo credit: S. Couturier

4 Our Lady of the Ark of the Covenant Church, Paris, France
  Photo credit: Gaston

5 University Residence, Paris, France
  Photo credit: P. Tourneboeuf

Assar

1

Belgium
Chaussée de La Hulpe 178
Brussels B-1170
Tel: +(32 2) 672 6824
Fax: +(32 2) 672 8337
E-mail: assar@assar.com
Website: www.assar.com

Person to Contact
Eric Ysebrant

Number of Employees
60

Selected Clients
Axa Belgium
Belgian Government
CDP, Compagnie de Promotion
CFE
Codic
CIB, Compagnie Immobilière de Belgique
Dow Corning
Fabrimetal
IP Benelux
NCC, Eurobalken
Robert Bosch
Sicabel
SmithKline Beecham Biologicals
Sofina
UCB
White Star

Design Philosophy and History
The ASSAR group, founded in 1985, is
comprised of approximately 60 architects and
interior designers committed to two professions:
architecture and urbanism, through ASSAR; and
interior design and facility management,
through Global Design. From the beginning,
ASSAR has been one of the first architectural
offices to invest heavily in computer aided
conception and design. In recent years, ASSAR
has won numerous competitions for the
construction of major administrative
headquarters, research centres and large scale
residential complexes. A permanent dialogue
with the client and the constant will to produce
quality architecture always come together with
the respect to timing and budgets within both
ASSAR and Global.

The work of ASSAR is varied in regard to both
building types and architectural style. ASSAR's
style is to create contemporary architecture,
while keeping in mind the context of the
project, the building technology and cost
effective solutions in response to the client's
needs.

In Brussels, well-known companies such as Axa
Belgium, UCB, Fabrimetal, IP, Weishaupt and
Sofina have entrusted ASSAR to design their
new headquarters. Axa Belgium, IP and
SmithKline Beecham among others have recently
asked ASSAR and Global to design their working
environments and interiors.

More than 150,000 square metres of office
space have been completed in the last decade
while more than 150,000 square metres of
housing are currently under construction today;
apart from the Royal Military academy of the
Belgian Armed Forces, a major development
covering 100,000 square metres of new and
renovated buildings, involving academic,
housing and sports facilities.

1 UCB Center, World Headquarters, Brussels, Belgium
   A new headquarters building for UCB built in a
   garden park on the edge of Brussels, finished in
   1998. The building is composed of short curved
   office wings around a central atrium space to
   encourage communication and contact within
   the company.
   Photo credit: Marc Detiffe courtesy ASSAR

2 Fabrimetal Headquarters, Brussels, Belgium
   The entry hall of an office building and conference
   centre finished in 1998 in Brussels. The use of
   varnished structural steel profiles for the spiral
   stair and waxed concrete floors give the interiors
   a masculine semi-industrial character.
   Photo credit: Marc Detiffe courtesy ASSAR

3 SmithKline Beecham Biologicals, Laboratories,
   Wavre, Belgium
   A winning competition project for a new
   headquarters and laboratory complex for
   SB Biologicals at the Wavre site in Belgium.
   The project is currently under study.
   Computer rendering: courtesy ASSAR

2

3

4 Novalis Apartments, Brussels, Belgium
An 80-unit social housing project located in central Brussels completed in 1998. The classically composed facades and rounded roofs create a memorable impression of a building type which is quite ordinary.
Photo credit: Marc Detiffe courtesy ASSAR

5 Weishaupt, Brussels, Belgium
A renovation project of the existing Belgian headquarters of the German firm Weishaupt, comprising office space, a showroom and training centre and a logistical centre for Belgium. The project was finished in early 1999.
Photo credit: Marc Detiffe courtesy ASSAR

6 UCB Center, Atrium lobby, Brussels, Belgium
Photo credit: Marc Detiffe courtesy ASSAR

4

5

6

Atelier d'Architecture de Genval

Belgium
43 place Communale
Genval B-1332
Tel: +(32 2) 653 0960
Fax: +(32 2) 654 1746
E-mail: genval@online.be

Number of Employees
25

Date of Establishment
1967

Project Types
Civic
Commercial
Educational
Hospitality
Landscape
Recreational
Residential
Retrofit
Town Planning
Transportation

Disciplines
Architecture
Interior Design
Feasibility Studies
Urban Planning

Recent Projects in Brussels
European Parliament 1998
Joseph II Tower 1998
North Area 1997
Stephanie Area 1993

Selected Clients
Asticus/IVG
Banimmo/AXA
Conrad Hotel
Eli - Lilly
European Parliament and Commission
Fortis
Générale de Belgique
Inter IKEA
Morgan Bank
Universities of Liege, Mons, Louvain-la-Neuve
Winterthur

Design Philosophy and History
Variety and lyricism are the hallmarks of the projects carried out by the Atelier de Genval. It seeks to make the most of this variety in its projects, so as to ensure each one stands out from the rest. The idea is to avoid repetition and duplication at all costs. The members of the Atelier boast a range of complementary skills where the individual lyricism develops a highly expressive form of architecture.

1

Joseph II Tower, Brussels, complete renovation
The 'dynamic' frontages feature of this building incorporates air-return systems, where the conditioning relies on the cold beam principle. The technical facilities in the roof have given rise to a cladding designed to give poetic expression to air movements (suction and expulsion) created by the machinery concealed therein.

1 Joseph II Tower, facades
  Computer graphics: Fabien de Cugnac
2 Impact of Joseph II in the city
  Photo credit: Fabien de Cugnac
3 Impact of the European Parliament in the city
  Photo credit: Paul Nemerlin
4 Facades of the parliamentarian offices
  Photo credit: Fabien de Cugnac
5 Parliamentarian building, interior street
  Photo credit: Fabien de Cugnac

2

3

European Parliament, Brussels

The Atelier d'Architecture de Genval has a 25 percent stake in the Atelier de l'Espace Leopold, the architect of the European Parliament in Brussels. The sheer size of the complex reflects the sensation of being part of a rapidly changing city and expresses the democratic openness of the European integration process. During the Parliamentary session the complex plays host to 4,500 people.

4

5

Atelier d'Art Urbain Architects

The Partners
Photo credit: Celine Lambiotte

Belgium
16 Brugmann Avenue
Brussels B-1060
Tel: +(32 2) 344 6464
Fax: +(32 2) 346 3600
E-mail: mail@atelier-art-urbain.com
Website: www.atelier-art-urbain.com

Partners
Sefik Birkiye, Founding Partner
Dominique Delbrouck
Grégoire de Jerphanion
Christian Sibilde

Person to Contact
Sefik Birkiye

Number of Employees
66

Date of Establishment
1979

Project Types
Corporate Headquarters
Hotels
Leisure
Mixed-use
Offices
Residential Buildings
Retail and Shopping Centres

Disciplines
Architecture
Feasibility Studies
Interior Architecture
Master Planning
Renovation and Preservation
Urban Planning

Selected Clients
Accor Group - Novotel
AG - Fortis Group
Banimmo
Besix Group
Compagnie Immobilière de Belgique
Crédit Communal de Belgique - Dexia Group
NCC-Eurobalken
Orascom
SAS Hotels
Société des Bains de Mer
Zurich Assurances

1

Current and Recent Projects
Belgium:
AG/Fortis Headquarters
Banco do Brazil
Boulevard Jacqmain Urban Redevelopment
City Center/City 2 Shopping Mall
Crédit Communal Bank
Green Island
Le Jardin des Fonderies
KBC World Headquarters (formerly Kredietbank)
Novotel Brussels City
Radisson SAS Hotel Brussels
Résidence de l'Abbaye
Villa Palladine
Zurich Assurances Belgium HQ
Former Zurich Assurances HQ Redevelopment

International:
Battery Park City Master Plan Study, New York, New York, USA
Cleveland Master Plan Study, Cleveland, Ohio, USA
Hôtel du Larvotto, Monte Carlo
Housing Project, Sedan, France
Klassis Hotel and Resort, Istanbul, Turkey
Nile City Financial Center, Cairo, Egypt
Hyatt Regency Cairo, Egypt

Design Philosophy and History
Created by Sefik Birkiye (44), who was joined by his student friends Dominique Delbrouck, Grégoire de Jerphanion and Christian Sibilde, the Atelier d'Art Urbain has been commissioned by some of the most important Belgian property developers to design projects of all types.

Its creative spirit, together with its adherence to the expectations of the developers, have quickly opened the doors to important instructions to this young team.

In the space of just 20 years it has become one of the biggest and best known architectural practices in Belgium, so that it is now considered a true reference point where major urban developments are concerned.

With the skilful use of natural materials such as stone, metal, marble and wood in the construction details, Atelier d'Art Urbain has a characteristic style which it is able to integrate into the existing architectural and stylistic environment of towns and cities, creating easily recognizable projects.

Major projects completed or underway in various areas demonstrate the capacities and skills of this team of architects and satisfy the expectations of the investors who wish to create buildings as convivial as they are timeless.

Nile City Financial Center in the heart of Cairo and in the spirit of the Pharaohs, Larvotto Beach Hotel in Monaco recalling the great summer palaces, Klassis Resort and Golf Club in Istanbul with its Byzantine and Ottoman influences are just some of the projects which demonstrate a style capable of adapting to the culture and influence of its surroundings.

3

4

5

1 Radisson Sas Hotel, Brussels; 285 guest rooms
  Photo credit: Yvan Glavie

2 Nile City Financial Center, Cairo; hotel, restaurant,
  office building and commercial mall
  Model Maker: Tetraedre
  Photo credit: Fabien de Cugnac

3 Klassis Hotel, Istanbul; 320 guest rooms and leisure
  sport
  Photo credit: Mehmet Mutaf

4 Loi 62, Brussels; refurbishment of an office building
  Photo credit: Yvan Glavie

5 Zurich Assurances, Brussels; Zurich Assurances
  Belgium HQ
  Photo credit: Yvan Glavie

ATELIER D'ART URBAIN
A R C H I T E C T S

Avery Associates Architects

UK
120 Wilton Road
London SW1V 1JZ
Tel: +(44 20) 7873 8568
Fax: +(44 20) 7233 5182
E-mail: enquiries@avery-architects.co.uk

Directors
Bryan Avery
John Dawson

Persons to Contact
Jenny Cochran
Bryan Avery

Number of Employees
10

Date of Establishment
1978

Project Types
Arts and Performance
Civic
Office
Commercial
Urban Design
Retail

Disciplines
Architecture
Interior Design
Product Design
Urban Design

Current and Recent Projects
Royal Academy of Dramatic Art (RADA), London
BFI London IMAX Cinema, London
No. 1 Neathouse Place, London
Museum of the Moving Image, London

Selected Clients
British Land Plc
The British Film Institute
Chesterfield Properties Ltd
De Montfort University
HMS Trincomalee Trust
Hewitt Associates
Horniman Museum
London Fire and Civil Defence Authority
National Film Theatre
Rank Xerox
Rohm & Haas (UK) Ltd
Royal Academy of Dramatic Art
Royal Artillery Regiment
The Commonwealth Institute

Design Philosophy and History
Avery Associates was founded in 1978 as a non-specialising, design-led practice. This background, along with a passion for innovative ideas and a lateral thinking capability, combine to generate a creative excitement behind each project.

The practice has experience in all stages of the design and implementation of a wide range of building types. These include commercial and residential buildings, arts and performance spaces, educational and university buildings, leisure, retail and museums.

Avery Associates' clients are equally diverse, including commercial developers, government organisations, national institutes, universities and charitable trusts. The practice has developed close and enduring relationships with many of their clients and are proud of the repeat work these relationships bring.

The clients are involved closely in the design process and find that they enjoy the friendliness of the team and appreciate the rigorous professionalism of the team's approach. For the practice, the client's brief is a starting point which, with dialogue, often leads to something which far exceeds the initial expectations.

Avery Associates' expertise ranges from small-scale refurbishments, building components and graphics right through to multi-million pound building projects and urban planning studies.

The practice has won many awards and has been extensively published both in the UK and abroad.

1

2

3

4

1 Model, general view, Royal Academy of Dramatic Art
  Photo credit: Bryan Avery

Neathouse Place
2 Southwest elevation and entrance rotunda
3 Rotunda detail
  Photo credit: Peter Cook

BFI London IMAX Cinema
4 482-seat auditorium
5 View looking west with Waterloo Station in background
6 Context view looking northwest

Photo credit: courtesy Avery Associates Architects (2,4); Richard Hottum (5,6)

5

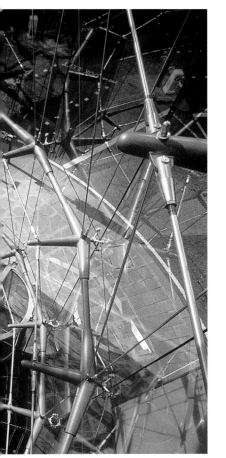

6

B3 Architects/Berkus Design Studio

Barry A. Berkus, AIA
President B3 Architects and Berkus Design Studio
Photo credit: courtesy Berkus Design Studio

USA
2020 Alameda Padre Serra, suite 133
Santa Barbara, California 93103
Tel: +(805) 966 1547
Fax: +(805) 966 1549
E-mail: inquire@b3architects.com

B3 Partners
Barry A. Berkus, AIA
Thomas E. Greer
Thomas C. McMahon, AIA
Art Sturz
David VanHoy

Person to Contact
Barry A. Berkus, AIA

Project Profiles
Resort and Community Planning
Golf Clubhouses
Urban Redevelopment and Adaptive Reuse
Mixed-use
Commercial/Retail
Residential Architecture

Partial Client Listing
Lyle Anderson
Jack Nicklaus
Santa Barbara Botanic Garden
Los Angeles Olympic Organizing Committee
Provincial Government of Vancouver
Transcontinental-Bass

Design Philosophy and History
The architects and planners of B3 Architects/ Berkus Design Studio practice the art of making place, creating community, and designing destination. They believe that good architecture is human in nature, human in scale and contextual, respecting geography and topography as well as regional historical and cultural traditions.

Throughout the world, whether the setting is an urban center, a rural enclave or a resort village, their focus is on understanding the client, the region and the site. Using the tools of technology, they translate the layers of requirements into a presentation that is an expressive characterization of community. The firm values the gesture of the hand, and the efficiency of the computer in its design process.

The B3 Architects/Berkus Design Studio design and planning portfolio illustrates versatility as well as expertise. Their teams are ever in pursuit of meaningful innovation:

- Creating vibrant mixed-use neighbourhoods out of decaying urban cores
- Integrating planning and architecture so that buildings draw on the strength of their sites, and sites are enhanced by the structures they host
- Bringing together recreation and residential amenities that continue to set the standard for destination resort environments.

Botanical Learning Center, Santa Barbara, California

Mixed-use redevelopment, Santa Barbara, California

A BERKUS DESIGN STUDIO

B³ ARCHITECTS

BERKUS DESIGN STUDIO

'Architecture is inhabited sculpture.' Constantin Brancusi

'Architecture of all the arts, is the one which acts the most slowly, but the most surely, on the soul.' Ernest Dimnet

'No house should ever be on a hill or on anything. It should be of the hill. Belonging to it. Hill and house should live together each the happier for the other.' Frank Lloyd Wright

Golf Clubhouse, Scottsdale, Arizona

Beach Club, Kona, Hawaii

Barton Phelps & Associates
Architects and Planners

Barton Phelps, FAIA
Photo credit: courtesy Barton Phelps & Associates

USA
5514 Wilshire Boulevard
Los Angeles, California 90036
Tel: +(323) 934 8615
Fax: +(323) 934 3289
Email: bpala@aol.com

Director
Barton Phelps, FAIA

Associates
David Haggerty
Rene Ilustre
Yvonne Yao
Ron Calvo

Persons to Contact
Barton Phelps, FAIA
David Haggerty

Number of Employees
12

Date of Establishment
1984

Project Types
Civic
Educational
Historic Retrofit
Industrial
Office Interiors
Parks and Recreation
Performing Arts
Residential

Disciplines
Architecture
Interior Design
Landscape Design
Master Planning

Recent Projects
Royce Hall Seismic Renovation, UCLA, USA
Cabrillo Marine Aquarium, Los Angeles, USA
Los Angeles Public Library, Los Feliz, USA
University Elementary School, UCLA, USA
Dimensional Fund Advisors Inc., Santa Monica, USA
Central District Headquarters, Department of Water & Power, Los Angeles, USA
Residences: California, Missouri, Virginia, USA

Selected Clients
University of California, Los Angeles
UCLA Medical Center
Los Angeles Public Library, Los Feliz
University Elementary School, UCLA
Dimensional Fund Advisors, Santa Monica
Department of Water & Power, Los Angeles

1

2

3

1 Los Angeles Department of Water & Power Central District Headquarters, Los Angeles, California
Photo credit: Tom Bonner courtesy Barton Phelps & Associates

2 Dimensional Fund Advisors Inc., Santa Monica, California
Photo credit: Tom Bonner courtesy Barton Phelps & Associates

3 Los Angeles Public Library, Los Feliz, Los Angeles, California
Photo credit: Tom Bonner courtesy Barton Phelps & Associates

4 East Building, Corinne A. Seeds University Elementary School, UCLA, Los Angeles, California
Photo credit: Grant Mudford courtesy Barton Phelps & Associates

5 Royce Hall Seismic Renovation, UCLA, Los Angeles, California
Photo credit: Tom Bonner courtesy Barton Phelps & Associates (with Anshen + Allen Los Angeles)

6 Epstein House, Los Angeles, California
Photo credit: David Glomb courtesy Barton Phelps & Associates

4

5

6

Design Philosophy
Simultaneity:
The presence of architecture as both utilitarian and expressive distinguishes it from artistic media that exist solely in the conscious realm of art. The firm exploits this anomaly in work that is both plain and expressive—meaningful without demanding special knowledge and open to divergent interpretations. Special concerns include:

- the primacy of experience - emphasizing perceptual differences between drawings and the actual experience of built form and materiality (using simple forms to produce complex results).
- transforming with light - altering perception of space through the use of specific lighting techniques.
- expedient elements verses 'principled form' - playing one against the other to engage perception and make ideas more accessible.
- buildings as landscape - allowing exterior spaces and events to shape buildings and treating enclosed and outdoor space as alike and connected.

Coming after: The firm investigates formal implications of earlier intentions, often reconstructing the lost history of a place and building upon those intentions, updating and redirecting them.

Data is good: In many good buildings function follows form (not the other way around). But the firm views programmatic data as a source of 'clues' to the society of a place and ways to represent it in architecture.

Allowing: Program changes, value engineering, code compliance, construction problems and organizational politics are valid modifiers of design concepts and can inform built results in meaningful ways. Design can take advantage of controversy.

Etiology: Developing a concept requires understanding sources and explaining where ideas come from. Barton Phelps & Associates works from observed conditions, looking for applicable ideas in locally recognizable vernacular models. Buildings always embody precedent and the creative changes/deformations they have undergone.

Practice: The firm has many repeat clients but avoids specializing in any one building type. Unbiased, first-time inquiry into sites, programs, and construction types is the heart of the design process. It often results in solutions that neither the architects nor the clients expect.

Bedaux de Brouwer Architecten B.V.

The Netherlands
Dr. Keyzerlaan 2
Goirle 5051 PB
Tel: +(31) 135 368 555
Fax: +(31) 135 364 585
E-mail: bedaux.debrouwer@inter.nl.net

Person to Contact
Drs G.J. Bedaux

Number of Employees
20

Date of Establishment
1938

Project Types
Educational Facilities
Office Buildings
Private Housing
Public Housing
Renovations
Social and Cultural Facilities
Town and City Planning
Villas

Current and Recent Projects
Housing project 'De Wijk', Tilburg
Music School, Roosendaal
Offices for law company in Tilburg and Breda
Restoration 'Het Cenakel', Tilburg

Selected Clients
Tilburg City Council
Dutch Government Building Management Services
Bouwfonds Housing Corporation
Rabo Real Estate
Various housing corporations in Tilburg, Breda, Utrecht and Eindhoven

Design Philosophy and History
Bedaux de Brouwer Architecten B.V., established in 1938, is a well-organized, medium sized architectural firm which has a continual high quality output. Its different projects are recognizable by the sharp architectural styling, supported by a unique choice of materials and clear, functional detailing. The range of architectural forms used is anchored within the environmental context by the use of typological variation.

The firm's architectural profile has a long tradition of deconstructing the elements of 'universal modernism'. The result—where local values and images are intermixed with foreign elements—is a milder, more humane form of modernism that is more attuned to the environmental context.

Bedaux de Brouwer Architecten B.V. has received prestigious national awards over the years. Various projects have been included in the architectural catalogues of a number of West European countries.

1 Villa City, the Netherlands
   Photo credit: Theo Krÿgsman

2 Villa in the City, Goes, the Netherlands
   Photo credit: Theo Krÿgsman

3 Tilburg Twin Towers, the Netherlands
   Photo credit: René De Wit

4 Social and Cultural Facility, Bergeyk, the Netherlands
   Photo credit: Marcel van Kerckhoven

5 Zwÿsencluster, Tilburg, the Netherlands
   Photo credit: Dorien Bedaux

6 Health Centre, Tilburg, the Netherlands
   Photo credit: Marcel van Kerckhoven

1

2

3

4

5

6

Bligh Voller Nield, Bligh Nield Health, Bligh Voller Nield Sports

Principals: Chris Clarke, Christopher Alcock, Graham Bligh, Michael Adams, Robert Gardner, Neil Hanson, James Grose, Lawrence Nield, Phillip Page, Phillip Tait, Shane Thompson, Jon Voller

Australia

Bligh Voller Nield
365 St Pauls Terrace
PO Box 801
Fortitude Valley
Brisbane, Queensland 4006
Tel: +(61 7) 3852 2525
Fax: +(61 7) 3852 2544
E-mail: brisbane@bvn.com.au

Level Two, 189 Kent Street
GPO Box N646 Grosvenor Place
Sydney, New South Wales 1220
Tel: +(61 2) 9252 1222
Fax: +(61 2) 9252 1776
E-mail: sydney@bvn.com.au

Bligh Voller Nield Sports Pty Ltd
Head Office
Level Two, 189 Kent Street
GPO Box N646 Grosvenor Place
Sydney, New South Wales 1220
Tel: +(61 2) 9252 1222
Fax: +(61 2) 9252 1776
E-mail: sydney@bvn.com.au
Website: www.blighvollernield.com.au

460 Bay Street
Port Melbourne
Melbourne, Victoria 3207
Tel: +(61 3) 9646 6188
Fax: +(61 3) 9646 6766
E-mail: melb@bvn.com.au

Level One, Sydney Building
121 London Circuit
GPO Box 2819
Canberra ACT 2601
Tel: +(61 2) 6249 8666
Fax: +(61 2) 6257 4958
E-mail: canberra@bvn.com.au

Bligh Nield Health Pty Ltd
Head Office
Level Two, 189 Kent Street
GPO Box N646 Grosvenor Place
Sydney, New South Wales 1220
Tel: +(61 2) 9252 1222
Fax: +(61 2) 9252 1776
E-mail: sydney@bvn.com.au

Persons to Contact

Shane Thompson, Brisbane
Neil Hanson or Chris Alcock, Sydney
Jon Voller, Melbourne
Phillip Page, Canberra

Project Types

Aged Housing
Building Systems
Commercial
Community
Conservation
Culture
Defence
Education
Environment
Entertainment
Government
Health
Hotel/Resort
Industrial
Institutional
Interior Design
Laboratories
Libraries
Licensed Clubs
Master Planning
Museums
Offices
Recreation
Refurbishment
Research
Residential
Restaurants
Rural
Sport & Leisure
Tourism
Transport
Urban Design

Current and Recent Projects

Ansett Australia Domestic Terminal, Sydney
Brisbane Airport International Terminal, Queensland
Docklands Stadium, Melbourne
Russell Offices, Canberra
Toowoomba Hospital, Queensland
University of Sunshine Coast Arts Faculty, Queensland
University of Sunshine Coast Library, Queensland
Queensland Clunies Ross Centre, Queensland
Queensland University of Technology, Queensland
   Built Environment Precinct
St Vincents Hospital, Sydney
Stadium Australia, Sydney
Sydney Olympic Tennis Centre, Sydney
Wellington Stadium, New Zealand

Clients

Ansett Australia
Australian High Commission
Australia Post
Barclay Mowlem Construction Ltd
Baulderstone Hornibrook Group
Boeing Australia Limited
Bovis, Australia
Brisbane City Council
Brisbane Grammar School
Brisbane International Airport
Coca Cola Amatil
CSR Limited
Department of Defence
Department of Environment
Department of Social Security
Deutsche Bank
Griffith University
IBM
Kumagai
Leighton Contractors Pty Limited
Lend Lease
Suncorp Metway Ltd
MLC
Multiplex Constructions Pty Ltd
New South Wales Government
Qantas Airways Limited
Olympic Tennis Centre
Optus Communications
Queensland Conservatorium
   of Music
Queensland Government
Queensland Police
Queensland University
   of Technology
SOCOG
South Australian Government
Telstra Corporation Limited
Thakral Holdings Limited
Thiess Contractors Ltd
University of New South Wales
University of Sunshine Coast
University of Sydney
University of Queensland
University of Western Sydney
Victorian Government
Walter Construction Group

Design Philosophy and History

Bligh Voller Nield was established during 1997–1998 with the merger of Bligh Voller Architects, Lawrence Nield and Partners Australia and Grose Bradley. These three prominent firms have brought together a powerful conjunction of design talent and professional expertise. They share the view that good architecture is not style-driven but reflects its region, culture and climate. Bligh Voller Nield is an expanded, enhanced architectural practice positioned to operate competitively throughout Australia and internationally.

This page:

Right: Russell Offices for Department of Defence, Canberra
Photo credit: Rodney Garnett
Bottom right: Ultimo Community & Childcare Centre, Sydney
Photo credit: John Gollings

Opposite page:

Top: Stadium Australia, Sydney
Photo credit: Patrick Bingham Hall
University of Sunshine Coast Library
Photo credit: John Gollings
Children's Hospital Westmead, Sydney
Photo credit: John Gollings
Centre: Stadium Australia, Sydney
Photo credit: courtesy Olympic Coordination Authority
Queensland University of Technology Built Environment Precinct, Brisbane
Photo credit: David Sandison
Bottom: Queensland Clunies Ross Centre, Brisbane
Photo credit: David Sandison

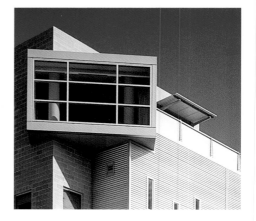

The attitude of the practice toward design is the belief that each commission at any scale is the opportunity to apply fresh ideas, innovative construction solutions and appropriate and human architecture. **Lawrence Nield**

The chief concern of the practice in the design process is understanding at the earliest possible moment the true needs and aspirations of the client. **Jon Voller**

The vigorous positive culture that is right throughout Bligh Voller Nield means that we bring an unmatched enthusiasm to all our projects. **Phillip Tait**

This practice acts very much as a collaborative. We maintain a studio atmosphere, with the emphasis on research and exploring ideas, methods and materials. It comes from a strong idea of the practice of architecture as craft. **Shane Thompson**

Bochsler + Partners Pty Ltd
Architects, Interior Designers, Planners

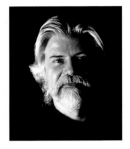

Australia
5 Edward Street
Toorak, Victoria 3142
Tel: +(61 3) 9827 2988
Fax: +(61 3) 9827 2722
E-mail: bochsler@netspace.net.au

Directors
Nicolas Bochsler
Graeme Ingrouille
Michael Rahill

Person to Contact
Nicolas Bochsler

Date of Establishment
1980

Project Types
Civic
Commercial
Conservation
Hospitality
Recreational
Residential

Disciplines
Architecture
Construction
Interior Design
Planning

Current and Recent Projects
Walgaoqiao Authority Headquarters,
  Shanghai, PRC
Shanghai City United Bank,
  Shanghai, PRC
Elf Atochem Administration Building,
  Shanghai, PRC
Jindun Mansions, Chongqing, PRC
Cliff House South Yarra, Melbourne, Australia
House Portsea, Melbourne, Australia
House Cape Schank, Melbourne, Australia
House Brighton, Melbourne, Australia
House Hawthorn, Melbourne, Australia

Design Philosophy and History
Nic Bochsler practised in Europe and Southern
Africa before establishing the company in
Melbourne in 1980. In 1992 Bochsler + Partners
expanded its activities to Shanghai where several
projects have been successfully completed.
Nic Bochsler's work is a continuing exploration
of the forms, light, scale and textures of the
spaces which house people and objects.

1

2

3

1 Exercise pool off main bedroom suite
  Photo credit: Neil Lorimer, Photographer

2 View from terrace through living and dining areas
  Photo credit: Neil Lorimer, Photographer

3 The sweep of views from city skyline, industrial areas
  through to parklands are framed to balance
  proportion of sky and light
  Photo credit: Neil Lorimer, Photographer

Opposite:
House on cliff overlooking Yarra River in Melbourne
Photo credit: Neil Lorimer, Photographer

Botti Rubin Arquitetos

Marc Rubin and Alberto Botti
Photo credit: courtesy Botti Rubin Arquitetos

Brazil
Hungria 888 - 7° Andar
São Paulo 01455-000
Tel: +(5511) 816 1055
Fax: +(5511) 870 8211
E-mail: bra@Bottirubin.com.br

Directors and Associates
Marc Rubin
Alberto Botti
Roberto De Castro Mello

Technical Staff and Architects
Agostino Landsmann
Antonio Dos Reis Noronha
Douglas Benincasa
Eduardo Patricio Suarez
Elzeli Carneiro
Gerson Bilezikjian
Jean Jacques Sendra
Luciana Amador Soto Barreiro
Maria Luisa Becheroni
Mãrio Humberto Guimarães
Mauro Martins
Mirian Butenas
Nilton Ueda
Paul Bringold
Renato Falzeta
Ricardo Hering
Sandro Rogërio Machado
Sërgio Ãlvaro De Oliveira
Sonia Maria Oliveira
Vania Zanocco

Persons to Contact
Marc Rubin
Alberto Botti
Roberto De Castro Mello

Number of Employees
55

Date of Establishment
1956

Project Types
Commercial Buildings
Hospitals
Recreational
Residential
Sport Facility
Shopping Centres
Theatres
Town Planning

Disciplines
Architecture
Town Planning

Current And Recent Projects
Centro Brasileiro Britãnico, São Paulo
Centro Empresarial Naçoes Unidas, São Paulo
Faria Lima Building, São Paulo
Office Tower Building, São Paulo
Shopping Patio Higienopolis, São Paulo

Selected Clients
Bolsa de Imoveis Do Estado De São Paulo
Construtora Better
Construtora Boghosian
Construtora Lider
Petros - Fundaçao Petrobras De Seguridade
  Social
Femco - Fundaçao Cosipa De Seguridade Social
Funcef - Fundaçao Dos Economiarios Federais
Hospital Alemao Oswaldo Cruz
Iguatemi Empresa De Shopping Centers
Imopar Participacoes Imobiliarias
Plaza Shopping Empreendimentos
Hochtief Do Brasil
Metodo Engenharia
Nestle
Racional Engenharia
America Properties
Serplan Desenvolvimento Imobiliario E Comercial
Tishman Speyer Metodo
Sesc Servico Social Do Comercio
Sesi Servico Social Da Industria
Senac Servico Nacional Aprendizagem Comercial

Design Philosophy and History
After working together for 40 years Alberto Botti and Marc Rubin can be proud not only of their long lasting partnership but also of their ample and diversified curriculum.

This curriculum shows an extensive series of programs - private houses, apartment buildings, headquarters for multi-national firms, hospitals, theatres, recreation centres, gymnasiums and a 270,000 square metre complex now being completed in São Paulo. The North Tower of this complex is the highest building in São Paulo and probably in South America.

An aesthetic refinement allied to great daring is evident throughout Botti Rubin's history.

The partnership was established in 1956. From the beginning, there was the clear indication that Botti Rubin was not going to become just another one among the many. Always at the forefront of their field, they were responsible for some of São Paulo's first exposed concrete high-rises. The path established by the firm was subsequently followed by many schools of architecture including tendencies towards brutalism, minimalism and deconstructivism.

Today, the result of a history of evolution of concepts becomes more evident when analyzing the firm's most recent projects. The transport of the stoke to a more advanced concept clearly stands out when looking at the four projects shown in these pages. The permanent use of geometrical forms in volumes of various proportions, along with the elements of rhythm, transparency and reflection applied to the buildings facades, captures the vibration and simultaneity of the current genres.

Globalization and local industry progress have made it possible to meet the challenge brought about by projects of major proportions and complexity so that state of the art technology has been associated with a personal revaluation to make these projects compatible with the most demanding standards in the world.

1 Centro Brasileiro Britanico
2 Centro Empresarial do Aco
3 Edificio River Park
Photo credit: Miguel Francisco Pacheoo E Chaves

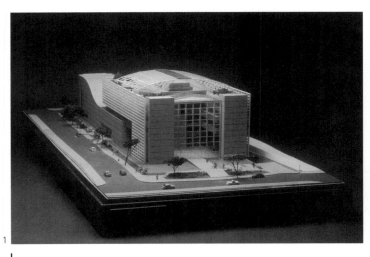

Building Design Partnership
Architects, Engineers and Cost Consultants

UK
BDP, PO Box 4WD
16 Gresse Street
London W1A 4WD
Tel: +(44 20) 7631 4733
Fax: +(44 20) 7631 0393
Website: www.bdp.co.uk

BDP, 5 Blythswood Square
Glasgow G2 4AD
Tel: +(44) 141 226 5291
Fax: +(44) 141 221 0720

BDP, 2 Bruce Street
Belfast BT2 7JD
Tel: +(44) 1232 243 394
Fax: +44 1232 329 337

BDP, PO Box 85
Sunlight House, Quay Street
Manchester M60 3JA
Tel: +(44) 161 834 8441
Fax: +(44) 161 832 4280

BDP, 38 Carver Street
Sheffield S1 4FY
Tel: +(44) 114 273 1641
Fax: +(44) 114 270 1878

Republic of Ireland
BDP Dublin Ltd
116 Lower Baggot Street
Dublin 2
Tel: +(3531) 676 5220
Fax: +(3531) 676 5232

Germany
BDP Gesamtplanung GmbH
Wilhelm-Leuschner Straße 7
60329 Frankfurt/Main
Tel: +(49) 69 2740 460
Fax: +(49) 69 2740 4620

Associate offices in Madrid, Grenoble, Osnabrück

Persons to Contact
Tony McGuirk, London, England
David Cash, Manchester, England
Sandy Fergusson, Glasgow, Scotland
Keith Pavey, Sheffield, England
Norman Bennie, Belfast, Northern Ireland
Donal Friel, Dublin, Republic of Ireland
Tim Williams, Frankfurt/Main, Germany

Project Types
Culture, Leisure & Sport
Education
Healthcare
Housing
Industrial
Offices
Public Buildings
Restoration
Retail
Transportation
Urbanism

Recent Projects (see photographs also)
Royal Albert Hall, London, England
Perth 2000 Arts Centre, Perth, Scotland
New No. 1 Court, Wimbledon, England
NikeTown, London, England
University of Sunderland, England
Hampden Gurney Primary School, London,
  England
Princess Louise Hospital, Erskine, Scotland
Seagate Industries, Limavady, Northern Ireland
Scottish Widows Headquarters, Edinburgh,
  Scotland
Trade Rows of Gum, Moscow, Russia
Marks & Spencer offices and stores including
  London, Manchester and Chester, England
White Rose Shopping Centre, Leeds, England
Via Catarina Centre, Porto, Portugal
Vasco da Gama Centre, Lisbon, Portugal
Channel Tunnel UK Terminal, Folkestone,
  England
City Airport, Belfast, Northern Ireland
CrossRail, London, England

Selected Clients
British Land
BT
Capital Shopping Centres
English Partnerships
Hammerson
Land Securities
Lend Lease
Marks & Spencer
Multi Development Corporation
Prudential
Railtrack
Rodamco
Scottish Widows
Sonae
Standard Life
University of Cambridge

Neptune Court, National Maritime Museum, Greenwich, UK
BDP and Rick Mather Architects
Photo credit: Dennis Gilbert

The Mall, Cribbs Causeway, Bristol, UK
Photo credit: Roger Ball

Glasgow Science Centre, Scotland

Building Design Partnership

Royal Opera House restoration, London, UK
Dixon Jones BDP
Photo credit: Hayes Davidson/Bill Cooper

Design Philosophy

Building Design Partnership was formed in 1961 as a multi-discipline practice of architects, engineers and cost consultants. The firm's goal is to be Europe's leading building design practice, delivering excellence in design and service through partnership. To service international clients BDP International SC has been created, an association of like-minded professionals across Europe, which today embraces 1,100 people.

BDP's philosophy is that design and performance are best when participants work creatively together in multi-disciplinary teams. This integrated approach is valued by clients for being both creative and economically effective. BDP designs are a direct response to the needs of clients and the community; they combine a concern and sensitivity for the environment and the people who live and work in it. Whether the challenge is to design a master plan, streetscape, a building, or an interior, the aim is for quality, appropriateness and added value.

The firm's continuing objectives for the next millennium are to create fine work, appreciated by clients, users, public and peers; and to advance the art of creating the built environment.

Adam Opel Haus, Rüsselsheim, Germany
Photo credit: Dennis Gilbert

Centerbrook
Architects and Planners, LLC

Centerbrook Partners
James C. Childress, William H. Grover,
Jefferson B. Riley, Chad Floyd, Mark Simon
Photo credit: Robert Benson Photography

USA
67 Main Street
PO Box 955
Centerbrook, Connecticut, 06409
Tel: +(1 860) 767 0175
Fax: +(1 860) 767 8719
E-mail: last name@centerbrook.com

Partners
William H. Grover, FAIA
Jefferson B. Riley, FAIA
Mark Simon, FAIA
Chad Floyd, FAIA
James C. Childress, AIA

Principal
James A. Coan, AIA

Number of Employees
78

Date of Establishment
1975

Disciplines
Architecture
Interior Design
Planning
Furniture Design
Light Fixture Design
Urban Design

Current and Recent Projects
Al-Ghurair Center, Dubai, United Arab Emirates
Town Lakes Park Community Events Center, Austin, Texas, USA
Briarwood College Master Plan, Southington, Connecticut, USA
Brooks School Dining Hall, North Andover, Massachusetts, USA
Cold Spring Harbor Laboratory, Imaging Laboratory, Cold Spring Harbor, New York, USA
Cold Spring Harbor Laboratory, Woodbury Sequencing Laboratory, Cold Spring Harbor, New York, USA
Colgate University Art Building, Hamilton, New York, USA
Dartmouth College, Master Plan for the Sciences, Hanover, New Hampshire, USA
First Congregational Church of Battle Creek, Battle Creek, Michigan, USA
Garde Arts Center, New London, Connecticut, USA
Heckscher Museum of Art, Huntington, Long Island, USA

Institute of Ecosystem Studies, New Research Laboratory, Millbrook, New York, USA
Jillson Hill Bridge, Windham, Connecticut, USA
Manchester Community-Technical College, Center for the Arts, Sciences and Applied Technology, Manchester, Connecticut, USA
Mark Twain Library, Redding, Connecticut, USA
Metropolitan Memorial United Methodist Church, Washington, DC, USA
MIT Center for Advanced Visual Studies, Cambridge, Massachusetts, USA
Nortel Networks Customer Briefing Center, Raleigh, North Carolina, USA
The Parrish Art Museum, Southampton, New York, USA
Phillips Exeter Academy, Science Classroom and Laboratory Building, Exeter, New Hampshire, USA
Quinnipiac College, Library, Hamden, Connecticut, USA
Simon's Rock Athletic Center and Library, Great Barrington, Massachusetts, USA
Stepping Stones Museum for Children, Norwalk, Connecticut, USA
Trudeau Institute, Immunology Laboratory, Saranac Lake, New York, USA
United Church of Christ World Headquarters Hotel and Sanctuary, Cleveland, Ohio, USA
University of Connecticut, Chemistry Building, Storrs, Connecticut, USA
University of Connecticut, School of Business Administration, Storrs, Connecticut, USA
University of Nebraska Ross Film Theater and Van Brunt Visitors Center, Lincoln, Nebraksa, USA
Worcester Railroad Bridge, Worcester, Massachusetts, USA
Yale Child Study Center, New Haven, Connecticut, USA
Yale University Dunham Laboratories, Yale Faculty of Engineering, New Haven, Connecticut, USA
Over 14 Single-Family Residences in Design or Recently Completed

Design Philosophy and History
Centerbrook has 27 years experience in architecture and planning. Located in a renovated factory on the Falls River in the rural town of Centerbrook, Connecticut, it has five partners and an overall staff of 78.

The firm's approach is distinctly American—its work is eclectic and its methods democratic. At the same time, Centerbrook has received over 170 awards for design excellence, including seven national AIA Honor Awards for a variety of projects. These range from highly crafted private residences and furniture to evocative institutional complexes and fully implemented city plans. In 1998, Centerbrook was named recipient of the National AIA Firm Award, the highest honour the AIA can confer on a firm.

Centerbrook pioneered large scale participatory design with users. Starting with six live, call-in TV 'Design-athons' planning Dayton, Ohio's riverfront in 1976, the firm has gone on to conceive 80 master plans, campuses, and buildings, collaborating with user and owner groups in programming and design.

The firm's work has been the focus of 250 articles and books and is the subject of the AIA Press book, by Michael Crosbie, *CENTERBROOK Reinventing American Architecture*, and a second book written by Andrea Oppenheimer Dean, *CENTERBROOK, Volume 2*.

Selected Recent Design Awards
American Institute of Architects, Architecture Firm Award, 1998
Quinnipiac College School of Law Library, AIA/ALA Award of Excellence, 1999
New Hearth Showroom, AIA Honor Award for Interiors, 1998
Pfizer Plant Master Plan, Pfizer USA Pharmaceutical Group, AIA New England Design Award, 1997
Metropolitan Home, Design 100 Hall of Fame, 1997
Shapiro Admissions Center, Brandeis University, AIA New England Design Award, 1996
McClintock Laboratory, Cold Spring Harbor Laboratory, AIA New England Design Award, 1995
Main Gate, Pfizer US Pharmaceutical Group, AIA New England Design Award, 1995
House in the Country, AIA Honor Award for Interiors, 1993
Reid House, New England Regional Council/AIA Design Award, 1992
Buchanan Residence, New England Regional Council/AIA Design Award, 1992
Architectural Digest's AD 100, List of Top 100 Architects, 1991
House in the Connecticut Hills, New England Regional Council/AIA Design Awards, 1990
McKim House, New England Regional Council/AIA Design Award, 1990
Wriston Art Center, Lawrence University, New England Regional Council/AIA Design Award, 1989
Watkins Glen Pier Pavilion, AIA Honor Award for Architecture, 1989
Watkins Glen Waterfront, AIA Honor Award for Urban Design, 1988
Hood Museum of Art, Dartmouth College, AIA Honor Award for Architecture, 1987
Jones Laboratory of Neurobiology, Cold Spring Harbor Laboratory, AIA Honor Award for Architecture, 1981

1 Miller House, Massachusetts, USA
   Photo credit: Jeff Goldberg/ESTO

2 Main Gate, Pfizer US Pharmaceuticals, Groton,
   Connecticut, USA
   Photo credit: Jeff Goldberg/ESTO

3 Lender School of Business Center, Quinnipiac
   College, Hamden, Connecticut, USA
   Photo credit: Jeff Goldberg/ESTO

4 Island House, New England Island, USA
   Photo credit: Jeff Goldberg/ESTO

5 Diebolt Offices, Old Lyme, Connecticut, USA
   Photo credit: Jeff Goldberg/ESTO

Cesar Pelli & Associates

Cesar Pelli, FAIA; Rafael Pelli, AIA; Fred W. Clarke, FAIA
Photo credit: Tracey Kroll

USA
1056 Chapel Street
New Haven CT 06510
Tel: +(1 203) 777 2515
Fax: +(1 203) 787 2856
E-mail: mailroom@cesar-pelli.com
Website: www.cesar-pelli.com

Cesar Pelli established the firm in New Haven, Connecticut in 1977 following his appointment as Dean of the School of Architecture at Yale University and after an already distinguished architectural career. Fred Clarke has been a Principal in the firm since 1981 and Rafael Pelli since 1993.

Cesar Pelli & Associates is a full service architectural practice of some 80 persons. The firm has worked with corporate, government and private clients to design major public spaces, museums, airports, laboratories, performing arts centres, academic buildings, hotels, office and residential towers and mixed-use projects. The number of commissions the firm accepts is carefully limited to ensure a high degree of personal involvement by the Principals.

Cesar Pelli & Associates seeks to produce the best possible building for each circumstance. The work of Cesar Pelli is not constrained by a personal style or a signature that would limit his architecture; instead, it tries to celebrate the unique characteristics of each project. With this approach, the firm has designed several exceptional buildings in the US and abroad. These projects have included the Museum of Modern Art Expansion and Renovation and the World Financial Center, both in New York City; Canary Wharf Tower and Docklands Light Railway Station in London; North Carolina Blumenthal Performing Arts Center in Charlotte; Frances Lehman Loeb Art Center at Vassar College; Aronoff Center for the Arts in Cincinnati; NTT Headquarters Building in Tokyo; Petronas Towers and Dewan Filharmonik Hall in Kuala Lumpur; and, currently under construction, the National Museum of Contemporary Art in Osaka, Japan.

The American Institute of Architects awarded Cesar Pelli the 1995 Gold Medal, which recognizes a lifetime of distinguished achievement and outstanding contributions. In 1989, it awarded Cesar Pelli & Associates its Firm Award in recognition of standard setting work in architectural design.

Concourse, Terminal B/C, Washington National Airport, USA
Photo credit: Jeff Goldberg/ESTO

View from Potomac River, Terminal B/C, Washington National Airport, USA
Photo credit: Jeff Goldberg/ESTO

Petronas Towers, Kuala Lumpur, Malaysia
Photo credit: Jeff Goldberg/ESTO

Chen Shi Min Architects Ltd

Chen Shi Min
Photo credit: courtesy Chen Shi Min Architects Ltd

Hong Kong
17/F Park Avenue Tower
5 Moreton Terrace
Causeway Bay, Hong Kong
Tel: +(852) 2886 0401
Fax: +(852) 2885 7349
E-mail: caarchitects@ctimail.com

P.R. China
31/F Dian zi Technology Building, Tower C
2070 Shennan Avenue
Shenzhen, P.R. China 518031
Tel: +(86 755) 368 3998
Fax: +(86 755) 368 3856
E-mail: caarch@public.szptt.net.cn

Directors
Chen Shi Min
Hon Lam
Chen Ting
Chen Liang

Person to Contact
Chen Ting, Deputy General Manager

Number of Employees
30

Project Profile
Urban design and master planning
Multi-function building complex with banking,
 office, hotel, residential and retails
Commercial and public buildings
High-rise residential

Disciplines
Architectural design
Design documentation
City planning
Project management and consultancy

Recent Projects
Shenzhen New Downtown Urban Design
Shajing Town Urban Design
Shenzhen Futian Residential Development of
 Huchison Whampoa
Shenye Garden Residential Design, Futian
 Shenzhen
Oriental Rose Garden, Shenzhen
Taizheng Garden, Chongqing
Shanghai Pingan Plaza, Shanghai
IBM ITP Manufacturing Facility, Futian FTZ
 Shenzhen

Selected Clients
Shenzhen Urban Planning & Land
 Administration Bureau
Hutchison Whampoa Properties Ltd.
Henderson (China) Investment Co. Ltd.
Shum Yip Holdings (Shenzhen) Co. Ltd.
Shajing Town Government
China Ping An Trust & Investment Company
IBM
Ove Arup & Partners Hong Kong Ltd.

Design Philosophy and History
Chen Shi Min, Design Master of China since 1994, has been at the forefront of architectural design for over 40 years. His unique innovative and pre-eminent design has been well-recognized in both China and overseas. In order to further his success and meet increasing demands for high quality architecture, a new specialized practice with a group of talented designers was formed in 1996 called Chen Shi Min Architects Ltd. (CA).

Over the past three years, CA has successfully secured the first class license from the Chinese government to practice both in China and Hong Kong. Due to the company's excellent design and quality services, CA has been successfully expanding its business activities to other regions across Mainland China.

CA provides diversified architectural services to its clients with a range of design skills. To date, its major projects have included urban design and master planning, design and design development for commercial and public buildings, large-scale multi-function building complexes for banking, hotel, office, residential and retail. CA also provides a range of architectural project consultancy and management to various departments of Chinese government as well as to domestic and international clients.

CA's mission is to apply Chinese and Western design philosophy and methodologies to create architecture with unique language as well as maintain international standards of high quality, building efficiency and cost effectiveness.

1

2

3

4

5

6

1 Shajing Town Urban Design
   Photo credit: courtesy Chen Shi Min Architects Ltd
2 Pinan Plaza
   Photo credit: courtesy Chen Shi Min Architects Ltd
3 Oriental Rose Garden
   Photo credit: courtesy Chen Shi Min Architects Ltd
4 New World Plaza
   Photo credit: courtesy Chen Shi Min Architects Ltd
5 Shen Ye Gorden
   Photo credit: courtesy Chen Shi Min Architects Ltd
6 Futian Residential Development of Hutchison
   Whampoa
   Photo credit: courtesy Chen Shi Min Architects Ltd

CJN Architects
Architects & Planners

Eero Valtiala, Juhani Jauhiainen, Kari Somma

Finland
Head Office
Tietäjäntie 4
Espoo 02130
Tel: +(358 9) 435 5300
Fax: +(358 9) 455 0986
E-mail: cjnarchitects@cjn.fi

Germany
Architecten CJN & Partners
Breite Strasse 37
Berlin 14199
Tel: +(49 30) 8909 2597
Fax: +(49 30) 8909 2598

Directors
Juhani Jauhiainen, M.Arch., SAFA
Kari Somma, M.Arch., SAFA
Eero Valtiala, M.Arch., SAFA
(SAFA: Association of Finnish Architects)

Persons to Contact
Juhani Jauhiainen
Kari Somma
Eero Valtiala

Number of Employees
14

Date of Establishment
1972

Project Types
Administration and Office Buildings
Congress Centre Design
Headquarters
Hospital Design
Hotel Design
Housing Areas
Schools
Shopping Centres
Stations and Terminals
Underground Spaces

Disciplines
Architecture
Interior Design
Renovation
Urban Planning

Current and Recent Projects
Hotel Inter-Continental, renovation, Helsinki,
   Finland
Hotel Marski, renovation, Helsinki, Finland
Jyväskylä Pavilion, Fair and Congress Centre,
   Jyväskylä, Finland
Jyväskylä Legal and Police Headquarters,
   extension and renovation, Jyväskylä, Finland
Neste Oy State Oil Company Headquarters,
   Espoo, Finland

1

Päijät-Häme Bank Headquarters and Shopping
   Centre, Lahti, Finland
Varma-Sampo Insurance Company Headquarters
   and Commercial Building, renovation, Helsinki,
   Finland
Congress Hall Complex, Sirt, Libya
Leisure and Training Centre, Darino, Russia
Vnesheconombank Headquarters, renovation,
   phase I, Moscow, Russia
NICE National Insurance Company Headquarters
   and Shopping Complex, Addis Ababa, Ethiopia

Selected Clients
The National Board of Building, Finland
The Association of Finnish Cities
Towns of Espoo, Jyväskylä, Helsinki
Pohjola Insurance Company
Neste Oy State Oil Company
Varma-Sampo Insurance Company
Merita Bank Plc.
Oy Nokia Ab
Nordic Hotels Ltd (Inter-Continental)
Scandic Hotels
The Industrialization Fund of Finland Ltd

Hewlett Packard Oy, Switzerland/Finland
Shell Company, Holland/Finland
Skanska Oy Construction Company, Sweden/
   Finland
Vnesheconombank, Moscow, Russia
NICE National Insurance Company, Ethiopia
NCB, National Consulting Bureau, Libya

Design Philosophy and History
With 30 years of ambitious architectural work,
CJN Architects have become part of the history
of modern Finnish architecture.

The design philosophy respected by all
associates has been developing during the
long process of working together: the essence
of all architectural endeavours must be striving
for high-class, aesthetically long-lasting quality,
based on confidence, where a perfect result is
gained through keen cooperation,
understanding and esteeming the client's
views. The firm's work can be characterized
by this attitude.

2

Throughout the firm's history, the designers have been trusted with large scale projects by the same clients, states, cities, banks, insurance companies, and more recently, in larger quantities by the hotel owning companies.

Following our clients' growing interest in historic building renovation, but also thanks to CJN Architects' earlier successful conservation and renovation projects, the office has recently been working in some of the most central blocks of Helsinki, renovating the prestigious buildings of Hotel Marski and Varma-Sampo Insurance Company, both of great importance for the Helsinki city character.

Studying and learning through design competitions has always been an essential part of the office's work, with many of the firm's most interesting projects resulting from winning proposals at architectural competitions in both Finland and abroad.

Projects of CJN Architects have been published widely in Europe, the United States, Japan, Saudi Arabia and Australia.

3

4

5

6

1 Päijät-Häme Bank Headquarters and Shopping Centre, Lahti, invited competition, first prize
Photo credit: Simo Rista

2 Neste Oy State Oil Company Headquarters and Extension Building, Espoo, Finland
Photo credit: Juhani Jauhiainen

3&4 Sirt Congress Hall Complex, Libya, invited competition, first prize
Photo credit: Jussi Tiainen

5 Hotel Inter-Continental Helsinki; renovation of 155 hotel rooms, interior architecture G.A. International Ltd, London
Photo credit: Voitto Niemelä

6 Jyväskylä Pavilion, Fair and Congress Centre; renovation of the existing fair spaces and congress centre new design, in conjunction with local architect Pekka Paavola Architects
Photo credit: Voitto Niemelä

Coop Himmelb(l)au
Wolf D. Prix, Helmut Swiczinsky

Austria
Zelinkagasse 2/5
Vienna A-1010
Tel: +(43 1) 532 5535
Fax: +(43 1) 532 5539
E-mail: chbl@aon.at

Directors
Wolf D. Prix
Helmut Swiczinsky

Associates
Frank Stepper
Sepp Weichenberger

Number of Employees
30

Date of Establishment
1968

Current and Recent Projects
Apartment Building Remise, Vienna 2, Austria, (1994–99)
Apartment Building Gasometer, Vienna 11, Austria, (1995–99)
SEG Apartment Tower, Vienna 22, Austria, (1994–1998)
UFA-Cinema Center, Dresden, Germany, (1993–1998)
Biennale-Pavilion, Biennale 95, Venice, Italy, (1995)
Research and Office Centre Seibersdorf, Seibersdorf, Austria, (1991–95)
Groninger Museum, East Pavilion, Groningen, the Netherlands, (1993–94)
Installation L'Object', Centre Pompidou, Paris, France, (1992)
Video Clip Folly, Groningen, the Netherlands, (1990)

Design Philosophy and History
Coop Himmelb(l)au was founded in 1968 in Vienna, Austria, by Wolf D. Prix and Helmut Swiczinsky and continues to work since then in the fields of architecture, design and art. In 1988, Coop Himmelb(l)au opened a second studio in Los Angeles, California.

Coop Himmelb(l)au has realized projects which range from remodelling, in Vienna to city planning projects in France. The most recognized projects are the Rooftop Remodelling in Vienna, Austria, the master plan for the city of Melun-Sénart in France and the Museum Pavilion in Groningen, Netherlands. In March 1998 the UFA-Cinema Center, a multi-functional cinema, was opened in Dresden, Germany. The 'SEG Apartment Tower' in Vienna, Austria, was completed in summer 1998.

Coop Himmelb(l)au is working on international projects in Germany, the Netherlands, France, the United States, Japan and Mexico. During the last five years Coop Himmelb(l)au received numerous awards including a recognition at the German Architecture Award 1999 and the Architekturpreis 1999 Beton (Architectural Award 1999 Concrete, Germany). Coop Himmelb(l)au is a member of the European Academy of Sciences and Arts.

Currently in planning are numerous projects including a complex in Hamburg (Hamburg Double Cone), a multi-functional office and educational center, multi-functional housing projects in Vienna (Apartment Building Gasometer Simmering and Apartment Building Remise) as well as exhibition designs and set

designs. In Guadalajara, Mexico, Coop Himmelb(l)au is planning a cinema and entertainment center as part of the JVC-Center and for the Expo 2001 they are creating the Arteplage in Biel, Switzerland.

The works of Coop Himmelb(l)au have been shown in many international exhibitions. Among them a solo retrospective at the Centre Georges Pomidou in Paris, France, and the Deconstructivist Architecture show at the Museum of Modern Art, New York, curated by Philip Johnson. In 1996, Coop Himmelb(l)au was invited as the Austrian representative to participate at the Sixth International Architecture Exhibition-Biennale in Venice. In 1998 the recent works of the team were presented at the gallery Aedes East in Berlin.

1

1–5
Views of the SEG Apartment Tower
Photo credit: Gerald Zugmann (2); Anna Blau (1,3–5)

2

3

4

5

The Cox Group Pty Ltd

Australia

Head Office
Cox Richardson Architects and Planners
Level 2, 204 Clarence Street
Sydney NSW 2000
Tel: +(61 2) 9267 9599
Fax: +(61 2) 9264 5844
E-mail: sydney@cox.com.au

Cox Rayner Architects and Planners
2 Edward Street
Brisbane Qld 4000
Tel: +(61 7) 3210 0844
Fax: +(61 7) 3210 0541
E-mail: brisbane@cox.com.au

Cox Sanderson Ness Architects and Planners
Level 3, 107-109 Flinders Lane
Melbourne Vic 3000
Tel: +(61 3) 9650 3288
Fax: +(61 3) 9650 2747
E-mail: melbourne@cox.com.au

Cox Howlett & Bailey Woodland Architects and Planners
61-65 King Street
Perth WA 6000
Tel: +(61 8) 9322 3644
Fax: +(61 8) 9322 1664
E-mail: perth@cox.com.au

Cox Humphries Moss Architects and Planners
22 Jardine Street
Canberra ACT 6200
Tel: +(61 8) 9322 1664
Fax: +(61 8) 6239 6260
E-mail: canberra@cox.com.au

Singapore

The Cox Group International
46B Tras Street
Singapore 078985
Tel: +(65) 226 2766
Fax: +(65) 324 3411
E-mail: singapore@cox.com.au

Contacts

Philip Cox, Sydney
Murray Etherington, Perth
Michael Rayner, Brisbane
Patrick Ness, Melbourne
Liu Kah Tek, Singapore

Number of Employees

200

Date of Establishment

1967 as Philip Cox & Partners
1996 re-titled The Cox Group

Project Types

Aquatic Centres
Casinos
Civic
Commercial
Cultural
Educational
Exhibition/Convention
Health
Heritage

Hotels and Resorts
Law and Order
Leisure
Public Buildings
Research/Technology
Residential
Sports and Recreation
Tourist Facilities
Transport

Disciplines

Architecture
Heritage Design
Interior Design
Master Planning
Urban Design

Selected Clients

Lend Lease
Leighton
Multiplex
Walker Corporation Ltd
Federal Government
State Government
Local Government

Current and Recent Projects

Star City, Pyrmont, NSW, Australia (as Cox/Hillier), 1997
New Sydney Showground, Homebush Bay, NSW, Australia (as CPTC), 1998
Eureka Stockade Interpretive Centre, Ballarat, Victoria, Australia, 1998
Asian Games Main Stadium and Aquatic Centre, Bangkok, Thailand, 1998
Singapore Expo, Changi, Singapore, 1999
Sydney SuperDome, Homebush Bay, NSW, Australia, 1999
Museum of Tropical Queensland, Townsville, Queensland, Australia, Current
No. 1 Figtree Drive, Homebush Bay, NSW, Australia, 1999
Cypress Lakes Resort, Pokolbin, Hunter Valley, NSW, Australia, Current
Theiss Headquarters, Brisbane, Queensland, Australia, Current
Hackett Hall, WA Museum, Perth, WA, Australia, Current
Midwest Museum, Geraldton, WA, Australia, Current
ABC Television Studios, Ultimo, Sydney, NSW, Australia, Current
King Street Wharf, Darling Harbour, NSW, Australia (with Crone Associates), Current
National Wine Centre, Adelaide, SA, Australia, Current
Princess Alexandra Hospital, Brisbane, Queensland, (as CoxMSJ), Current
CSIRO Research Complex, North Ryde, NSW, Australia, Current

Design Philosophy and History

Beginning as Philip Cox & Partners in 1966, the Cox Group has offices throughout Australia and in Singapore, and has a reputation for providing innovative architectural responses to regional contexts. Buildings designed by architects of the Cox Group embody the principles of the Australian vernacular architecture with its direct response to climate, its integration of structure and form, and its intrinsic relationship between building and landscape.

The Cox Group's reputation internationally has been established through major awards such as the inaugural IOC Olympic Award and the Sir Robert Matthew Award for Innovative Architecture in Commonwealth countries, and their work is represented by projects in Venice, Durban and throughout southeast Asia.

The Cox Group is perceived as one of the most prominent of Australia's architectural firms from both a national and international perspective. The reputation of the practice has been largely earned from its large scale structures such as convention and exhibition centres and its Olympic and other major sports venues, but it is one of only a few international firms with significant projects of every type and scale to its credit.

1

2

3

4

5

1 Interior view, Asian Games Aquatic Centre, Bangkok,
Thailand
Photo credit: Graham Sands

2 Eureka Stockade Interpretive Centre, Ballarat,
Australia
Photo credit: Patrick Bingham-Hall

3 Asian Games Main Stadium, Bangkok, Thailand
Photo credit: Graham Sands

4 Maritime Museum, Fremantle, Australia
Photo credit: Graham Sands

5 Singapore Expo Exhibition and Convention Centre,
Changi, Singapore
Photo credit: Graham Sands

Daryl Jackson Architecture
Master Planners and Interior Designers

Australia

Daryl Jackson Pty Ltd
35 Little Bourke Street
Melbourne, Victoria 3000
Tel: +(61 3) 9662 3022
Fax: +(61 3) 9663 5239
E-mail:
djmelb@daryljackson.com.au

Daryl Jackson Pty Ltd Architects
212 Boundary Street
Springhill, QLD 4000
Tel: +(61 7) 3832 0666
Fax: +(61 7) 3832 0676
E-mail:
djbris@qld.daryljackson.com.au

Daryl Jackson
Alastair Swayn Pty Ltd
49 Jardine Street
Kingston, ACT 2604
Tel: +(61 2) 6295 2000
Fax: +(61 2) 6295 0964
E-mail: djas@spirit.com.au

Daryl Jackson
Robin Dyke Pty Ltd Architects
64 Rose Street
Chippendale, NSW 2008
Tel: +(61 2) 9319 2955
Fax: +(61 2) 9698 1116
E-mail: djrd@s054.aone.net.au

UK

Jackson Architecture International Limited
Broadcourt
43 Drury Lane
London WC 2b 5RT
Tel: +(44 171) 497 2212
Fax: +(44 171) 497 2330
E-mail: architect@djiuk.demon.co.uk

Germany

Jackson Architecture International Limited
Charlottenstrasse.95
Berlin 10969
Tel: + (49 30) 2529 7864
Fax: + (49 30) 2529 7865
E-mail: djb@berlin.snafu.de

Directors

Daryl Jackson AO (Principal)
Alastair Swayn
Bill Ryan
Bill Sydlik
Bob Sinclair
David Trott
Lyndon Hayward
Peter Quigley
Peter Cole
Robin Dyke
Tim Jackson

Associate Directors

Gary Carter
Jonathan Gardiner
Lincoln Barker
Mark Roehrs
Philip Chadwick

Associates

Sara Jackson
Andrew Hipwell
Manfred Lobert

Number of Employees

150

Date of Establishment

1965

Project Types

Commercial Architecture: Offices
Education: Schools and Universities
Health: Hospitals and Health Centres
Masterplanning: City and Institutional
Public Architecture: Libraries, Arts and Museums
Retail
Sports Architecture: Stadia, Recreation and
  Lifestyle
Tourism: Hotels and Hospitality

Current and Recent Projects

Cannon's Gymnasium, London, UK
Pyrmont Housing, Sydney, Australia
Conservatorium of Music, Sydney, Australia
Cedars' Health Club, Richmond, London, UK
Australian Ambassador's Residence,
  Berlin, Germany
Melbourne University Masterplan, Australia
University of Northern Territory Masterplan,
  Australia
Couran Cove Resort, Stradbroke Island,
  Queensland, Australia
C.S.I.R.O. Plant Services Research/Discovery
  Centre, Canberra, Australia
Colonial Stadium, Melbourne, Australia
Royal Prince Alfred Hospital, Sydney, Australia
Royal Brisbane Hospital, Brisbane, Australia
Western Australian Police Academy, Perth,
  Australia
Old Customs House, Museum of Immigration,
  Melbourne, Australia
Georges Redevelopment, Melbourne, Australia
School of Business, University of Melbourne,
  Australia
School of Management, Swinburne University of
  Technology, Melbourne, Australia
Woollangabba Cricket Ground, Brisbane,
  Australia

Selected Clients

Sydney Organising Committee for the Olympic
  Games (SOCOG)
Australian Institute of Sport
Australian Department of Foreign Affairs and
  Trade
Brisbane Cricket Ground Trust
New South Wales Department of Works &
  Services
Australian National University
Wesley College
Methodist Ladies College
Commonwealth Scientific and Industrial
  Research Organisation
Menzies Centre for Medical Research
Queensland Health Department
Lend Lease Corporation
Kosciuszko Thredbo Pty Ltd
LEG Brandenburg, Germany

Design Philosophy and History

Daryl Jackson is an influential Australian
Architect whose work has earned him
distinguished awards both in his own country
and abroad.

Over the past 30 years the originality and
diversity of his designs for large-scale projects in
education, sport, commerce and housing have
earned him an international reputation.

Daryl Jackson's offices see architecture as a
visionary design medium and as a problem
solving discipline. Architectural talent,
philosophic and technical, caring and sensible,
imaginative and operational, is always necessary.

Designers work in a host of different ways;
imagining and correlating, reviewing, and
dismissing the unwanted, to further develop
those images that offer the most significant
prospects. Design only reaches fruition when the
user requirements work with the desired images
to consolidate the compositional expression and
form.

Daryl Jackson's office consults openly and
equitably; the client is a vital component of the
team, so too may be the project manager, the
contractor and of course other significant
consultants and design disciplines. All work is

undertaken by a Director or an Associate, and
teams are assembled to enable the leaders to
remain with the project until completion.

Daryl Jackson works in collaboration with other
architects. As an international practice he
understands the need to pursue local objectives
in legal, technical, heritage and planning
matters. Requisite specialist talents are engaged
wherever a project is to be constructed, simply
to ensure as smooth a passage as possible into
the field. Much of the work involves estate
management and feasibility; cost planning (both
capital and recurrent) and of understanding the
environmental content and context.

Daryl Jackson travels widely and retains a critical
watching eye on all aspects of design. The
success of the practice may be found in the
design principles established by him.

Seeing design as a process of exploration and
resolution, the working method is propositional;
formal ideas are developed for discussion with
clients and relevant authorities; evaluation and
testing is welcomed as a fundamental part of
the process; other ideas may emerge before real
synthesis can occur. This way of working ensures
that a particular identity is established for each
project.

1

1&4 Masterplan proposal, Mukim, Tebrau, Johor
    Darul Takzin, Malaysia
    Photo credit: Daryl Jackson Pty Ltd Architects,
    AbRAZ Arkitek

2 120 Collins Street, Melbourne, Australia
   Photo credit: Daryl Jackson Pty Ltd Architects,
   Hassell Pty Ltd

3 Great Southern Stand, Melbourne Cricket
   Ground, Melbourne, Australia
   Photo credit: Daryl Jackson Pty Ltd Architects,
   Thomkins Shaw + Evans Pty Ltd

5 Colonial Stadium, Docklands, Melbourne,
   Australia
   Photo credit: Daryl Jackson, Bligh Lobb Sports
   Architecture Pty Ltd

2

3

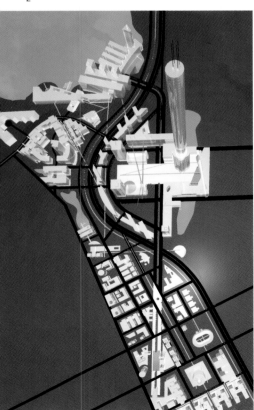

4

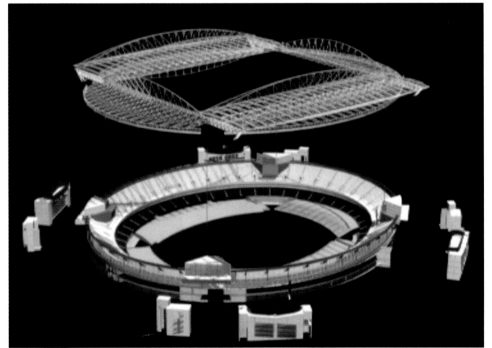

5

David M. Schwarz/Architectural Services, Inc.

USA

Suite 800
1133 Connecticut Avenue, NW
Washington, DC 20036
Tel: +(1 202) 862 0777
Fax: +(1 202) 331 0507
E-mail: info@dmsas.com

600 Texas Commerce Bank Tower
201 Main Street
Fort Worth, Texas 76102
Tel: +(1 817) 339 1133

Persons to Contact
David M. Schwarz
Thomas H. Greene

Project Types
Arenas/Convention Centres
Commercial/Offices
Healthcare
Hospitality
Residential
Retail

Current and Recent Projects
Nancy Lee and Perry R. Bass Performance Hall,
  Fort Worth, Texas, USA
American Airlines Center Arena, Dallas, Texas,
  USA
Yale Environmental Sciences Building,
  New Haven, Connecticut, USA
Severance Hall Restoration and Addition,
  Cleveland, Ohio, USA
National Cowgirl Museum and Hall of Fame,
  Fort Worth, Texas, USA
Southlake Town Center, Southlake, Texas, USA

Selected Clients
The Cleveland Orchestra
Performing Arts Fort Worth
Texas Rangers Ball Club
CarrAmerica
Cook Children's Medical Center

Design Philosophy and History
David M. Schwarz/Architectural Services, Inc. is
a Washington, DC based design firm established
in 1976 with a second office in Fort Worth,
Texas.

The design-oriented firm emphasizes
architecture as both a service and an art.
Designs must interpret and positively impact the
built environment. They must satisfy the client's
desire for excellence that will inspire people and
be spoken of positively. Pragmatically, they must
work for all users and be affordable to build.

A healthy respect for the past is a key to
understanding the present and helps define
directions for the future. David M. Schwarz/
Architectural Services is deeply committed to
historic preservation. While the majority of the
firm's work is new construction, a substantial
amount involves historic structures, landmark
buildings and historic districts. Design solutions
include accurate restorations, adaptive reuse,
facade preservation, and sympathetic,
contextual, new construction.

Designs must relate both to the occupants and
to the passive users, those who pass by the
building daily, by creating a human scale
enriched through an appropriate level of detail
and the juxtaposition of a broad palette of
ornament and material.

With the belief that a good design firm can
design any building type, the projects of David
M. Schwarz/Architectural Services encompasses
a broad range of building types.

1

2

3

4

5

6

7

1 Office space for an investment firm, Washington, DC, USA
  Photo credit: Hedrich–Blessing

2 1718 Connecticut Avenue, an office building, Washington, DC, USA
  Photo credit: Fred Sons

3 Entry facade, Cook Children's Medical Center, Fort Worth, Texas, USA
  Photo credit: Hedrich–Blessing

4 1133 Connecticut Avenue, an office building, Washington, DC, USA
  Photo credit: Hedrich–Blessing

5 Interior stairway, Sundance 11 AMC Cinemas, Fort Worth, Texas, USA
  Photo credit: Hedrich–Blessing

6 Penthouse apartment, Washington, DC, USA
  Photo credit: Hedrich–Blessing

7 Nancy Lee and Perry R. Bass Performance Hall, Fort Worth, Texas, USA
  Photo credit: Hedrich–Blessing

8 Home Plate entrance, The Ballpark in Arlington, Texas, USA
  Photo credit: Hedrich–Blessing

8

Development Design Group, Inc.

USA
7 St. Paul Street
Baltimore, Maryland, 21202
Tel: +(1 410) 962 0505
Fax: +(1 410) 783 0816
E-mail: ddg@ddg-usa.com

Directors
Roy H. Higgs, CEO
John B. Clark, President
Ahsin Rasheed, Senior Vice President
Michial C. Alston, Vice President
James P. Andreone, Vice President

Number of Employees
95

Date of Establishment
1979

Disciplines
Architecture
Graphics
Interior Design
Landscape Design
Planning
Urban Design

Design Philosophy and History
Development Design Group is an international
architecture, planning and design firm with a
history of achievements that span the globe.
The firm is a world leader in the creation of
high profile, high quality environments and has
received over 60 international design awards in
the last decade. Development Design Group's
multi-disciplinary interactive approach to
planning and design allows the team to create
places that are economically successful,
integrated with their surroundings,
architecturally harmonious and culturally
attuned to the lifestyles of clients and their
customers.

PLANNING
RETAIL
ENTERTAINMENT
TOWN CENTRES
MIXED USE
HOSPITALITY
GRAPHICS

1 Easton Town Center, Columbus, Ohio, USA
  Photo credit: Development Design Group, Inc.

2 CocoWalk, Miami, Florida, USA
  Photo credit: Forrer

3 Dubai Blue Coast, Dubai, United Arab Emirates
  Photo credit: Development Design Group, Inc.

4 Urban Development, Jakarta, Indonesia
  Photo credit: Development Design Group, Inc.

5 Muvico 'Drive-In', Pompano Beach, Florida, USA
  Photo credit: Development Design Group, Inc.

6 Holiday Inn Bali Hai, Bali Indonesia
  Photo credit: Development Design Group, Inc.

7 Muvico 'Paradise 24', Davie, Florida, USA
  Photo credit: Muvico Theaters

منتزه مواجهة للبحر
BEACHFRONT PROMENADE

جزيرة الخيال
FANTASY ISLAND

منارة الرأس
LIGHTHOUSE TOWER

R A B I A N   G U L F

3

4

POMPANO
Beach

Arcade
Videos
Games

MOTEL

5

6

MUVICO 24

7

Durbach Block Murcutt
Architecture; Urban Design

Australia
Level 3, 441 Kent Street
Sydney, NSW 2000
Tel: +(612) 9261 3941
Fax: +(612) 9261 2207
E-mail: neild@ozemail.com.au

Persons to Contact
Neil Durbach
Camilla Block
Nicholas Murcutt

Project Types
Institutional
Interior Design
Landscape Architecture
Residential
Urban Design

Selected Recent Projects
Building 3 – 36 apartments, community hall and
  commercial development, Sydney
Hunters Hill House, Sydney
Foster Street Apartments, Sydney
RMIT Student Housing, Melbourne

Featured Project
Four Amenities Buildings for the Olympic
Co-ordination Authority, Homebush Bay, Sydney

Project Team
Neil Durbach, Camilla Block, Nicholas Murcutt,
Joseph Grech, David Jaggers, Lisa Le Van,
James McGrath, Jenny Grigg

Competitions
Winning urban design proposals include:
Headquarters for The Royal Australian Institute
  of Architects, Sydney with Harold Levine
RMIT Student Housing, Melbourne
Civic Centre for Council of Wagga Wagga
Overseas Passenger Terminal Competition
Honeysuckle Housing Ideas Competition,
  Newcastle
Model Urban Housing, St Clair
Rocks Square Competition, Sydney
South Sydney Ideas Competition, Bicentennial
  Travelling Exhibition
Cronulla Main Street and Mall
First Government House Tower competition with
  JTCW and SOM (USA)

Publications
(inside) magazine; *The Australian*; *Architecture
Australia*; *Architecture B* (Denmark); *The
Architecture Bulletin*; *Architecture Now*
(Craftsman Press); *Australian Architecture
Review*; *Australian Houses* (Thames & Hudson -
UK); *Belle*; *Betoni* (Finland); *Blueprint* (United
Kingdom); *Casa Viva* (Italy) *Document*; *Durbach
Block, The Luminous Space of Abstraction*
(Pesaro Press); *Financial Review Magazine*; *HQ
Magazine*; *Guide to Sydney Architecture*
(Watermark Publications); *Houses*; *The
Independent Magazine* (UK); *Interior
Architecture*; *Monument*; *Newsweek Bulletin*;
New Australia Style (Thames & Hudson);
Olympic Architecture Building Sydney 2000
(Watermark Press); *RIBA Journal* (UK); *Sydney,
A Guide to Recent Architecture* (Konemann
Publications Edition Habit UK); *Sydney Morning
Herald*; *Transitions*; *Vogue*; *Picturing
Architecture* (Thames & Hudson); *Quay Visions*;
200 Years of Australian Architecture (Watermark
Press); *Wohn/Design* (Germany)

Awards
Nominated artist for the Seppelt Contemporary
  Art Awards, (Museum of Contemporary Art
  NSW), Australia, 1998
RAIA National Robin Boyd Award for the Foster
  Street Penthouse Apartment, Surry Hills,
  Australia
RAIA Wilkinson Award for Housing in NSW the
  Foster Street Penthouse Apartment, Surry Hills,
  Australia, 1997
RAIA Merit Award for Interior Architecture for
  Apartment Einfeld, Darling Point, Australia

Exhibitions
Work has been exhibited and presented in
  Sydney, Melbourne, Perth, (Australia), Stuttgart
  (Germany), Innsbruck (Austria), Graz (Austria),
  The RIBA Gallery (United Kingdom)
'Project A' Penthouse was featured in 'Sydney
  Open 98' and the Einfeld Apartment in the
  RAIA Houses Tour in 1999
Photo credits: Patrick Bingham Hall

*By day, the spaces are light filled and spacious. By night, they invert, as the fabric glows
and magnifies their presence, taut luminescent islands in eddying flows of spectators.*

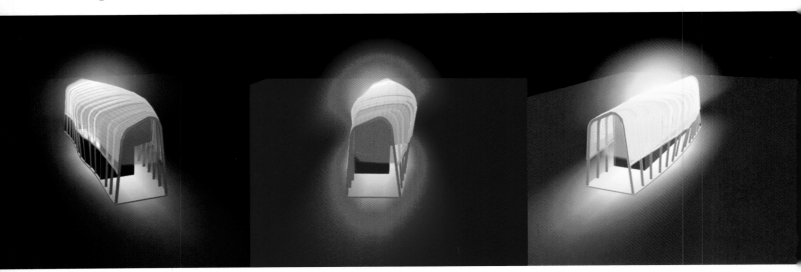

Edward R. Niles Architect F.A.I.A.

USA
Suite 9, 29350 Pacific Coast Highway
Malibu, California 90265
Tel: +(1 310) 457 3602
Fax: +(1 310) 457 3376

Associates
Lisa Niles
James Corcoran
Steve Fernandez

Person to Contact
Edward Niles

Number of Employees
3

Current and Recent Projects
Gillis Residence, Beverly Hills, California, USA
Schneider Residence, Malibu, California, USA
Klein Residence, Hermosa Beach, California,
 USA
Yuen Residence, Pasadena, California, USA
McKay Residence, California, USA
Luskin Residence, Brentwood, California, USA

Selected Clients
Milton Sidley
Meyer Luskin
Heather McKay
Bob Whitham

Design Philosophy and History
To characterize the interrelation between natural
forms found in nature and the synthesis of these
forms into the built environment.

This characterization derived from nature forms
a constant search, not only of form but the
beauty inherent in the rigour of making and
experiencing its product. The process is never a
slave to the dogma of style but a dynamism of
endless expression whose limits are only the
capacity of the architect as creator.

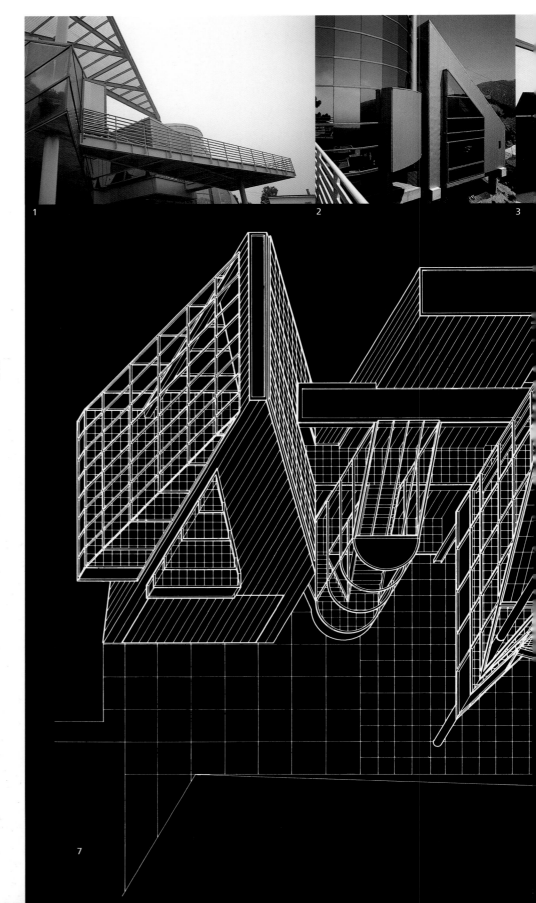

1 Observation deck and sun canopy, McKay Residence,
 Malibu, California
 Photo credit: Edward Niles

2 Bedroom tower, master bath tower, McKay
 Residence, Malibu, California
 Photo credit: Leif Wivelsted

3 Living room, McKay Residence, Malibu, California
 Photo credit: Leif Wivelsted

4 View from entry drive, McKay Residence, Malibu,
 California
 Photo credit: Edward Niles

5 View from street, McKay Residence, Malibu,
 California
 Photo credit: Leif Wivelsted

6 View from loft above bedroom, McKay Residence,
 Malibu, California
 Photo credit: Leif Wivelsted

7 Axonometric, McKay Residence, Malibu, California

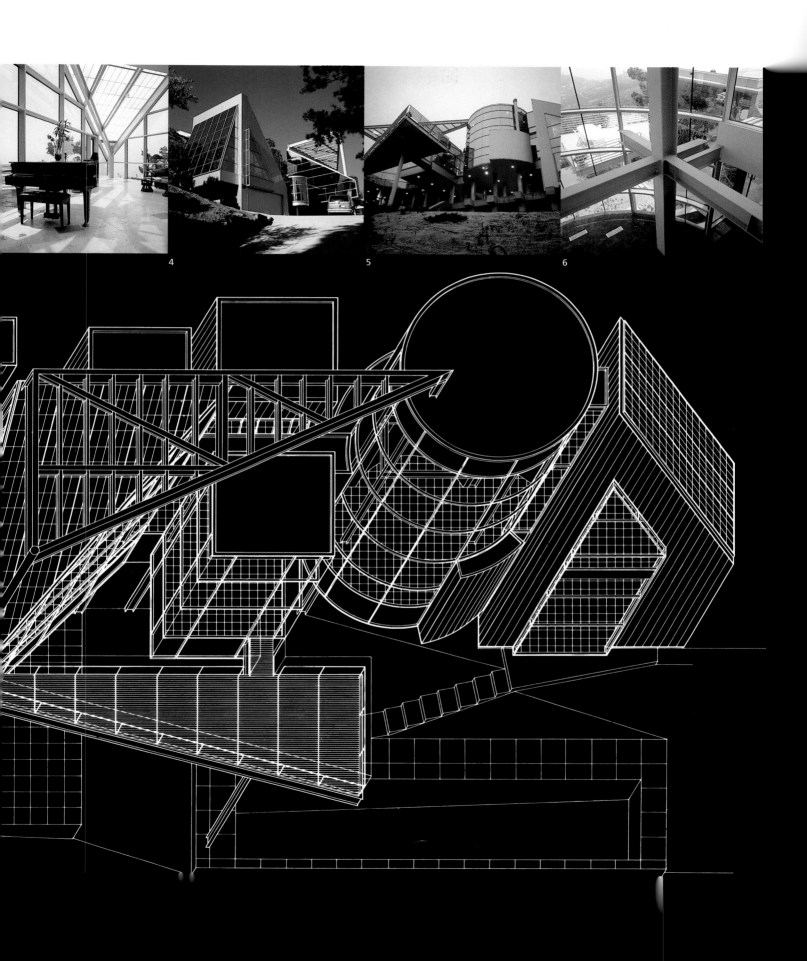

4   5   6

Elizabeth Wright Ingraham & Associates
Architects & Planners

Elizabeth Wright Ingraham, Joseph Miller, Lou Wynne
Photo credit: courtesy Elizabeth Wright Ingraham Associates

USA
111 1/2 East Pikes Peak Avenue
Colorado Springs, Colorado 80903
Tel: +(1 719) 633 7011
Fax: +(1 719) 603 1733

Directors
Elizabeth Wright Ingraham, Principal
Lou Wynne, Assistant, Archivist
Joseph Miller, Production Architect (CADD)

Person to Contact
Elizabeth Wright Ingraham

Number of Employees
3

Date of Establishment
1983

Project Types
Commercial
Corporate
Cultural Facilities
Housing
Light Industrial
Redevelopment
Residences
Resorts
Site Planning
Suburban Renewal
Urban Design

Current and Recent Projects
Senior Housing Blocks
University Arts Complex Studies

Selected Clients
Dr Brian and Genean Cole, Cole Heights
Dr's Michael and Constance Wehling Wood,
 La Casa
Bradford and Dawn Wilde, Solaz
Board of Directors, Vista Grande Community
 Church
Wright-Ingraham Institute Running Creek Field
 Station Board of Directors

1 Solaz, Maitou Springs, Colorado Residence, USA
  Photo credit: Thorney Lieberman
2 Cole Heights, Colorado Springs, Colorado
  Residence, USA
  Photo credit: Ed LaCasse
3&5 Vista Grande Community Church, USA
  Photo credit: Ed LaCasse
4 Decorative exterior detail, Vista Grande
  Community Church, USA
  Photo credit: Ed LaCasse
6 La Casa, Pueblo West, Colorado, USA
  Photo credit: Thorney Lieberman

1

2

3

4

5

6

Design Philosophy and History

Elizabeth Wright Ingraham was a partner in Ingraham & Ingraham from 1950 to 1970. In 1971, Ms Ingraham founded and directed the Wright-Ingraham Institute in Colorado. The institute was an interdisciplinary graduate level think-tank for students and faculty studying environmental impacts on a 640 acre grasslands campus. In 1983 Ms Ingraham returned to the practice of architecture as a sole proprietor of a small firm dedicated to contemporary work.

In 1995, Elizabeth Wright Ingraham was elevated to a Fellow of the American Institute of Architects, and was awarded a Doctor of Humane Letters from the University of Colorado that same year. She has been active in public affairs at both the regional, national and international levels. She has held elected public office and has authored papers on architecture, land use, conservation, environmental concerns, integrative education, public affairs and women's issues. Ms Ingraham has travelled and lectured widely and was visiting professor of architecture at the University of Colorado in 1980–83. Ms Ingraham is the grand-daughter of Frank Lloyd Wright, and daughter of architect John Lloyd Wright. She is active in the Richard Lloyd Jones family endeavours in America. In 1996 she joined an international effort to save Myonichikan, the last of Frank Lloyd Wright's standing work in Japan.

"History has borne out that 'architecture is the message a civilization sends about itself to the future'. Let us respond to this challenge with the reservoirs of new knowledge we possess. While there may be a place for contextualism in architecture, the larger thrust forward today and tomorrow for architects will be to intervene in a manner that is environmentally sensitive, structurally sound and aesthetically compelling within a global culture."

Elizabeth Wright Ingraham & Associates is organized to create a team of practitioners, engineers, builders and artists for each individual project. The design emphasis is on strong form, natural light and the use of industrial materials coupled with a selective palette of colour. The firm maintains a close architect/client relationship throughout the design and construction process.

Eric Owen Moss Architects

USA
8557 Higuera Street
Culver City, California 90232
Tel: +(1 310) 839 1199
Fax: +(1 310) 839 7922

History

Eric Owen Moss opened his office in 1973 in Los Angeles. Moss was educated at Berkeley and Harvard. He has recently held professional chairs at Yale, Harvard, and appointments in Copenhagen and Vienna, in addition to Sci-Arc, where he began teaching in 1973 and is currently on the Board of Directors.

His work has been recently exhibited in Duren, Germany; Barcelona, Spain; Tokyo, Japan; Glasgow, Scotland; Copenhagen, Denmark; and he was one of the four American architects invited to represent the US at the 1996 Venice Biennale. A second Rizzoli monograph, *Eric Owen Moss: Buildings and Projects 2* was published in 1995, along with *The Box*, published by Princeton Architectural Press in 1996, *The Lawson/Western House* published by Phaidon Press is 1994, and *PS* published by The Images Publishing Group in 1998. His most recent book is *Gnostic Architecture*, a statement/manifesto of Moss' theory of design, published by Monacelli Press. Upcoming books include *10 Years and the New City* to be published by Phaidon Press in 1999, and *Buildings and Projects 3*, to be published by Rizzoli.

Current projects include work in Vienna, Spain, France, New York, Los Angeles, and Culver City. The latest completed buildings are the 100-metre long Samitaur office block, headquarters for Eastman Kodak, situated over a road in Los Angeles; and, 3535 Hayden Ave., the headquarters of an international digital design firm (both buildings were for Samitaur Constructs of Culver City). The Umbrella, the headquarters for a film projection compant is under construction. Upcoming projects include high-rise towers in Los Angeles, the Stealth building in Culver City, and residential projects in Hollywood and Calabassas.

Moss is the recipient of 35 design awards from *Progressive Architecture* and the American Institute of Architecture as well as the 1999 Award in Architecture from the American Academy of Arts and Letters. He is a fellow of the American Institute of Architecture.

Design Philosophy

'If I were to argue that architecture can interpret and re-direct the culture, then a sense of the world advancing by jumps, not according to a single synchronized system, should find its way into the architecture. It's plausible to argue that architecture should not deal with painful subjects, that its job ought to add solace and comfort and stability, and put its occupants at ease. That might be part of the job, part of the time, but if that were all of the job all of the time, architecture would divorce itself from subject matter that might lead the culture somewhere else, and would make architecture reactionary, not progressive. To hide as opposed to seek. And architecture is not a place to hide.'

1

2

3

4

5

6

1–6   Hayden Avenue
Photo credit: Paul Groh

Estudio BC, Javier Barba

Javier Barba
Photo credit: Michael Webb

Spain
Plaza Eguilaz 10
Entresuelo 3a
Barcelona
Tel: +(34 93) 204 4206
Fax: +(34 93) 204 2697
E-mail: javbarba@ctv.es,text

Design Philosophy and History

Javier Barba was born in Barcelona, Spain in 1948. The son and grandson of architects, Barba grew up immersed in the world of architecture. After graduating from secondary school, Barba did not doubt his choice of careers and enrolled in the Barcelona School of Architecture in 1967.

In 1972 he joined his father's firm, where he gained experience but yearned for a different type of architecture, breaking off from the rationalist tradition of Le Corbusier and feeling more inspired by Frank Lloyd Wright. His development as an architect came from his work; each building was in itself an experiment and an evolution, leading to the next so that one can see a progression of forms, with his master being the natural environment itself. In 1980 he formed his own practice, Estudio BC. In a time of mass production of impersonal buildings, Barba has been faithful to the idea of *haute couture* instead of *prêt a porter* architecture, fitting each site with a building appropriate to its characteristics. Recognized as one of the leaders of the Green Movement of Integrated Architecture, Barba has lectured at home at the University of Barcelona and the University of Seville, and abroad at the Ben Gurion University in Israel, at the Congress on Sustainable Architecture in Crete, at the International Congress on Sustainability and at the University of Monterrey, Mexico.

In 1989 the commission of the European Community chose the Llavaneras semi-buried house to feature in *Project Monitor* as an example of one of the best bioclimatic constructions in Europe. In 1993 Barba contributed an article on Integrated Bioclimatic Architecture to the George Wright Forum and has been invited to participate in international competitions amongst which was the Cathedral of St Vibiana in Los Angeles. Barba's work has been published in many international magazines and has been featured on the covers of several. Currently, Barba is living in Barcelona when not travelling to far ends of the globe to work on his growing number of commissions.

1

2

1 Tsirigakis House, living room
   Photo credit: Eugenio Pons

2 Mora House, view from southwest at night
   Photo credit: Eugenio Pons

3 Monjo house from below
   Photo credit: Luis Casals

Opposite:
   Rothschild Summer Pavilion, Roman pool
   Photo credit: Eugenio Pons

3

Fentress Bradburn Architects
Architecture, Interiors, Planning

Curtis W. Fentress and James H. Bradburn
Photo credit: courtesy Fentress Bradburn Architects

USA
421 Broadway
Denver, Colorado, 80203
Tel: +(1 303) 722 5000
Fax: +(1 303) 722 7293
E-mail: studio@fentressbradburn.com

Directors
Curtis Worth Fentress
James Henry Bradburn

Persons to Contact
Curtis W. Fentress
Karen Gilbert

Number of Employees
83

Date of Establishment
1980

Project Types
Civic
Commercial
Corporate
Educational
Historical
Recreational
Residential
Transportation

Disciplines
Architecture
Interiors
Planning

Current and Recent Projects
David Skagg's Research Center, Boulder,
  Colorado
Denver Broncos Professional Athletic Stadium,
  Denver, Colorado
Denver International Airport, Denver, Colorado
National Museum of Wildlife Art, Jackson,
  Wyoming

Associates
Denver Broncos Stadium
HNTB Sports Architecture in association with
  Fentress Bradburn Architects and Bertram
  A. Bruton Associates

Selected Clients
General Services Administration/National
  Oceanic and Atmospheric Administration
Metropolitan Stadium District
City and Country of Denver
National Museum of Wildlife Art

Design Philosophy and History
Fentress Bradburn Architects strives to practice architecture, interior design, and planning with the highest degree of excellence in design, as defined by the qualities of creative problem solving and original thinking in regard to technical and aesthetic excellence for each individual project. Careful consideration of specified users allows the firm to produce designs that portray a humanist continuity between exteriors and interiors.

The firm is committed to engaging in challenging design opportunities both nationally and internationally while keeping the goal of contextual regionalism in mind at all times. Each design is unique, drawing upon a region's urban, cultural, natural, and historical essence. Members of Fentress Bradburn Architects function as a team that promotes creativity, communication and innovative, diverse ideas. To date, the firm has received 137 awards and has completed the design of 35 public sector buildings, 42 office buildings, 4 airport terminals, 40 renovation and preservation projects, 10 museum projects, 61 interior projects and 18 mixed-use residential projects.

From left to right:
Aerial view of David Skagg's Research Center, Flatiron Mountains, Boulder, Colorado
Photo credit: Nick Merrick
Exterior detail of David Skagg's Research Stadium
Photo credit: Nick Merrick
Model of new Denver Broncos' Stadium
Photo credit: Ron Johnson
Denver Broncos' open-air stadium model featuring natural anodized aluminium facade
Photo credit: Ron Johnson
Interior view of south wall at Denver International Airport
Photo credit: Timothy Hursley
Denver International Airport's terminal, featuring parking structure as seen at night
Photo credit: Timothy Hursley
Aerial view of Denver International Airport
Photo credit: Timothy Hursley
Exterior view of National Museum of Wildlife Art as an outcropping of its natural surroundings
Photo credit: Nick Merrick
Exterior view from east side of National Museum of Wildlife Art
Photo credit: Nick Merrick, Hedrich-Blessing
Main entrance to National Museum of Wildlife Art
Photo credit: Nick Merrick

Fentress Bradburn
ARCHITECTS LTD.
Architecture • Interiors • Planning

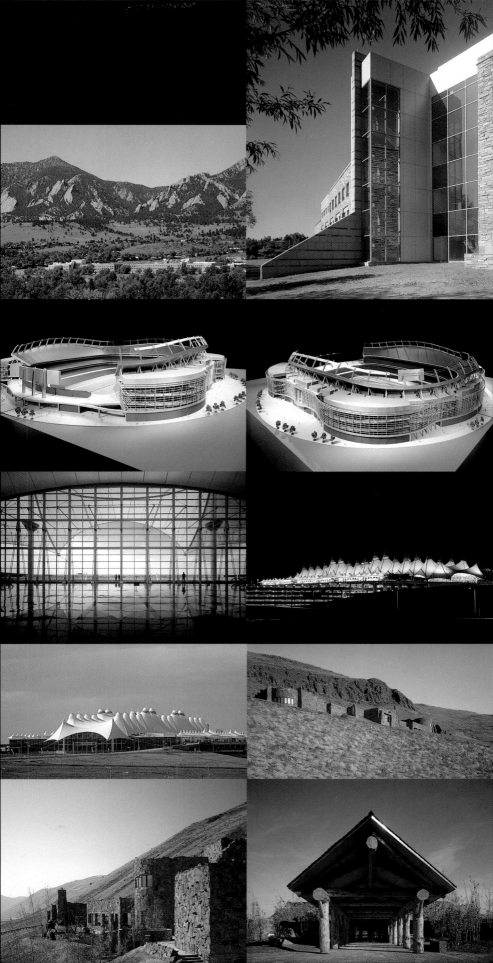

Foster and Partners
Architects and Planners

Lord Foster
Photo credit: Andrew Ward

UK
Head Office
Riverside Three
22 Hester Road
London SW11 4AN
Tel: +(44) 171 738 0455
Fax: +(44) 171 738 1107
E-mail: enquiries@fosterandpartners.com
Website: www.fosterandpartners.com

Germany
Giesebrechtstrasse 10
D.10629 Berlin
Tel: +(49 30) 88 67 360
Fax: + (49 30) 88 67 3688
E-mail: berlin@fosterandpartners.com

Singapore
29 Whitchurch Road
Singapore 138835
Tel: (65) 43 06 603
Fax: (65) 43 06 601

Partners
Lord Foster
Spencer de Grey
David Nelson
Ken Shuttleworth
Graham Phillips
Barry Cooke

Person to Contact
Graham Phillips, London

Number of Employees
480

Date of Establishment
1967

Project Types
Government/Education/Cultural
Infrastructure/Transportation
Healthcare
Leisure/Entertainment
Convention Centre/Trade Fairs
Hotels/Resorts/Restaurants
Offices/Work Environments
Retail
Multi-Unit Housing
Sports Facilities

Disciplines
Architecture
Interior Design
Industrial and Furniture Design
Planning

Current and Recent Projects
Headquarters for Hongkong and Shanghai
 Banking Corporation, UK 1998–2000
New Parliament building for Greater London
 Authority, UK, 1998*
London Bridge City Masterplan, UK 1998
Regional Music Centre, Gateshead, UK 1997*
World Squares for All Master Plan for Central
 London, UK 1996*
Millennium Bridge, London, UK 1996–2000*
Headquarters for Citibank, Canary Wharf,
 London, UK 1996–1999
Oxford University Library, Oxford, UK 1996
Transport Interchange, North Greenwich,
 London, UK 1995–1998*
Medical Research Laboratory, Stanford
 Universtiy, California, USA 1995–1999*
Multimedia Centre, Hamburg, Germany 1995–
 1999*
National Botanic Gardens for Wales, Middleton
 Hall, Wales, UK 1995–2000
Headquarters for Daewoo Electronics, Seoul,
 Korea 1995–2001
Conference Centre and Industrial Theatre for
 SECC, Glasgow, Scotland 1995–1997
Jiu Shi Tower, Shanghai, China 1995–1999
Faculty of Management, Robert Gordon
 University, Aberdeen, Scotland 1994–1998
Sir Alexander Fleming Building, Medical
 Research Faculty, Imperial College, London, UK
 1994–2000
Great Court, British Museum Redevelopment,
 London, UK 1994–2000*
Viaduct, Millau, France 1993–
Al Faisaliah Complex, Riyadh, Saudi Arabia
 1993–2000*
Headquarters for ARAG 2000, Düsseldorf,
 Germany 1993–2001
London School of Economics Library, London,
 UK 1993–*
Congress Centre, Valencia, Spain 1993–1998

* Denotes winner of national or international
 competition

Recent Clients
Airport Authority Hong Kong
British Museum
Commerzbank Ag
Daewoo
HSBC
J-C Decaux
King Faisal Foundation
Land Transport Authority Singapore
London Underground Ltd
Citibank
Oxford University
Petronas
Prudential
Stanford University
TAG McLaren Holdings Ltd

Design Philosophy and History
Foster and Partners is an international
architecture and design practice led by Lord
Foster and five partners. Norman Foster's
philosophy of integration can be seen in the
way the practice's London design studio works;
it is essentially one large open space, shared
equally by everyone, and free of subdivision to
encourage good communication between the
many people who work there.

Projects range in scale from master plans for
regeneration and expanding cities to individual
buildings, furniture and product design, signage
and exhibitions.

The practice has major projects in the United
Kingdom, Japan , Hong Kong, China, France,
Germany, the Netherlands, Spain, the United
States and Saudi Arabia. Current projects under
construction include: the redevelopment of the
British Museum, the Millennium Bridge for
London and the Citibank Headquarters in
London's Docklands.

Principal completed projects include the Willis
Faber Dumas office, Ipswich; the Sainsbury
Centre for Visual Arts, Norwich; the Hongkong
and Shanghai Banking Headquarters, Hong
Kong; the third London Airport, Stansted;
Century Tower in Tokyo; the Carré d'Art, Nîmes;
the Bilbao Metro; Cambridge University Law
Faculty; the American Air Museum in Duxford;
the Commerzbank Headquarters in Frankfurt; a
Congress Centre in Valencia, the new airport at
Chek Lap Kok, Hong Kong and the new German
Parliament, Reichstag in Berlin.

The central concern of the practice is design
excellence, achieved through active
collaboration with clients. A wide range of
supporting skills underpins the work of the
practice, including modelmaking, CAD drawing
and visualization, and in-house audio-visual,
photographic and printing systems.

Foster and Partners has received more than 160
awards and citations for design excellence, and
won 50 national and international design
competitions. Norman Foster was appointed by
the Queen to the Order of Merit, is a Royal
Designer for Industry, a Fellow of the Chartered
Society of Designers, an Honorary Fellow of the
Royal Academy of Engineering, and a Gold
Medalist of both the Royal Institute of British
Architects, and the American Institute of
Architects. In 1999 he became the 21st Pritzker
Architecture Prize Laureate and was honoured
with a Life Peerage in the Queen's Birthday
Honours. The practice has been awarded the
Queen's Award for Export Achievement.

1

1 Interior CAD view of The Great Court, British Museum, London, UK
Photo credit: Foster and Partners visualization

2 Exterior view of Reichstag with new dome, Plenary Building in Converted Reichstag, Berlin, Germany
Photo credit: Dennis Gilbert/VIEW

3 Exterior general view from market, Commerzbank Headquarters, Frankfurt, Germany
Photo credit: Ian Lambot

4 Exterior view showing canopy over departures road, Hong Kong International Airport, Chek Lap Kok, Hong Kong
Photo credit: Dennis Gilbert/VIEW

2

3

4

Frank O. Gehry & Associates

USA
1520 B Cloverfield Boulevard
Santa Monica, California 90404
Tel: +(1 310) 828 6088
Fax: +(1 310) 828 2098

Current and Recent Projects
Guggenheim Museum, Bilbao, Spain
Samsung Museum of Modern Art, Seoul, Korea
Pariser Platz 3, Berlin, Germany
Der Neue Zollhof, Düsseldorf, Germany
Experience Music project, Seattle, USA
Bard College Center for the Performing Arts,
  New York, USA
University of Cincinnati Center for Molecular
  Studies, Cincinnati, Ohio, USA
Team Disneyland Administration Building,
  Anaheim, California, USA
Nationale-Nederlanden, Prague, Czech Republic
EMR Communication and Technology Center in
  Bad Oeynhausen, Germany
Frederick R. Weisman Art Museum, University of
  Minnesota, USA
University of Toledo Center for Visual Arts in
  Toledo, Ohio, USA
Vila Olimpica Retail an Commercial Complex,
  Barcelona, Spain
Walt Disney Concert Hall, Los Angeles, USA
American Center in Paris, France
EuroDisney Retail and Entertainment Center,
  outside of Paris, France
University of Iowa Laser Laboratory, Iowa, USA
Chiat/Day Office Building, Venice, California,
  USA
Vitra International Furniture Museum and
  Factory, Weil am Rhein, Germany
Vitra International Headquarters, Basel,
  Switzerland

Design Philosphy and History
Frank Gehry established the architectural firm of
Frank O. Gehry & Associates in 1962. Since that
time, Frank O. Gehry & Associates has grown
into a full service firm with broad international
experience in museum, theatre, performance,
institutional, commercial and residential
projects. The three principals of the firm, Frank
Gehry, James Glymph, and Randolph Jefferson,
work as a team in the development of all
projects undertaken by the firm, with Frank
Gehry working as Design Principal and James
Glymph and Randolph Jefferson complimenting
the work of Frank Gehry with their extensive
experience in project management and in the
development of technical systems.

Located in Santa Monica, California, the
architecture studio has a staff of over 120
people, which includes a group of senior
architects who are highly qualified in project
management and in the technical development
of building systems and construction
documents, as well as extensive model-making
facilities and a model building staff capable of
executing everything from scale architectural
models to full size mock-ups. The firm employs a
network of sophisticated computer aided design
workstations in the development of projects and
in the translation of design ideas for the
technical documents required for construction.
The firm uses CATIA, a 3-dimensional computer
modelling program originally designed for the
aerospace industry. This program is
supplemented by more traditional 2-dimensional
CAD programs.

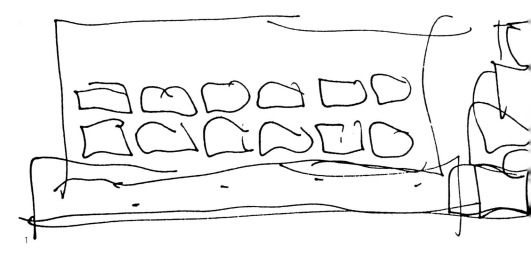

1

2

3

1 Chiat/Day Building
   Sketch by Frank Gehry

2 Chiat/Day West Coast HQ, Venice, California, USA
   Photo credit: Michael Webb

3 Vila Olimpica, Barcelona, Spain
   Photo credit: Michael Webb

4 Loyola University Law School, Los Angeles, USA
   Photo credit: Michael Webb

5 Metal Crafts Building, Univeristy of Toledo, Ohio, USA
   Photo credit: Michael Webb

6 Former American Center (now Maison du Cinema) Paris, France
   Photo credit: Michael Webb

7 Vitra Design Museum, Weil-am-Rhein, Germany
   Photo credit: Michael Webb

5

7

Frank Williams & Associates Architects

USA

154 West 57th Street
New York, New York 10019
Tel: +(1 212) 582 4685
Fax: +(1 212) 974 5471
E-mail: archfwa@aol.com

Joseph F. Galea
Joseph Navarro
Emad Michael
Ernesto Fong
Santiago Aulestia
Veronica Williams

Frank Williams & Associates Architects' practice has primarily focused on hotels, urban residential and mixed-use commercial buildings in New York and around the world. The firm is committed to providing excellence in design at all the stages of building an edifice.

Frank Williams and IM Pei are the associated architects for the Four Seasons Hotel, New York, between Madison and Park Avenues on East 57th Street.

Currently, the firm has under construction in New York: a 55-storey Planet Hollywood— Sheraton Hotel in Times Square at 47th Street and Broadway; a 42-storey luxury residential tower at 515 Park Avenue at 60th and Park Avenue; and, The Century in San Francisco, a 51-storey residential complex.

Internationally, the firm is designing the Four Seasons Hotel in Shanghai, and a 40-storey residential complex Lang Suan Ville in Bangkok, Thailand.

Mr Williams is a Fellow of the American Institute of Architects. Rockport Press recently published a book of his works, *The Architecture of Frank Williams*.

Planet Hollywood—Sheraton Hotel

Owner/Developer:
 Times Square Partners

This 55-storey Times Square hotel has 550 hotel rooms and a major Planet Hollywood restaurant within the first three levels of the complex and a sky lobby on the fourth floor. A major new design element is the 300-foot high sign tower. This sign tower fronts on the major northerly open space of Times Square and will be a dramatic example of the new signage proposed for the Times Square district.

The Century

Owner/Developer:
 Swig-Burris Equities
Associated Architects:
 Heller-Manus Architects, San Francisco

The Century, which is currently under construction, will be the largest and most luxurious residential building in San Francisco. The Century will introduce an entirely new level of residential luxury living to the dramatically evolving cultural, hospitality, and entertainment/ retail transformation taking place in the Yerba Buena district south of Market. At 51 storeys it will be the tallest residential building west of the Mississippi. The Century will add 505 new residential units—170 condominiums and 335 rental apartments—to the San Francisco housing market. As part of the development project, 51 units will be reserved for affordable housing. Residents will have full access to a variety of amenities.

1

515 Park Avenue

Owner/Developer:
 Zeckendorf Realty

515 Park Avenue is New York's most important new residential tower in decades—a 40-unit, 43-storey luxury condominium at 515 Park Avenue featuring duplex residences as well as full-floor apartments, private wine cellars, staff apartments, and private gym.

515 Park Avenue is the first true luxury residence to be built on Park Avenue in over 60 years, marking the resurgence of a look and style of the lavish, pre-war building that characterized the avenue in the 1920s. The new structure will reflect in fine detail the grandeur and workmanship of the classic Park Avenue apartment house supported by all the amenities and technology of state-of-the-art living today. The architectural form is a series of graceful setbacks, forming the base, middle, and top elements. French (Magny) limestone with brick comprises the exterior materials. Architecturally, the residential tower complements Park Avenue. It does not stand out as a new building; rather a Park Avenue tower that has evolved over time.

2

3

5

4

1 Times Square Hotel, New York, USA
   Rendering: David Williams

2&3 The Century, San Francisco, USA
     Rendering: David Williams

4 515 Park Avenue, New York, USA
   Rendering: David Williams

5 515 Park Avenue, conceptual architectural model,
   New York, USA
   Photo credit: Jock Pottle Photography

gmp-Architekten von Gerkan, Marg und Partner

Germany
Elbchaussee 139
Hamburg, D - 22763
Tel: +(49 40) 88 151 0
Fax: +(49 40) 88 151 177/178
E-mail: Hamburg-E@gmp-architekten.de

Directors
Professor Meinhard von Gerkan
Professor Volkwin Marg

Key Personnel
Professor Meinhard von Gerkan, Chairman
Professor Volkwin Marg, Chairman
Klaus Staratzke, Partner
Uwe Grahl, Partner
Joachim Zais, Partner
Hubert Nienhoff, Partner
Nikolaus Goetze, Partner
Jürgen Hillmer, Partner
Wolfgang Haux, Associate Partner

Disciplines
Culture buildings
Exhibition and conference buildings
Healthcare
Hotels
Housing
Industrial buildings
Infrastructure and transportation
Interior design
Master planning
Office buildings
Public buildings
Research and teaching buildings
Shopping malls
Urban planning

Current and Recent Projects
New Trade Fair, Leipzig
Trade Fair, Hanover Hall 4
Trade Fair, Hanover Hall 8/9
Dresdner Bank, Pariser Platz, Berlin
The Christian Pavilion, Expo 2000 Hanover
Conference Hall, Weimar
Lecture Theater Centre, University of Oldenburg
Lecture Theater Centre, Technical University of
  Chemnitz
Railway Station, Berlin-Spandau
Lehrter Bahnhof, New Central Station Berlin

Selected Clients
Deutsche Bahn AG
Deutsche Lufthansa AG
Deutsche Telekom AG
Hapag Lloyd AG
Kajima Development GmbH
Allianz Insurance Co
Gerling Insurance Co
EXPO 2000, Hanover
Dresdner Bank
Hypo Bank
Bertelsmann AG
City of Berlin, Lübeck, Bielefeld, Oldenburg
Tishman Speyer Properties, New York
Deutsche Messe AG
Leipziger Messegesellschaft mbH
Bundesrepublik Deutschland
Airport Authorities Stuttgart, Hamburg, Munich
Government of Algeria

Design Philosophy and History
In the past 30 years von Gerkan, Marg and
Partners have planned and constructed buildings
in most major German cities.

The range of their projects is not limited to any
one type of building. They have designed small
scale homes, the interior of the Metropolitan
Express Train, hotels, theatres and concert halls,
office buildings and commercial centres,
hospitals and research facilities, jumbo-hangars
and car parks, EXPO 2000 and the New Trade
Fair Leipzig.

Von Gerkan, Marg and Partners became
internationally known as a team of airport
architects when, in 1975, they designed the
Berlin-Tegel building with its drive-in airplane
terminal for 'stacked parking'. This innovative
design has been further developed to transform
the departure and arrival halls at Stuttgart and
Hamburg airports.

They are internationally recognized not only for
their completed projects, but also for their
designs, of which 330 have scored prizes, more
than 130 as first. Key examples are their designs
for the 'Lehrter Bahnhof'– the new central
railway station in Berlin, which is currently under
construction; the Christian Pavilion for the Expo
2000; the reconstruction of the Olympic
Stadium in Berlin; and their visionary proposals
for the urban master plan of Bucharest 2000 as
well as Munich 21, Stuttgart 21 and Frankfurt
21.

In their understanding of the design process,
question and answer mingle in close correlation:
'Architecture as an art with social application is
in the need of obviousness in an economic,
constructive and formal way. Architecture has to
reveal causality towards its content, reference
towards its aim.'

1 'Lehrter Bahnhof', New Central Station, Berlin,
  Germany
  Photo credit: Archimation

2 Dresdner Bank, Pariser Platz, Berlin, Germany
  Photo credit: H-Chr. Schink

3 Conference Hall, Weimar, Germany
  Photo credit: H-Chr. Schink

4 The Christian Pavilion, Expo 2000, Hanover,
  Germany
  Photo credit: H. Leiska

5 New Trade Fair Leipzig, Leipzig, Germany
  Photo credit: Busam/Richter

1

2

3

4

Information

Graham Gund Architects

Graham Gund

USA
47 Thorndike Street
Cambridge, Massachusetts 02141
Tel: +(1 617) 577 9600
Fax: +(1 617) 577 9614
E-mail: bethm@grahamgund.com

Directors
Graham Gund, FAIA, Principal
John A. Prokos, AIA, Managing Principal

Associates
Marianne Beagan
George Coon, RIBA
James Cullion, RA
Laura Sanden Cabo, AIA
Youngmin Jahan, AIA
F. Daniel Rutledge, RA
Elizabeth Fitch Mac Alpine
Maria R. Fernandez-Donovan, AIA
Doris Nelson
Stephen P. Dadagian, AIA

Persons to Contact
Elizabeth Mac Alpine
John A. Prokos, AIA

Number of Employees
55

Date of Establishment
1971

Project Types
Commercial
Educational
Hotels
Housing
Institutions
Museums
Performing Arts Facilities

Disciplines
Architecture
Feasibility Studies
Interior Design
Master Planning
Planners
Programming
Urban Design

1

Current and Recent Projects
University of North Carolina Fine and Performing
 Arts Center, Chapel Hill, North Carolina, USA
Taft School Math & Science Center and Library,
 Watertown, Connecticut, USA
Holy Cross Center for Religious Ethics,
 Worcester, Massachusetts, USA
North Shore Center for the Performing Arts,
 Skokie, Illinois, USA
University of New Hampshire Dimond Library,
 Durham, New Hampshire, USA
Cleveland Botanical Gardens & Conservatory,
 Cleveland, Ohio, USA
Disney Coronado Springs Resort & Convention
 Center, Orlando, Florida, USA
Western Carolina University Fine & Performing
 Arts Center, Cullowhee, North Carolina, USA
Hathaway Brown School Campus Center, Shaker
 Heights, Ohio, USA

Selected Clients
Walt Disney Company
Cleveland Botanical Gardens
Cheekwood Botanical Gardens
College of the Holy Cross
University of North Carolina
The Taft School
St. Paul's School
The Lawrenceville School
Fernbank Museum of Natural History
Mt. Holyoke College
University of New Hampshire

2

3

4

5

6

Design Philosophy and History

Graham Gund Architects is an award-winning professional practice which provides services in architecture, planning and interior architecture. Founded in 1971, the firm has been honored with over 100 national and regional awards for design excellence and has received wide critical acclaim and professional recognition for its work.

In short, the firm is noted for the following:

- A national reputation for creative and distinguished architectural design.
- A solid track record in the design, project management and construction of projects, both large and small.
- A client and user-oriented design approach which reveres the collaborative process.

- A design philosophy which looks to understand how layers of history and qualities of nature combine to define and enrich a place and inform the development of physical form and detail.
- A group of architects who have been with the firm for a number of years and who have worked together successfully on many projects.
- A design team persona which combines strong project management skills with a thoughtful and intimate collaborative working spirit.

1 Hathaway Brown School, Shaker Heights, Ohio, USA

2&6 North Shore Center for the Performing Arts, Skokie, Illinois, USA
Photo credit: Hedrich-Blessing

3 University of New Hampshire Dimond Library, Durham, New Hampshire, USA
Photo credit: Nick Wheeler

4 The Lawrenceville School Visual Arts Center, Lawrenceville, New Jersey, USA
Photo credit: Warren Jagger

5 The Taft School Math and Science Center and Library Expansion, Watertown, Connecticut, USA
Photo credit: Peter Aaron, Esto Photographics

Gwathmey Siegel & Associates Architects, *llc*

USA
475 Tenth Avenue
New York 10018
Tel: +(1 212) 947 1240
Fax: +(1 212) 967 0890
E-mail: info@gwathmey-seigel.com

Principals
Charles Gwathmey, FAIA
Robert Siegel, FAIA

Associates
Jacob Alspector, RA (Senior Associate)
Nancy Clayton, RA
Steven Forman, AIA
Gerald Gendreau, AIA
Dirk Kramer, AIA
Thomas Levering, AIA
Joseph Ruocco, RA
Elizabeth Skowronek, AIA
Lilla Smith, RA

Persons to Contact
Charles Gwathmey and Robert Siegel

Number of Employees
75

Date of Establishment
1968

Project Types
Auditoria/Theatres
Colleges and Universities
Cultural Facilities
Government Facilities
Gymnasiums and Athletic Facilities
Hospitals
Libraries
Master Planning
Museums
Residential

Disciplines
Adaptive Reuse
Architecture
Interior Architecture
Master Planning
Renovation

Current and Recent Projects
City University of New York (CUNY), USA
Henry Art Gallery Addition and Renovation,
 University of Washington, USA
James S. McDonnell Hall Physics Building,
 Princeton University, USA
Levitt Center for University Advancement,
 University of Iowa, USA
Lutheran World Relief Center, Baltimore,
 Maryland, USA
Naismith Memorial Basketball Hall of Fame,
 Springfield, Massachusetts, USA
Nanyang Polytechnic, Singapore
US Mission to the United Nations, New York,
 USA

Selected Clients
City University of New York
Cornell University
Guggenheim Museum
Harvard University
New York Public Library
Princeton University
United States Government
University of Iowa

1

4

2

3

5

Nanyang Polytechnic, Singapore

1　Aerial view of model from south
　　Photo credit: Albert Lim

2　View of School of Business Management from
　　the central garden looking north
　　Photo credit: Albert Lim

3　Reflecting pool with campus centre beyond.
　　The six-level campus centre building acts as
　　the focal point of the Polytechnic
　　Photo credit: Albert Lim

4　Swimming complex with nine-lane competition
　　pool, spectator seating and instructional pools
　　Photo credit: Albert Lim

5　Atrium in campus centre building
　　Photo credit: Albert Lim

Design Philosophy and History
Founded in 1968, Gwathmey Siegel and
Associates Architects has completed over three
hundred projects for educational, cultural,
corporate, government and private clients.
The firm offers master planning, architecture,
interior architecture and product design services.

Charles Gwathmey and Robert Siegel are
responsible for the conceptual design direction
and actively participate in the development
process of each project, which is managed on
a daily basis by the associates. Ten in number,
the associates are senior architects who have
been with the firm from 10 to 25 years. They

6

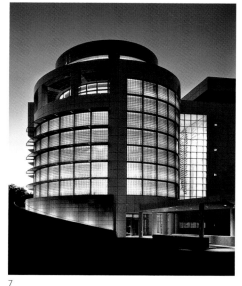

7

8

9

10

11

Levitt Center for University Advancement, University of Iowa

6 Southeast view from across the Iowa River. Exterior materials include Indiana limestone, white and silver aluminium panels and glass
Photo credit: Farshid Assassi

7 Rotunda at dusk from northeast. The triple-height rotunda marks a visual and literal edge to the University of Iowa's Performing Arts Campus
Photo credit: Farshid Assassi

8 Southwest view of limestone and metal 'bar' element containing administrative offices
Photo credit: Farshid Assassi

9 Two-storey circular boardroom at the top of the rotunda. This flexible assembly space, capped by an inverted dome, is finished in cherry and features concentric, custom-designed conference tables.
Photo credit: Farshid Assassi

10 Interior of rotunda seen from below. This three-storey public reception lobby integrates works of art by faculty, students and local artists. It is encircled by a ceremonial stair and cantilevered bridges that create a promenade, leading visitors to the public assembly spaces located at the top of the building
Photo credit: Farshid Assassi

11 Detail of promenade stair
Photo credit: Farshid Assassi

supervise the teams established for each project, are responsible for the selection and coordination of outside engineering and specialized consultants, and act as the liaison between the firm and its clients. Teams are assembled from a technical staff of 70 architects and draftspeople. The nucleus of the group remains on the project team from the beginning through the design development and construction phases.

The firm's clients are valued collaborators in shaping the program and determining the design direction. Their approach is to synthesize from interaction and analysis. The firm is sensitive to the nuances of place and precedent. A substantial portion of the firm's work consists of projects in campus and urban centres, as well as additions to historic buildings.

The firm is known for its holistic approach, which integrates interior design details and site-related improvements as integral parts of the architectural solution.

T. R. Hamzah & Yeang Sdn. Bhd.

Malaysia
No. 8 Jalan Satu
Taman Sri Ukay
Ampang, Selangor Darul Ehsan 68000
Tel: +(6 03) 457 1966
Fax: +(6 03) 456 1005
E-mail: trhy@tm.net.my
Website: www.trhamzah-yeang.com

Directors
Tengku Robert Hamzah, AA Dip, APAM
Dr Kenneth Yeang, AA Dip, PhD (Cantab),
 APAM, RIBA, FSIA, Hon. FAIA

Date of Establishment
1975

Number of Employees
45

Disciplines
Architecture
Urban Design
Master Planning
Interior Design
R&D (Building Systems)
Building Technology

Current and Recent Projects
Completed Projects
Menara Boustead, 31 storeys
IBM Plaza, 24 storeys
Plaza Atrium, 24 storeys
Wisma SMI, 17 storeys
Menara Mesiniaga, 14 storeys
SEDC Kelantan, 20 storeys
Wangsa Ukay Condominium, 16 storeys
Leisure Bay Condominium, 16 storeys
Casa Del Sol, 10 storeys
Central Plaza, 27 storeys
Menara UMNO, 21 storeys
Menara TA, 40 storeys
Sheraton Towers, 33 storeys
Guthrie Pavilion, 4 storeys
Roof-Roof House, 3 storeys
Selangor Turf Club, Sungai Besi, 3 storeys
KESDA Headquarters, 4 storeys
BBMB Training Campus, 4 storeys

Under Construction
Wirrina, Australia, 4 storeys
Gamuda Headquarters, 12 storeys

Under Design
TTDI Apartments, Kuala Lumpur, 28 storeys
Menara Pan Global, Kuala Lumpur, 25 storeys
National Library Board Building, Singapore,
 14 storeys
ADO Head Office, Germany, 5 storeys

1

2

3

4

5

6

7

9

8

10

11

Partial Client's List
IBM World Trade Corporation
Mesiniaga Sdn. Bhd.
Standard Chartered Bank
Dunlop Industries Malaysia Bhd
Sime Darby
Deutsche Bank (Asia)
Embassy of Switzerland
BP British Petroleum
The World Bank
Philip Morris Asia Inc.
MBf
The Bank of Canton Limited
Bank of Nova Scotia
DHL

Expertise
High-tech building
High-rise office building
High-rise apartment building
High-rise hotel building
High-rise low-cost apartments
High-rise M&E systems coordination
Curtain-wall and sunshading design
Low-energy design

Partial Awards List
1999
Asia Pacific Distinguished Scholar Award at the
  Third International Symposium on Asia Pacific
  Architecture
UIA Auguste Perret Prize, for Applied
  Technology in Architecture
1998
URA (Urban Redevelopment Authority)
  Ecological Design in the Tropics Design Award
  for EDITT Tower, Singapore (Second Prize)
SIA Award (Honorable Mention) for Menara
  UMNO, Penang Overseas Category
PAM Architecture Award for the Central Plaza
  for excellence in design and building, Malaysia
Aga Khan Award for Architecture for Menara,
  Mesiniaga, Geneva, Switzerland
SIA Design Award (Overseas Category) Honorary
  Mention, Selangor Turf Club Grandstand
1995
3rd Prize, Taichung Civic Centre International
  Competition (UIA), Taichung, Taiwan

Work Published In
Architectural Review
London Financial Times
RIBAJ
Blueprint
Kenchiku Bunka
Architecture Record
World Architecture

1 Guthrie Pavilion
2 Menara UMNO
3 Menara UMNO, skycourt-balcony details
4 Central Plaza
5 Central Plaza, entrance details
6 Menara TA
7 Menara TA, roof-top tent structure
8 Menara Mesiniaga
9 Menara Mesiniaga, rooftop poolside and sun-roof
10 MBf Tower
11 MBf Tower penthouse jacuzzi
Photo credit: T. R. Hamzah & Yeang Sdn. Bhd.

Hardy Holzman Pfeiffer Associates
Architecture, Planning and Interior Design

Partners and Associates

Seated: Robert Almodover, Pam Loeffelman, Daria Pizzetta, William Murray, Robin Kunz, David Saviola, Nestor Bottino, Jean Gath

Standing: Hugh Hardy (Partner), James Brogan, Cleveland Adams, Stewart Jones, Doug Moss, Stephen Johnson, Sharon Lasoff, Edward Carfagno, Norman Pfeiffer (Partner), Jack Martin, Malcolm Holzman (Partner)

Missing: Maya Schali, Caroline Bertrand, David Hart, Anthony Poon

Main wing extension, Cleveland Public Library, Cleveland, Ohio
Photo credit: courtesy Cleveland Public Library Archives, Don Snyder

USA
902 Broadway
New York, New York 10010
Tel: +(1 212) 677 6030
Fax: +(1 212) 979 0535

811 West 7th Street, Suite 430
Los Angeles, California 90017
Tel: +(1 213) 624 2775
Fax: +(1 213) 895 0923

Partners
Hugh Hardy, FAIA
Malcolm Holzman, FAIA
Norman Pfeiffer, FAIA

Associate Partner
Stephen Johnson, AIA

Senior Associates
Robert Almodovar, AIA
Jean Gath
Stewart Jones, AIA
Robin Kunz
Pamela Loeffelman, AIA
Jack Martin, AIA
William Murray, AIA

Associates
Cleveland Adams, AIA
Caroline Bertrand
Nestor Bottino, AIA
James Brogan, AIA
Edward Carfagno, AIA
David Hart, AIA

Sharon Lasoff
Douglas Moss, AIA
Daria Pizzetta, AIA
Anthony Poon, AIA
David Saviola, AIA
Maya Schali, AIA

Persons to Contact
Jkolleeny@hhpa.com
Slasoff@hhpa.com

Number of Employees
136

Date of Establishment
1967

Project Types
Civic
Commercial
Educational
Historic/Restoration
Hospitality
Libraries
Museums
Recreational
Theatre/Entertainment
Transportation

Disciplines
Architecture
Interior Design
Planning and Urban Design

Current and Recent Projects
Colburn School of Performing Arts, Los Angeles
Cleveland Public Library, Cleveland, Ohio
United States Toll Plaza at Rainbow Bridge, Niagara Falls, New York
Lucille 'Lupe' Murchison Performing Arts Center University of North Texas, Denton, Texas
Soka University of America, Aliso Viejo, California
Radio City Music Hall, New York City
San Angelo Museum of Fine Arts and Education Center, San Angelo, Texas
Central Synagogue Reconstruction, New York
Gateway Cultural Campus, Salt Lake City, Utah

Selected Clients
Walt Disney Imagineering
General Services Administration
Princeton University
Scholastic, Inc.
Brooklyn Academy of Music
The Shubert Organization
City University of New York
Los Angeles Community Redevelopment Agency

Design Philosophy and History
Established in 1967, Hardy Holzman Pfeiffer Associates is a nationally recognized planning, architectural and interior design firm. Highly respected for some of the country's most innovative architecture, the firm is particularly well-known for its design of buildings for public use. The firm has created a reputation for diversity – both in the type of projects completed and the variety of design solutions employed. HHPA's work features a wide range of design because it is made in response to the needs and imagery of each project. This versatile aesthetic approach, coupled with HHPA's inquiring attitude, is seldom matched in present American architecture.

Hardy Holzman Pfeiffer Associates has received more than 100 national design awards, including Honour Awards from the American Institute of Architects (AIA) in 1976, 1978, 1979, 1981, 1983, 1994, 1995, 1996, 1997, and 1998. In 1992, in recognition of their significant contributions to interior design and architecture, Hugh Hardy, Malcolm Holzman, and Norman Pfeiffer were inducted into the Interior Design Magazine Hall of Fame. In 1981, HHPA received the Architectural Firm Award from the American Institute of Architects, the highest honour conferred on an American architectural practice.

View from Canadian side at night, United States Toll Plaza at Rainbow Bridge, Niagara Falls, New York
Photo credit: Michael Moran Photography

New Amsterdam Theatre, New York
Photo credit: Whitney Cox / Disney Enterprises, Inc.

Interior of Zipper Hall, Colburn School of Performing Arts, Los Angeles
Photo credit: Foaad Farah

HARRY SEIDLER & ASSOCIATES
Architects & Planners

Australia
2 Glen Street
Milsons Point, NSW 2061
Tel: +(61 2) 9922 1388
Fax: +(61 2) 9957 2947
Email: hsa@seidler.net.au

Principals
Harry Seidler
Penelope Seidler
Peter Hirst
Henry Feiner
Greg Holman
Gil. Williams
John Curro

Design Philosophy and History
The office of Harry Seidler & Associates has been in practice for 50 years and has completed a great variety of large projects in Australia, Europe, America and Asia. The design philosophy is based on a consequential methodology emanating from Seidler's teachers and mentors: Gropius and Breuer in the USA and Niemeyer in Brazil with whom he worked before commencing practice in the 1950s. The completed work has consistently pushed frontiers of structural and construction technology forward, particularly during a 15 year collaboration and consultancy with Nervi in Rome. The resulting aesthetic impact of buildings in recent years has expanded the early minimalist approach into greater richness of form and expression by maximising advanced technology. The design aim is to achieve the most, practically and aesthetically, with the least possible means. Design achieves added long term value and maximises profit for clients at no added cost. The firm's buildings are planned to focus on exposure to views; concrete towers are built at the rate of one floor per week without external scaffolding; long span interiors are column free and, integrate mechanical services within the structural floor depth.

Minimum energy consumption is ensured by external solar protection.

The skilful urban planning of large scale projects ensures that they become assets to the city by the design of public spaces which attract people and tenants.

Major Awards
- Companion, Order of Australia, 1987
- Royal Gold Medal, RIBA, 1996
- Gold Medal, RAIA, 1976
- Gold Medal, City of Vienna, 1989
- 1st Class Cross of Honour Arts & Sciences, Austria, 1996
- Honorary Doctorates:
  - University of Manitoba, 1988;
  - University of Technology, Sydney, 1991;
  - University of NSW, 1999;
  - University of Sydney, 1999

Photo credit: courtesy Harry Seidler & Associates

The 42 storey Horizon Apartments, Sydney, 1998

Along the Danube: City of Vienna housing is built over a covered expressway, 1999

Angled planning ensures all apartments have water views

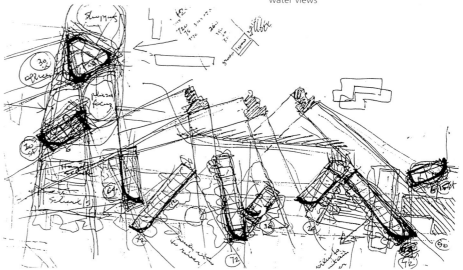

Harry Seidler's first sketch

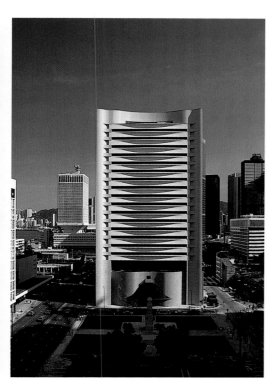

Hong Kong Club and Offices, 1985

Residence with opposing richly curved roof profile, 1999

Hartman-Cox Architects

USA
1074 Thomas Jefferson Street, N.W.
Washington, DC. 20007
Tel: +(1 202) 333 6446
Fax: +(1 202) 333 3802
E-mail: hca2@aol.com

Senior Partners
George E. Hartman, Jr. FAIA
Warren J. Cox, FAIA
T. Lee Becker, FAIA
Mario H. Boiardi, FAIA
D. Graham Davidson, FAIA

Person to Contact
Warren J. Cox, FAIA

Number of Employees
30

Date of Establishment
1965

Project Types
Adaptive reuse
Civic
Commercial
Cultural
Educational
Governmental
Planning
Preservation
Residential
Restoration

Disciplines
Architecture
Planning
Historic Preservation
Interior Design
Programming

Current and Recent Projects
Federal Courthouse, Corpus Christi, Texas
Concert Hall, Kennedy Center, Washington, DC.
Kelvin Smith Library, Cleveland, Ohio
Special Collections Library, University of Virginia
Renovation of Lincoln and Jefferson Memorials,
 Washington, DC.
Student Center, St. Mary's City, Maryland
Office Complexes, Washington, DC.
Museum Renovation, Smithsonian Institution,
 Washington, DC.
Law School, Washington University, St. Louis,
 Missouri

Selected Clients
Smithsonian Institution
National Park Service
Universities of Virginia, Connecticut, Tulane,
 Brown, Washington and Georgetown
Lincoln Properties
Cadillac Fairview
Prentiss Properties
Thomas Jefferson Memorial Foundation
General Services Administration
Foreign Building Office
Department of State
Saul Properties
Winterthur and Chrysler Museums

Georgetown University Law Center Library, Washington, DC.

Kelvin Smith Library, Case Western Reserve University, Cleveland, Ohio

National Permanent Building, Washington, DC.

Folger Shakespeare Library, Washington, DC.

Design Philosophy and History

Hartman-Cox's goal is to design appropriate buildings. The firm endeavours to tailor each project specifically to its client, budget, program and site. As a result, the firm has worked in a wide variety of styles and no two buildings resemble each other. The firm does not do 'signature' buildings: one style does not fit all. Whether it is of major civic importance, simply a 'background' building, or part of an urban complex, they strive to design the right building for the right place.

The firm undertakes projects from five million dollars to 100 million dollars in size, ranging from small libraries to concert halls to full block developments. Current projects range all across the United States.

Hartman-Cox has received over 100 design awards for their work including the AIA Architectural Firm Award, the highest design award a firm can receive in the United States.

Entrance Rotunda, Georgetown University Law Center Library, Washington, DC.
This full-block building accommodates one of the largest law libraries in the country and forms the first component of a new complex which doubles the size of the existing law centre. The library stands to the north of Edward Durrell Stone's existing 1960s law centre and both complements and contrasts with it. The building can accommodate up to 500,000 volumes and study seating for 1,200 students.
Photo credit: Robert Lautmam

Entrance facade, Kelvin Smith Library, Case Western Reserve University, Cleveland, Ohio
The site of this new main university library is one of the most prominent in the city, bounded on the south by the classical concert hall, on the west by a major park, on the northwest by the classical museum of art and to the northeast by the student centre. The library is configured to serve as the focus of a new open space called the 'Heart of Campus'. It is intended to reinforce the existing complex of buildings and is completely site specific. It is as much urban design as architecture on the exterior.
Photo credit: Robert Lautman

Detail of facade, National Permanent Building, Washington, DC.
The scale, grey and black colour, and degree of forcefulness of the National Permanent Building were tailored to its prominent location on a triangular Pennsylvania Avenue site located two blocks from the White House. Intended as 'a relatively tame foreground structure', it can be seen for over a mile up the Avenue to the west. It alludes to the nearby Old Executive Office Building with its multitude of exterior columns.
Photo credit: Robert Lautman

New reading room addition, Folger Shakespeare Library, Washington, DC.
Renovations and additions to Paul Cret's 1920s stripped classical library, housing the foremost collection of Shakespearean material in the world, progressed over a period of seven years in three stages. The Reading Room addition consists of a long, rectangular volume topped by a barrel-vaulted ceiling which admits natural light through a central opening and narrow clerestories along the sides. At each end of this room are apse-like rounded sections, again lit around their perimeter.
The room is used as a picture gallery for the library's extensive collection of Shakespeare-related paintings.
Photo credit: Peter Aaron/ESTO

Helin & Siitonen Architects

Finland
3 Tammasaarenlaituri
Helsinki 00180
Tel: +(358 9) 4137 1300
Fax: +(358 9) 4137 1400
E-mail: info@archs.fi

Directors
Pekka Helin, Architect SAFA
Tuomo Siitonen, Professor, Architect SAFA

Persons to Contact
Pekka Helin and Tuomo Siitonen

Number of Employees
50

Date of Establishment
1979

Project Types

City Planning	Offices
Commercial	Public Buildings
Government	Sports Facilities
Multi-storey Housing	Transportation

Disciplines
Architecture
City Planning
Interior Design

Current and Recent Projects
Nokia House, Espoo, Finland
Nokia Research Center, Helsinki, Finland
Ministry of Social Affairs and Health, Helsinki, Finland
Baltic Square Offices, Helsinki, Finland
Finnish Embassy, extension and restoration, Moscow, Russia
Housing Services Center Wilhelmiina, Helsinki, Finland
Laivapoika Housing, Helsinki, Finland
Kellosaarenkatu Housing, Helsinki, Finland

Selected Clients
Nokia
Aleksia
Realinvest
State Real Property Authority
Miina Sillanpää Foundation
Wärtsila NSD
City of Helsinki
All the major contractors in Finland

Design Philosphy and History
Since the firm's founding in 1979 its work has included cultural institutions, offices, commercial and recreational development and housing. The scale of projects range in size from summer cottages to corporate headquarters of 50,000 square metres and master plans for multifunctional centres.

The work is committed to creative design, backed up by particular research in every project, and thorough knowledge of processes and technology in the field of building.

The emphasis is on the quality of the design, careful supervision of the execution and close collaboration with the client.

Each project is given the same individual attention and is treated as an unique opportunity to improve conditions of space for a certain function.

The office is fully equipped with modern CAD facilities.

1

1 Facade to east, Ministry of Social Affairs and Health, Helsinki, Finland
Photo credit: Tiita Lumio

Opposite:
Entrance hall with wooden auditorium, Nokia Research Center, Helsinki, Finland
Photo credit: Matti Pyykkö

Helliwell + Smith•Blue Sky Architecture

Kim Smith and Bo Helliwell
Photo credit: Alan Fletcher

1

2

Canada
4090 Bayridge Avenue
West Vancouver V7V 3K1
Tel: +(1 604) 921 8646
Fax: +(1 604) 921 0755
E-mail: blue.sky@pro.net

3815 Shingle Spit Road
Hornby Island V0R 1Z0
Tel: +(1 250) 335 2703
Fax: +(1 250) 335 2703
E-mail: blue.sky@pro.net

Directors and Persons to Contact
Bo Helliwell
Kim Smith

Number of Employees
2

Date of Establishment
1992

Project Types
Commercial
Institutional
Residential Custom Home
Multi-family

Disciplines
Architecture
Interior Design
Planning

Current and Recent Works
Bowen Island Library, Bowen Island, Canada
South Chesterman Beach Homes, Tofino,
  Canada
Pemberton Revitilization Plan, Pemberton,
  Canada
Greenwood 'Fishbones' House, Galiano Island,
  Canada
Harvey 'Bridge' House, Denman Island, Canada
U.B.C. Wilderness Conference Center, Maple
  Ridge, Canada

Selected Clients
Bowen Island Library Association
R & L Properties Ltd
Village of Pemberton
Barry and Sophie Greenwood

Design Philosophy and History
Blue Sky was born out of the ferment of the late 1960s and early 1970s, but it has proved to have much more staying power, talent and guts than most other idealistic initiatives of the time. Helliwell and Smith are inheritors and interpreters of the organic tradition of modernism.

They have been deeply involved with the ecology and topography of southern British Columbia and its wonderful interweave of sea, forest, and rock. At the same time, they have always been open to ideas and influences from the rest of the world, translating and adapting them to their area, so making architecture that is far more than provincial.

Blue Sky's work so far has shown how, in our time, the principles of Arts and Crafts Modernism can be brought to houses on the West Coast and enriched: ecological consciousness; deep respect for site and user program; craftsmanly involvement with process to generate buildings that are constructively coherent both tectonically and intellectually.

Blue Sky's volumes certainly flow into each other, but they form an interconnected tissue of internal and external places, simultaneously specific and capable of many individual interpretations.

The buildings are kindly, and tender to humankind and nature, which are both enriched by their existence.

Exerts from the Preface by Peter Davey, Editor of *The Architectural Review*, London by the recently published book on Helliwell + Smith by The Images Publishing Group Pty Ltd, Australia.

3

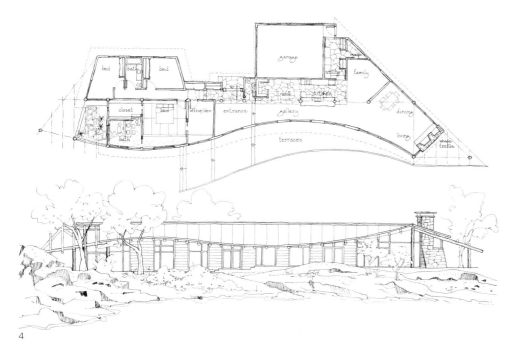

1 Collins House, street elevation in snow, Canada
  Photo credit: Leanna Rathkelly
2 Harvey House, stair detail, Canada
  Photo credit: Patrizia Menton
3 Greenwood House, interior gallery, Canada
  Photo credit: Peter Powles
4 Greenwood House floor plan and southwest
  elevation
5 Fishbones, Galiano Island, B.C., Canada
  Photo credit: Peter Powles
6 Harvey House, beachside elevation, Canada
  Photo credit: John Fulker
7 Harvey House exploded axonometric

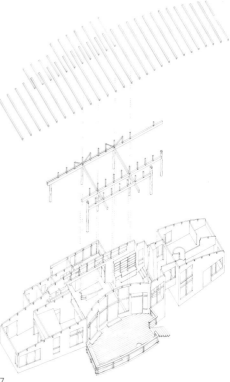

Hellmuth, Obata + Kassabaum, Inc.
Architecture, Engineering, Interiors, Planning, Graphics, Consulting

HOK Executive Committee
Front: Gyo Obata, FAIA Co-Founder and Co-Chairman;
Jerome J. Sincoff, FAIA President and CEO
Back: William E. Valentine, FAIA Co-Chairman;
Larry D. Self, FAIA Executive Vice President;
Patrick E. Maclemay, Executive Vice President
Not pictured: Ronald Labinski, FAIA, Senior Vice
President

USA
Suite 600, 211 North Broadway
St. Louis, Missouri 63102
Tel: +(1 314) 421 2000
Fax: +(1 314) 621 0944
E-mail: contact@hok.com

Additional Offices
Atlanta, Berlin, Brisbane, Chicago, Dallas,
Greenville, Hong Kong, Houston, Kansas City,
London, Los Angeles, Mexico City, Moscow,
New York, Newport Beach, Orlando, Ottawa,
Prague, San Francisco, Seattle, Sydney, Tampa,
Tokyo, Toronto, Warsaw and Washington, DC

Person to Contact
Dawn O'Malley, Corporate Communications,
  St. Louis

Number of Employees
1,600

Date of Establishment
1955

Project Types
Aviation
Conservation and Preservation
Convention Centres
Corporate
Education
Healthcare
Hospitality
Justice
Military
Mixed-use and Hospitality
Public and Institutional
Retail and Entertainment
Science and Technology
Senior Living
Sport
Urban Planning

Disciplines
Architecture
Engineering
Consulting
Graphics
Interiors
Planning

1

2

1 Reorganized Church of Jesus Christ of Latter Day
   Saints World Headquarters Independence, Missouri,
   USA
   Photo credit: Balthazar Korab

2 Long Beach Aquarium, Long Beach, California, USA
   Photo credit: Marvin Rand

3 Sendai International Airport, Domestic and
   International Passenger Terminal, Sendai, Japan
   Photo credit: Yukio Futagawa

4 Oriole Park at Camden Yards, Baltimore, Maryland,
   USA
   Photo credit: Jeff Goldberg/ESTO

5 Arena Central, Birmingham, England, UK

3

Current and Recent Projects
Japanese American National Museum,
 Los Angeles, California, USA
The Sharnoti Dead Sea Resort, Jordan
Toronto Hospital, Toronto, Canada
Ministry of Defence, London, UK
Chep Lap Kok International Airport, Hong Kong
Eason Field, Houston, Texas, USA
Enron Field, Houston, Texas, USA

Selected Clients
Microsoft
Northwestern Memorial Hospital
Nortel Networks
Sun Microsystems

Design Philosophy and History
Hellmuth, Obata + Kassabaum (HOK), Inc. is a global provider of architectural, engineering, planning, interior, graphics and consulting services for the built environment. With more than 1,600 employees in 27 cities worldwide, HOK is one of the world's most influential design firms. HOK is committed to delivering design excellence and quality service that enables clients to achieve their goals and enrich their lives.

HOK manages the total planning, design and construction process of any size and scope, anywhere in the world. The firm's regional offices are linked with specialty design groups, allowing them to meet the growing client demand for specialized expertise in specific facility types.

HOK's core belief in integrating design excellence with client needs is based on the philosophy that built environments must go beyond pure function to enhance the quality of life for those who live and work in them. Each HOK project is approached individually, without preconceptions and designed to serve the particular needs of the clients, always with the goal of achieving design excellence.

4

5

Herbert S Newman and Partners

USA
300 York Street
New Haven, Connecticut 06511
Tel: +(1 203) 772 1990
Fax: +(1 203) 772 1997
E-mail: pnewman@hnsparch.com

Partners
Herbert S. Newman, FAIA, Principal
Joseph C. Schiffer, AIA
Robert Godshall, AIA
A. Michael Raso, AIA
Richard Munday, AIA
Mavis Terry, Business Partner

Associates
Carl Weis, AIA, Senior Associate
Howard Hebel, AIA, Senior Associate
James Elmasry, AIA
Gwen Wood Emery
Joseph Huether, AIA
Peter Newman, Associate AIA

Persons to Contact
Herbert S. Newman, FAIA, Principal
Peter J. Newman, Assoc. AIA, Director of
Business Development

Number of Employees
50

Date of Establishment
1964

Project Types
Civic/Government
Commercial
Education
Residential

Disciplines
Architecture
Design/Build
Historic Preservation/Renovation
Interior Architecture
Master Planning
Sustainable Design

Current and Recent Projects
Duracell World Headquarters, Bethel
  Connecticut, USA
Goodspeed Opera House Master Plan, East
  Haddam, Connecticut, USA
Greenwich Academy, Performing Arts and
  Athletic Center, Greenwich, Connecticut, USA
New Dormitory and Dining Hall, Middlebury
  College, Middlebury, Vermont, USA
Pocantico Conference Center of the Rockefeller
  Brothers' Fund, Tarrytown, New York, USA
Richard's of Greenwich, Greenwich.
  Connecticut, USA
The Maritime Aquarium, Norwalk, Connecticut,
  USA
Northwest Quad Dormitory and new Dining
  Hall, University of Connecticut, Storrs,
  Connecticut, USA
Westport Public Library Addition and
  Renovation, Westport, Connecticut, USA
Yale University New Residence Hall, New Haven,
  Connecticut, USA
Yale University Law School Dormitory, New
  Haven, Connecticut, USA
Yale University Power Plant, New Haven,
  Connecticut, USA

1

2

3

4

5

6

1 Conard High School, West
Hartford, Connecticut, USA
Photo credit: Robert Benson 1999

2 Richard's of Greenwich, Greenwich,
Connecticut, USA
Photo credit: Robert Benson 1999

3&5 Yale University, New Residence Hall,
New Haven, Connecticut, USA
Photo credit: Robert Benson 1999

4 Greenwich Academy, New
Performing Arts Center and
Athletic Center, USA
Photo credit: Robert Benson 1999

6 Greenwich Academy, New
Performing Arts Center, Theater,
Connecticut, USA
Photo credit: Jeff Goldberg/ESTO

HKS Inc.
Architecture Engineering Interiors

Directors:
Ronald L. Skaggs, C. Joe Buskuhl,
Ronald M. Brame and H. Ralph Hawkins

USA

Head Office
1919 McKinney Avenue
Dallas, Texas 75201
Tel: +(1 214) 969 5599
Fax: +(1 214) 969 3397

Suite 1030
5401 W. Kennedy Blvd
Tampa, Florida 33609
Tel: +(1 813) 287 2140
Fax: +(1 813) 286 8969

Suite 180
901 E. Bird Street
Richmond, Virginia 23219
Tel: +(1 804) 644 8400
Fax: +(1 804) 644 8469

Suite 275
2440 S. Sepulveda Blvd
Los Angeles, California 90064
Tel: +(1 310) 966 1520
Fax: +(1 310) 966 1524

Suite 405
225 E. Robinson Street
Orlando, Florida 32801
Tel: +(1 407) 648 9956
Fax: +(1 407) 648 9976

Principals
Ronald L. Skaggs, FAIA
C. Joe Buskuhl, FAIA
Ronald M. Brame, FAIA
H. Ralph Hawkins, FAIA
Thomas L. Amis, Jr., AIA
James B. Atkins, AIA
Noel Barrick, AIA
J. Craig Beale, FAIA
Robert E. Booth, AIA
E. Davis Chauviere, AIA
Ronald W. Dennis, AIA
Nunzio M. DeSantis, AIA
Ronald E. Gover, AIA
Ernest W. Hanchey, Jr., AIA
Thomas E. Harvey, Jr., AIA
Thomas R. Holt, AIA
Daniel L. Jeakins, AIA
Owen E. McCrory, AIA
James L. Mitchell, PE
Jack D. Price, Jr., AIA
John H. Richardson, AIA
Fredric D. Roberts, AIA
Grant A. Simpson, AIA
Joseph G. Sprague, FAIA
Jack R. Yardley, FAIA

Persons to Contact
Ronald L. Skaggs, FAIA
  Chairman and CEO
C. Joe Buskuhl, FAIA
  President

Number of Employees
480

Date of Establishment
1939

Project Types
Commercial
Office, Corporate, Hotel, Retail, Data Processing
Educational
School, College, University
Governmental
Civic, Criminal Justice, Institutional
Healthcare
Hospital, Ambulatory Care, Research, Extended
  Care
Aviation
Terminal, Distribution Centre, Control Centre
Sports/Entertainment
Sports Facility, Stadium, Arena, Performing Art,
  Auditorium, Theme Park, Gaming

Disciplines
Architecture
Computer Aided Drafting and Design
Environmental Graphics
Equipment Planning
Facility Programming
Facility Evaluations
Facility Management
Graphic Design
Interior Design
Master Planning
Model Services
Structural Engineering

Current and Recent Projects
Commercial
American Express Financial Headquarters,
  Minneapolis, Minnesota
World Com Operation Center, Washington, DC
Educational
Shenandoah University Master Plan,
  Winchester, Virginia
Widtsoe Hall Chemistry Building,
  Utah State University, Logan, Utah
Governmental/Criminal Justice
Colorado Department of Corrections Special
  Needs Unit, Pueblo, Colorado
DFW International Airport Terminal B Expansion
  and Renovation, Irving, Texas
Healthcare
University of Texas M.D. Anderson Cancer
  Center, Houston, Texas
Methodist Hospital of Southern California,
  Arcadia, California
Resorts/Entertainment
Atlantis Resort Phase II,
  Paradise Island, Bahamas
Melia Chateau Montry, Montry, France
Sports
Miller Park, Milwaukee, Minnesota
Lone Star Park Race Track, Grand Prairie, Texas

Selected Clients
Baylor University Medical Center
Dallas Fort Worth Airport
Disney Development Company
Dresser Industries, Inc.
Electronic Data Systems
Four Seasons Hotels
General Motors Corporation
Hyatt Regency Hotels
IBM Corporation
Integris Health Systems
Intermountain Healthcare
JCPenney Company, Inc.
Lincoln Property Company
Marriott Hotels
Milwaukee Brewers Baseball Club
Trammell Crow Company
United States Federal Bureau of Prisons
University of North Carolina Hospitals
Xerox Corporation

Design Philosophy and History
Founded in 1939, HKS Inc. has executed
commissions for structures valued in excess of
nine billion dollars. Since its inception, HKS has
grown to be one of the largest architectural and
engineering firms in the US.

HKS' business philosophy emphasizes
performance in achievement of client goals. The
deliberate and effective application of this
philosophy of service has resulted in the ability
to consistently deliver successful projects that
are well designed, technically executed, and
completed within budget and on schedule.

1

2

3

4

5

6

1 Valley Children's Hospital, Madera, California, USA
   Photo credit: Kaled AlKotob

2 Las Ventanas al Paraiso, Los Cabos, Mexico
   Photo credit: Tom Fox

3 University of Texas M.D. Anderson Cancer Center, Houston, Texas, USA
   Photo credit: Beryl Striewski

4 Citigroup Regional Headquarters, Tampa, Florida, USA
   Photo credit: Michael Lowry

5 Lone Star Park, Grand Prairie, Texas, USA
   Photo credit: Wes Thompson

6 American Stores Company, Salt Lake City, Utah, USA
   Photo credit: Wes Thompson

House + House Architects

Steven and Cathi House

USA

1499 Washington Street
San Francisco, California 94109
Tel: +(1 415) 474 2112
Fax: +(1 415) 474 2654
E-mail: house@ix.netcom.com

Firm Profile

Steven and Cathi House and their associates endeavour to create beauty, serenity and awe in their work. Their greatest inspiration comes from the subtleties of each site and the deepest recesses of their client's souls. Through intimate analysis, they mould each project into a unique, magical and harmonious environment. They strive to lift themselves and their clients to a higher level of perception of the world through skillful manipulation of form, light and texture. The poetic quality of their work derives from the simpler side of life: the magic sparkle of sunlight raking across a textured wall, the drama of surprise in turning a corner, the luminous glow of colour at the moment of twilight.

Since 1982 House + House Architects have produced a diverse body of work that demonstrates their passion for site specific, well choreographed buildings throughout the San Francisco Bay Area, the Sierra Nevada mountains, Florida, Hawaii, Mexico, and the Caribbean. Recognized for their innovative work, House + House Architects have received numerous design awards including AIA, ASID Design Excellence, the Gold Nugget Grand Award and the Builder's Choice 'Project of the Year Award' for their own home in Mexico.

Their work has been exhibited widely and has been featured in national and international publications including *Architecture, Architectural Record, House Beautiful, Metropolitan Home, Brava Casa, DBZ, Eigen Huis* and *The New York Times*. Their work is also featured in the monograph *House + House Architects - Choreographing Space,* as well as *West Coast Wave - New California Houses, The American House, San Francisco Houses - After the Fire,* and *Expressive Details*. Steven and Cathi House created a major exhibition entitled *'Mediterranean Indigenous Architecture - Timeless Solutions for the Human Habitat',* which has travelled throughout the United States. They have lectured extensively and both serve on the Advisory Council for the College of Architecture and Urban Studies at Virginia Tech.

1 Forest View Residence, Hillsborough, California, USA
Photo credit: Christopher Irion courtesy of *House Beautiful*, © July 1992, The Hearst Corporation, All Rights Reserved

2 Telegraph Hill Residence, San Francisco, California, USA
Photo credit: Alan Geller

3 A House for Two Architects, San Miguel de Allende, Mexico
Photo credit: Steven House

4 Jarvis Residence, Oakland, California, USA
Photo credit: Steven House; Portrait by William Helsel

Opposite: Grandview Residence, Oakland, California, USA
Photo credit: Steven House

ILKUN C&C ARCHITECTS INC.

Kwan Young Choi, Dong Myeong Cheong

Korea
1665-14, Seocho-Dong, Seocho-Ku
Seoul 137-070
Tel: +(82 2) 525 8271
Fax: +(82 2) 525 8038
E-mail: ig4@chollian.net

Directors
Kwan Young Choi was born in 1941 and received a Bachelor of Architecture in 1965 and Master in Environmental Landscape Architecture in 1979 from the Seoul National University. He founded his own architectural firm 'Dongkuk Architects' in 1973 (now ILKUN C&C ARCHITECTS INC.); taught architecture at Chungang University from 1981 to 1988; and, taught at Seoul National University from 1989 to 1994 as an invited professor. He is an honourary director of the Korean Institute of Architects, a member of the Korean Institute of Registered Architects and the Korean Association of Landscape Architects.

Partner Dong Myeong Cheong was born in 1951 and received a Bachelor of Architecture from the Seoul National University in 1974. He was Officer of Construction in ROKAF, and then joined with Kwan Young Choi in 1978. Since 1984, he has served as a design partner on many projects. He is a member of the Korean Institute of Architects and the Korean Institute of Registered Architects.

Persons to Contact
Kwan Young Choi or Dong Myeong Cheong

Number of Employees
30

Date of Establishment
1973

Project Types
Athletic
Broadcasting and Communication
Education and Research
Exhibition
Hotels and Resort Condominiums
Housing
Industrial
Office Buildings
Commercial
Transportation

Disciplines
Architectural Design
Construction Administration
Feasibility Studies
Landscape Design

1

Current and Recent Projects
Welfare facility for Korea Development Bank, Seoul, Korea
Han's Obstetrics & Gynaecology, Seoul, Korea
Lotte Duksan Condominium, Chungchongdo, Korea
BMW Seoul Service Center, Seoul, Korea
C &C Building, Seoul, Korea
Lotte Sky Complex, Seoul, Korea
Taegu Munhwa Broadcasting Corporation Building, Taegu, Korea
Headquarters of Credit Union, Taejon, Korea
Anyang Station Complex, Anyang, Korea
International Education Center for Kookmin University, Seoul, Korea
College of Art & Music for Kookmin University, Korea

Selected Clients
Anyang Station Co., Ltd
Bigway Co., Ltd
Credit Union
Gyeongsang National University
Kolon Group
Kookmin University
Korea Development Bank
Korea Federation of Textile Industries
Lotte Construction Co., Ltd
Lotte Shopping
Munhwa Broadcasting Corp.
Pohang University of Science & Technology
Seoul Broadcasting Systems
Tongkook Synthetic Fibers Co., Ltd

1 Taegu Munhwa Broadcasting Corporation Building, Taegu, Korea
  Photo credit: ILKUN C&C ARCHITECTS INC.
2 College of Art & Music, Kookmin University, Seoul, Korea
  Photo credit: ILKUN C&C ARCHITECTS INC.
3 International Education Center, Kookmin University, Seoul, Korea
  Photo credit: ILKUN C&C ARCHITECTS INC.
4 Anyang Station Complex, Anyang, Korea
  Photo credit: ILKUN C&C ARCHITECTS INC.
5 C&C Building, Seoul, Korea
  Photo credit: ILKUN C&C ARCHITECTS INC.

2   3

4

Design Philosophy and History

Based in Seoul, ILKUN C&C ARCHITECTS INC. was established as Dongkuk Architects in 1973, was renamed as ILKUN Architects & Planners in 1979, and then became ILKUN C&C ARCHITECTS INC., in 1995. Since its founding, the firm has designed and constructed over 130 buildings in Seoul and other major cities in Korea.

By winning numerous competitions and by providing a professional practice satisfying the existing clients, the firm has grown by gaining wide experience on a variety of building types with accumulated know-how & technology. The firm's design achievements have been accomplished through the accurate analysis of

each project and the pertinent solution of the site, plus a deep understanding of the client's needs.

For ILKUN C&C ARCHITECTS INC., architecture is seen as part of the creative activity of inheriting and developing culture, and this is reflected in its architectural style. The firm believes that a sound society creates a sound city which in turn is an aggregate of sound architecture. It has striven for perfection and freshness in its design, harmonized with the existing environment and individual project location. The firm has received many awards including: KIA; KIRA; Seoul Metropolitan Government; Korean Society of Steel Construction; and, Architectural Institute of Korea.

5

J.J. Pan and Partners
Architects and Planners

Taiwan, R.O.C.
21, Alley 12, Lane 118, Ren Ai Road, Sec.3
Taipei 106
Tel: +(886 2) 2701 2617
Fax: +(886 2) 2700 4489
E-mail: jjpan@ms2.hinet.net

Associates
Tatung Chou, Senior Vice President,
　Development
Chung-Tsai Huang, Senior Vice President,
　Construction Adm.
Tse-Hsiung Cheng, Vice President,
　Quality Assurance
Lung-Yue Cheng, Vice President, Design

Number of Employees
95

Date of Establishment
1981

Project Types
Commercial	Industrial
Educational	Landscape
Healthcare	Recreational
Hospitality	Residential

Disciplines
Architecture
Construction Management
Interior Design
Planning

Current and Recent Projects
Holistic Education Village, Chung Yuan Christian
　University, Chungli
QDI TFT/LCD Plant, Quanta Display Inc., Taoyuan
Truth Lutheran Church Reconstruction, Truth
　Lutheran Church, Taipei
Training & Activity Center, Macronix
　International Co., Ltd., Hsinchu
Logefeil Memorial Hospital Reconstruction,
　Logefeil Memorial Hospital, Taitung
Master Plan for Social Welfare Park of Suanglien
　Presbyterian Church, The Presbyterian Church
　in Taiwan, Taipei County
National Museum of Marine Biology &
　Aquarium, Pingtung
Cheng-Du Business School Complex, Feng Chia
　University, Taichung

Selected Clients
Science-based Industrial Park Administration,
　Hsinchu
Chung Yuan Christian University, Chungli
Feng Chia University, Taichung
Philips Electronics Industries (Taiwan) Ltd.,
　Hsinchu
Taiwan Semiconductor Manufacturing Company,
　Hsinchu
Winbond Electronics Corp., Hsinchu
Macronix International Co., Ltd., Hsinchu
Merck Taiwan Ltd., Taoyuan
Shin-Etsu Handotai Taiwan Co., Ltd., Hsinchu
ScinoPharm Taiwan, Ltd., Taiwan
Development Center for Biotechnology, Taipei
　County
Pingtung Christian Hospital, Pingtung
Taiwan Mennonite Christian Hospital, Hualien
Acer Property Development, Inc., Taoyuan
Makro Taiwan Ltd., Taipei
Primax Electronics Ltd., Taipei
Chinese Culture University, Taipei
Etron Technology, Inc., Hsinchu
Acer Display Technology, Inc., Taoyuan
Quanta Display Inc., Taoyuan

Design Philosophy and History
J.J. Pan and Partners is an architectural and
planning firm dedicated to providing creative
solutions in the design and planning of human
environments. The firm believes in a holistic
approach to architectural design maintaining a
harmonious balance between heaven, earth and
man. For clients in Taiwan and from around the
globe, the firm has, since its inception in 1981,
offered a comprehensive service package
combining a proven track record, advanced
education, talented creativity, diversified
technical experience, and a wide range of
professional, teaching, and research
backgrounds.

Regarding its professional commitment, J.J. Pan
and Partners believes that innovative design,
considerate service and reliable delivery are
important aspects in producing a successful
work of architecture. Because of this ideology,
the firm has consistently provided top quality,
meticulously co-ordinated and smoothly
delivered projects to its clients over the years.
As a result, the firm has earned the trust of
repeat clients and walk-in referrals, as well as
having received scores of design awards from
government, professional associations and
journals.

In recognition of a career of distinction, Mr. Pan
was elected a Fellow by the American Institute
of Architects in 1994 and has been named an
Outstanding Architect by the Government of
the R.O.C.

1

2

3

4

5

6

7

8

9

10

11

12

1 Headquarters Building for Etron Technology, Inc., view from southwest
Photo credit: Chun-Chieh Liu

2 Fab III and IV, Taiwan Semiconductor Manufacturing Company, approach to main entrance
Photo credit: Min-Hsiung Tseng

3 Student Center, National Chiao Tung University, amphitheater at night
Photo credit: Gina Lin

4 Multiple-stage renewal of National Taiwan Ocean University, view from campus green

5 Headquarters Building for Macronix International Co., Ltd., front elevation at sundown
Photo credit: Chuan-Jim Chang

6 Cerebral Palsy Education Center Phase I & II, Pingtung Victory House, side view of Phase I from plaza

7 Grace Gospel Center, The Mon-Eng Presbyterian Church, corner front facade
Photo credit: Min-Hsiung Tseng

8 Phase I Plant, Zyxel Communications Corporation, upper atrium
Photo credit: Min-Hsiung Tseng

9 Gymnasium and Indoor Swimming Pool, Chung Yuan Christian University, front entrance of swimming pool
Photo credit: Gina Lin

10 Founder's Memorial Library, Chinese Culture University, entry plaza from southwest
Photo credit: Min-Hsiung Tseng

11 Research and Development Center, Development Center for Biotechnology, view of building B from west
Photo credit: Min-Hsiung Tseng

12 Cherry Grove Housing, My-House Group, night view
Photo credit: Min-Hsiung Tseng

Jestico + Whiles
Architects

Tom Jestico, John Whiles, Tony Ingram,
Heinz Richardson, Tony Ling and Śniez Torbarina

UK
1 Cobourg Street
London NW1 2HP
Tel: +(44 20) 7380 0382
Fax: +(44 20) 7380 0511
E-mail: j+w@jesticowhiles.co.uk

Czech Republic
Americka 35
Prague 120 00 Praha 2
Tel: +(42 02) 2425 1561
Fax: +(42 02) 2425 1558
E-mail: imbryan@czn.cz

Germany
Bodenseestrasse 311
Munich, Munchen 81249
Tel: +(49 89) 871 4417
Fax: +(49 89) 871 4827

Directors
John Whiles, AA Dip RIBA
Tom Jestico, Dip Art RIBA
Tony Ingram, D Arch RIBA
Heinz Richardson, BSc Dip Arch RIBA

Associates
Tony Ling, B Arch MRAIC
Suzanne Gilmour, Dip Bus Admin
Eoin Keating, BA(Hons) Dip Arch Tech
David Perera, B Arch (RMIT) RAIA

Head of Interior Architecture
Śniez Torbarina, Dip Ing Arch

Persons to Contact
Rachel Butterworth, London
Tony Ingram, London

Number of Employees
40

Date of Establishment
1977

Project Types
Educational
Industrial
Leisure
Mixed-use
Offices

Public
Residential
Retail
Transportation

Disciplines
Architecture
Environmental Design
Furniture Design
Interior Design

Lighting Design
Project Management
Space Planning
Urban Design

Current and Recent Projects
One Aldwych, London
Equitable House, City of London
Ocean Wharf, Docklands, London
Vinopolis, City of Wine, London
Village, 12 Cinemas, Prague
Hilton Hotel (Terminal 4), Heathrow, London
Open University Business School, Milton Keynes
House for the Future, Cardiff
Camden Town Station, London
The Mailbox, Malmaison, London

Selected Clients
Foreign and Commonwealth Office
Hilton International
National Museums and Galleries of Wales
PolyGram International
London Underground
National Westminster Bank
British Council
Greycoat plc

Design Philosophy and History
At Jestico + Whiles, the practice of architecture goes beyond the design of buildings. It's about approaching every project with a fresh mind, and leaving it with a distinctive, innovative and practical solution for the client's needs. It's about releasing all the potential the project has to offer, for the client, the community and the environment. And it's about making sure, through systematic management with the latest technology, that the firm's creativity delivers results on time, to budget.

The service is total, and at its heart is a design approach that is all-embracing: we develop imaginative, cost-effective solutions at every level of scale in the built environment. The architects, interior designers and project managers at Jestico + Whiles are engaged on commissions that span urban masterplanning, transport infrastructure, corporate headquarters, hotels, housing and furniture.

The firm listens, manages, and designs. The firm never takes the responsibility of designing buildings lightly, but believes architecture—its process and product—should be enjoyed. Clients in the UK, Europe and the Far East have come to share the firm's view. Most importantly, it's a philosophy that yields results. Every year since its foundation, Jestico + Whiles has won at least one national or international architectural award. And, as the clients acclaim, they have been rewarded with buildings of stature, value and invention.

1 Exterior, Jestico House, London
   Photo credit: Jo Reid and John Peck

2 Lobby bar, One Aldwych, London
   Photo credit: Paul Ratigan

3 Glazed atrium, Burswood BV, London
   Photo credit: Jo Reid and John Peck

4 Reception and exhibition space, British Council, Prague
   Photo credit: Radovan Bocek

5 Internal stair topped by oval rooflight, British Council, Madrid
   Photo credit: Reto Halme

1

2

3

4

5

Johnson Fain Partners
Architecture Planning Interiors

USA
800 Wilshire Boulevard
Los Angeles, California 90027
Tel: +(1 213) 622 3500
Fax: +(1 213) 622 6532
E-mail: mgershen@jfpartners.com
Website: www.jfpartners.com

Person to Contact
William H. Fain, Jr., FAIA

Number of Employees
50

Date of Establishment
1931

Partners
Scott Johnson, FAIA
William H. Fain, Jr., FAIA

Associate Partners
Larry R. Ball, AIA
Mark R. Gershen, Associate AIA
Daniel J. Janotta, AIA

Senior Associates
Jeffrey Averill, AIA
Juan Carlos Begazo, AIA

Associates
Stephen E. Levine, AIA
Srinivas Rao
Albert H. Sawano, AIA
Robert P. Shaffer, AIA
Kevin Tyrrell, AIA
Gregory Verabian, AIA

Project Types
Architecture
Corporate/office, governmental and public buildings, mixed-use retail, residential/condominiums, hotel-resort, large-scale high-rise, educational-university, medical facilities-technical and research laboratories including new construction, building modernization, renovation and restoration.

Interiors
Corporate office environments, film studios, stage sets, art galleries, museums, resorts, condominiums, wineries and restaurants.

Planning and Urban Design
New town plans, master plans, facilities master planning, general and specific plans, site feasibility, and land use analysis for a variety of clients and diverse industries including: aviation; universities; film industry; public agencies; cities; the United States and international governments; resorts; recreation; private and public development; and redevelopment.

Disciplines
Architecture, Interior Design, Planning and Urban Design

Current and Recent Projects
Amgen Center, Thousand Oaks
Capitol Area East End Complex, Sacramento
City National Bank, Burbank
Constellation Place, Los Angeles
Junipero Serra, State of California Office Building, Los Angeles
LAX Master Plan Update Urban Design, Los Angeles
Mondavi Winery, Monterey County
NBC 4 Newsroom, Burbank
Oklahoma Native American Museum and Cultural Center, Oklahoma City
Twenty First Century Insurance, Woodland Hills
Warner Bros. International Recreation Enterprises, Glendale

Selected Clients
American Airlines; Lockheed; Amgen; Nestle USA; Unocal; Charernkit; Sunflower Group; Dreamworks SKG; JMB/Urban; Sheraton International; Westin; Hilton; Italian-Thai Development Co.; LaSalle Partners; Trump Org.; Los Angeles International Airport; Giorgio of Beverly Hills; CBS; MCA; NBC; Paramount; Citibank; Home Savings of America; Guam Housing Corporation; People's Construction Bank/China; Kingdom of Saudi Arabia; State of Qatar; Sumitomo Ltd.; Miyama Development International; Estate of James Campbell; Baron Philippe de Rothschild, Inc.; Patramas Adhiloka; Perini L+D; SunAmerica; Warner Bros.

Design Philosophy
With nearly 70 years of professional experience in the United States and overseas, Johnson Fain Partners, a California Corporation, and JFP International, a Guam Corporation, have an established record as an architecture and planning office known for its creative approach in the design of buildings, building complexes and new communities. The firm has been awarded many awards for design excellence.

Attention to all levels of detail and close client communications ensure the best match of client needs, design intent and cost effectiveness.
A flexible management structure, experienced staff, innovative design and advanced CAD technology enable the firm to respond to concurrent projects with proficiency.

Fox Plaza, Los Angeles, California, USA
Photo credit: John Gaylord

Rincon Center, San Francisco, California, USA
Photo credit: Steve Whittaker

Amgen Center, Thousand Oaks, California, USA
Photo credit: Erhard Pfeiffer

Patramas Adhiloka Oil Plaza, Jakarta
Photo credit: Erhard Pfeiffer

1999 Avenue of the Stars, Los Angeles, California, USA
Photo credit: Mark Lohman

LeoPalace Resort, Guam
Photo credit: courtesy Johnson Fain Partners

Dreamworks SKG Studios, Playa Vista, California, USA
Photo credit: Mark Lohman

Warner Bros. Inc. Headquarters, Burbank, California, USA
Photo credit: Erhard Pfeiffer

Joseph Wong Design Associates
Architecture, Planning, Interior Design

Joseph O. Wong, Herbert Shear, Tony Fan,
Edgardo Celestino, Tomás Vega-Tapia and
Richard Rounds

USA
Head Office
2359 Fourth Avenue
San Diego, California 92101-1606
Tel: +(1 619) 233 6777
Fax: +(1 619) 237 0541
E-mail: jwda@jwdainc.com

China
No. 2570 Xietu Road
Shanghai 200030
Tel: +(8621) 6468 7179
Fax: +(8621) 6468 7180
E-mail: jwdasha@online.sh.cn

Directors
Joseph O. Wong, Principal
Herbert Shear, Associate Principal
Tony Fan, Associate

Associates
Edgardo Celestino
Tomás Vega-Tapia
Richard Rounds
Michael Fraire
Hector Zuniga
Pete Rose
Jason J.S. Hu

Persons to Contact
Joseph O. Wong, San Diego
Herbert Shear, San Diego
Tony Fan, Shanghai

Number of Employees
35

Date of Establishment
1977

Project Types
Corporate/Offices
Educational
Government
Hotels and Resorts
Medical
Mixed-use
Residential

Disciplines
Architecture
Interior Design
Planning
Urban Design

Current and Recent Projects
International Tennis Center and Regal Hotel,
 Shanghai
San Diego International Airport Expansion, San
 Diego
San Diego State University Foundation KPBS/
 Gateway Building,
 San Diego
San Diego Convention Center Expansion, San
 Diego
Maintenance Warehouse Corporate Offices, San
 Diego
Pacific Bell Network Operations Center, San
 Diego
Hilton Hotels, Carlsbad Beach and San Diego
Station B Hotel, San Diego
Marriott Hotels, San Diego and Burbank
Regents Park Place (Residential), La Jolla
ICBC Bank, projects at Bund & Pudong,
 Shanghai
Shanghai Telecommunications Building,
 Shanghai

Selected Clients
AT&T
BRE Properties
San Diego Unified School District
Waterford Development Company
Department of the Navy
Union Bank of California
Centre City Development Corporation
City and County of San Diego
San Diego State University Foundation
University of California
Port of San Diego
Pacific Bell
Hilton Hotels
Beijing University
Shanghai Telephone Company
Industrial & Commercial Bank of China
Maintenance Warehouse/Home Depot
US Department of Housing & Development
McDonald's Corporation

Design Philosophy and History
Joseph Wong Design Associates, Inc. (JWDA) is
an architectural design and planning firm with
offices in San Diego, California and Shanghai,
which was established in 1977 to provide a full
spectrum of professional services in architecture,
master planning and interior design. JWDA
takes pride in its reputation for on-time and on-
budget delivery of services and believes that a
client's success is the key to its success. Excellent
design, creative planning and technical expertise
provides the basis of the design system.
Evidence of this commitment to consistent
quality, cost and design is the fact that most
projects in the last five years have been with
repeat clients.

JWDA is a full service, multi-disciplinary firm
offering proven experience and personal
commitment on all types of projects, evidenced
by more than 50 local and national awards of
excellence. JWDA's diversified practice has
developed an impressive breadth of experience
in a broad range of projects for both the public
and private sectors. These projects while varied
are united by a commitment to excellence. They
include community facilities, state-of-the-art
educational, institutional and public complexes,
world-class mixed-use developments, and
medical facilities as well as master planning for
residential communities and internationally
recognized hotels and resorts. Each project
comes to fruition under the constant personal
attention of a project manager supported by the
guidance of the principal designer, Mr. Joseph
Wong.

The choice of an architect is based upon
professional trust vested in the principals, key
employees, and staff of the firm. The JWDA
team includes the creative talents of experienced
architects, highly trained planners, interior
designers, specification writers and business
support personnel. The JWDA staff takes pride
in a solid record of delivering architectural
services in a manner consistent with each client's
pragmatic concerns. Each staff member views
his or her work not as a means to an end, but as
a service to a valued client, creating a lasting
contribution to society through the development
of a client's vision. JWDA is sensitive to the
importance of the client's needs and
understands that the continued success of the
firm depends on the record of client satisfaction.

1 Marriott Hotel, Carmel Valley Gateway, Waterford
 Development Inc., San Diego, USA
 Photo credit: courtesy Joseph Wong Design
 Associates

2 San Diego Convention Centre Expansion,
 San Diego, USA
 Photo credit: courtesy Joseph Wong Design
 Associates

3 Shanghai International Tennis Center and Regal
 Hotel, Shanghai East-Asia Group, China
 Photo credit: courtesy Joseph Wong Design
 Associates

4 Shanghai Telecommunications Building, Shanghai
 Telephone Company, China
 Photo credit: courtesy Joseph Wong Design
 Associates

5 Station B Hotel, Monaghan Company LLC, San
 Diego, USA
 Photo credit: courtesy Joseph Wong Design
 Associates

JWDA
Joseph Wong Design Associates

1

2

3

4

5

Kanner Architects

USA
10924 Le Conte Avenue
Los Angeles, California 90024
Tel: +(1 310) 208 0028
Fax: +(1 310) 208 5756
E-mail: kannerarch2@earthlink.net

Date of Establishment
1946

Project Types
Commercial
Entertainment
Institutional
Recreational
Residential

Disciplines
Architectural Design
Interior Design
Planning

Design Philosophy and History

Kanner Architects is an internationally recognized office located in Los Angeles, California. Their buildings have won numerous significant awards including honours for design given by the American Institute of Architects. Their work has been widely published, with feature articles in *Abitare*, *Architecture*, *Architecture Record*, *Architectural Digest* and *Metropolis* magazines. A monograph on the firm's work, *POP Architecture*, was published by The Images Publishing Group in 1998.

Kanner Architects believes that every project is a special endeavour and that superior architecture will be achieved through applying the core values of fulfilling the client's needs, sound planning, cost-effectiveness, and sensitivity to site. The firm's design philosophy embraces the notion that buildings are meant to be places of joy – open and accessible, colourful and inspirational. No project is too small. Every project must enhance the built environment.

1

2

3

4

5

1 High Rise Auto Mall, Los Angeles, California
2 Bright Child, Santa Monica, California
3 IN-N-OUT Burger, Los Angeles, California
4 Copeland Residence, Los Angeles, California
5 Christina Development Offices, Malibu, California

6 China Airport, Beijing, China
7 Greer Residence, Palm Springs, California
8 Harvard Apartments, Los Angeles, California
9 Men in Black attraction, Universal Studios Florida, Orlando, Florida

Photo credits: courtesy Kanner Architects

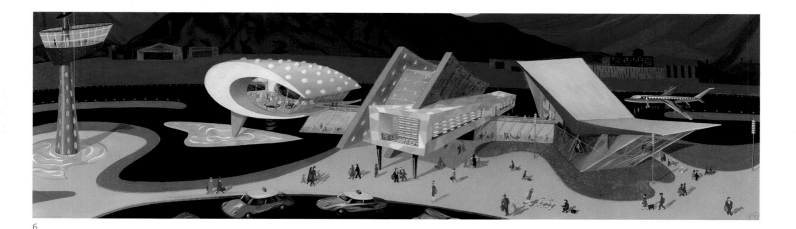

6

7

8

9

Kengo Kuma & Associates

Kengo Kuma
Photo credit: Mitsumasa Fujitsuka

Japan
2-12-12-9F Minamiaoyama Minatoku
Tokyo 107-0062
Tel: (81 3) 3401 7721
Fax: (81 3) 3401 7778
E-mail: Kuma@baz.sonet.ne.jp

Number of Employees
13

Date of Establishment
1990

Project Types
Commercial
River/Filter, Tamagawa-mura, Fukushima
   prefecture, Japan, 1996
Guest House
Water/Glass, Oiso-cho Naka-gun, Kanagawa
   prefecture, Japan, 1997
Observatory
Kiro-san Observatory, Yoshiumi-cho Ochi-gun,
   Ehime prefecture, Japan, 1994
Public
Noh Stage in the Forest, Toyama-machi Tome-
   gun, Miyagi prefecture, Japan, 1997

Current and Recent Projects
Museum of Ando Hiroshige, Batoh-cho Nasu-
   gun, Tochigi prefecture, Japan, 2000
Kitakami Canal Museum, Ishinomaki City, Miyagi
   prefecture, Japan, 1999
Stone Museum, Nasu-mach, Nasu City, Japan,
   1999

Selected Clients
Japanese Ministry of Construction
Tokyo City
Bandai, Co., Ltd
Suntory Co., Ltd

1

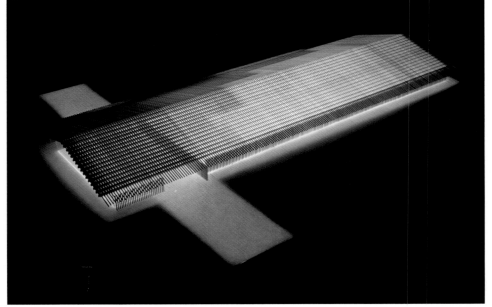

2

Design Philosophy and History

Kengo Kuma founded Kengo Kuma & Associates in 1990 and the firm is based in Tokyo. Its work concentrates on creative architectural design and planning, and on close supervision of execution. It emphasizes experimentation with techniques and material to create unique spaces for each project. Kuma's work has won many prizes, most recently the Grand Prize for the Architectural Institution of Japan and First Prize for the Residential Dupont Benedictus Award, both in 1997.

Experience of the firm is varied, including office buildings, public amenity buildings, corporate headquarters, residential buildings, and sports and entertainment facilities. Its approach is mainly derived from the traditional Japanese concern of interior and exterior relationships. Kengo Kuma & Associates aim to provide design solutions that are primarily concerned with the relation of man-to-nature, consequently resulting in an architecture that seeks to mediate between the architectural object and landscape through the play on screens and frames, and on the intricate inter-layering of spaces and landscape, achieving a sort of transparency that blurs clear edge, melts architecture to its surroundings and defies the 'containing' nature of architectural space as we know it.

Kengo Kuma's theoretical works have a definite influence on the firm's approach to design, especially in its use of multi-media tools in both process and presentation (virtual and CAD projects combined with other media-like videos) and in its constant experimentation on space and on the interior and exterior relationships that are at the core of its work.

1 Water/Glass
   Photo credit: Mitsumasa Fujitsuka
2 Museum of Ando Hiroshige
   Photo credit: Mitsumasa Fujitsuka
3 Kiro-san Observatory
   Photo credit: Mitsumasa Fujitsuka
4 Noh Stage in the Forest
   Photo credit: Mitsumasa Fujitsuka
5 River/Filter
   Photo credit: Mitsumasa Fujitsuka
6 Bamboo
   Photo credit: Mitsumasa Fujitsuka

3

4

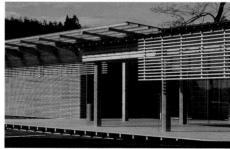

5

6

Kim Young-Sub
Architects & Associates

President, Young Sub Kim

Head Office
Korea
287-3 Yang-Jae Dong
Secho-Ku, Seoul 137-130
Tel: +(81 2) 574 3842
Fax: +(81 2) 579 4172
E-mail: Kunchook@hanmail.net

Person to Contact
Young Sub Kim, President

Number of Employees
25

Date of Establishment
1982

Project Types
Commercial
Educational
Religious
Residential

Recent Projects
Korea Life Insurance, Kangnam Building, Seoul, Korea
SungKyunKwan University, Lecture Building, Seoul, Korea
Balan Catholic Church, Balan City, Korea
ChungYang Catholic Church, ChungYang, Korea

Selected Clients
Catholic Church Archdiocese in Suwon
Korea Life Insurance
SungKyunKwan University

Design Philosophy and History
Kim Young-Sub is well known for his innovative work in the design of catholic churches. He is famous for not only maintaining a delicate harmony between his architectural works and its surroundings, but also for successfully blending traditional Korean elements with Western architectural concepts.

Kim Young-Sub's portfolio is not limited to the many catholic chuches, which has brought him fame worldwide. He has also worked on diverse projects ranging from residences to high-scale modern office buildings, all of which incorporate his unique design philosophy.

Having established his architectural firm, Kunchook-Moonhwa ('The Culture of Architecture') in 1982 in Seoul, Korea, he has since then garnered major architectural awards for his outstanding works. His works were shown at SIAC in Rome in 1986, and he was invited to participate as the Korean representative at the Innovative Architecture International Symposium that was held in Bangalore, India in 1998.

1

2

3

4

5

1 KangNam Building, Sechodong, Seoul, Korea
  Photo credit: Joe-Kyeong Kim

2 Chung's Residence, Seodaeshindong, Pusan, Korea
  Photo credit: Joe-Kyeong Kim

3 Ikchunggak & Crystal House, Samchungdong,
  Seoul, Korea
  Photo credit: Joe-Kyeong Kim

4 ChungYang Catholic Church, ChungYang,
  Chongchungnam-do, Korea
  Photo credit: Joe-Kyeong Kim

5 ChungAng Catholic Church, Anyang City,
  Kyungki-do, Korea
  Photo credit: Joe-Kyeong Kim

Kisho Kurokawa
architect & associates

Japan
11F, Aoyama Building
1-2-3 Kita Aoyama, Minato-Ku
Tokyo 107-0061
Tel: +(81 3) 3404 3481
Fax: +(81 3) 3404 6222
E-mail: kurokawa@kisho.co.jp

9F, Shinsaibashi Nt Building
1-11-17 Higashi-Shinsaibashi, Chuo-Ku
Osaka 542-0083
Tel: +(81 6) 6251 5789
Fax: +(81 6) 6251 5791
E-mail: kkaaosak@kisho.co.jp

3F 1-2, Misonoza Kaikan
1-6-14 Sakae, Naka-Ku
Nagoya 460-0008
Tel: +(81 52) 222 4491
Fax: +(81 52) 218 3181

Directors
Kisho Kurokawa, President
Tadao Shibata, Executive Managing Director
Hank Cheriex, Managing Director
Naotake Ueki, Managing Director
Ichiro Tanaka, Managing Director
Yoshiyuki Umebayashi, Director
Masahiro Kamei, Director
Iwao Miura, Advisor
Wataru Honda, Auditor

Associates
Kurokawa Cad Center Inc, Tokyo
Urban Design Consultant Inc, Tokyo
Institute for Social Engineering Inc, Tokyo

Person to Contact
Yukari Miyanaga, Tokyo

Number of Employees
205

Date of Establishment
1962

Disciplines
Architectural
Structural
Mechanical & Electrical
Landscape
Interior Art Work & Furniture
Specification
Bills of Quantities
Cost Estimation

Current and Recent Projects
New Wing of the Van Gogh Museum,
 Amsterdam, the Netherlands
Kuala Lumpur International Airport,
 Kuala Lumpur, Malaysia
Fukui City Museum of Art, Fukui, Japan
Museum of Modern Art, Wakayama, Japan
Wakayama Prefectural Museum, Wakayama,
 Japan
Ehime Prefectural Museum of General Science,
 Ehime, Japan
Amber Hall (Kuji City Cultural Hall),
 Iwate, Japan

Selected Clients
Van Gogh Museum New Wing Foundation,
 the Netherlands
Government of Malaysia
Government of the Republic of Kazakhstan,
 Astana, Kazakhstan
Shenzhen Urban Planning & Land
 Administration Bureau, Shenzhen, China
CDL Properties Pet Ltd, Singapore
Hotel Lotte Co. Ltd, Korea
Osaka Prefectural Government, Japan
Fukui Prefectural Government, Japan
Wakayama Prefectural Government, Japan
Ehime Prefectural Government, Japan
Toyota Municipal Government, Japan
Sony Corporation, Japan
Central Japan Railway Company, Japan
Fukuoka Bank Co. Ltd, Japan

Design Philosophy and History
The Kurokawa Group represents the merger of
two professional design firms: Kisho Kurokawa
architect & associates, established in 1962 and
Urban Design Consultants, Inc., established in
1969 by Professor Kisho Kurokawa, together
with the Institute for Social Engineering, Inc.,
which was also established in 1969. During its
brief history the Group has grown to include
more than 200 professional staff plus
administrative personnel. The Group has
provided technical expertise in the fields of
architecture, urban design, regional and new
town planning, landscape design, social-
economic planning, long-range development
planning, and futures forecasting for
government and private agencies both in Japan
and abroad.

When approaching a particular project, the
architects, planners and engineers comprising
the Group focus on the concepts of the
'symbiotic theory', postulating that architecture
as well as urban and social structures should
enhance the ambivalent, heterogeneous nature
of man. This theory, which has inherently been
manifest in every culture, aims to probe the
interrelationship between architecture and
nature, man and technology, history and the
future, and various differing cultures by creating
intermediacy and having these elements
supplement each other. In applying these
concepts, the practicing consultant includes in
each project plan an understanding of how the
structural and causal variables are integrated
within a constantly changing environment.

1

2

1 Ehime Prefectural Museum of General Science
  Photo credit: Tomio Ohashi

2 Kuala Lumpur International Airport, Kisho Kurokawa
  Architect & Associates in association with Akitek
  Jururancang
  Photo credit: Tomio Ohashi

3 New Wing of the Van Gogh Museum
  Photo credit: Sels-Clerbourt

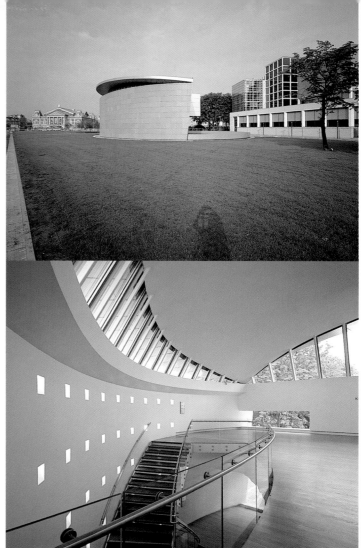

3

KPF Kohn Pedersen Fox Associates

USA
111 West 57th Street
New York, New York 10019
Tel: +(1 212) 977 6500
Fax: +(1 212) 956 2526
E-mail: info@kpf.com
Website: www.kpf.com

Japan
Akasaka Annex Building 3F
2-17-42 Akasaka
Minato-Ku, Tokyo 107-0052
Tel: +(813) 3585 8822
Fax: +(813) 3585 8824
E-mail: pkatz@kpf.com
Contact: Paul Katz

UK
13 Langley Street
Covent Garden
London WC2H 9JG
Tel: +(44 171) 836 6668
Fax: +(44 171) 497 1175
E-mail: info@kpf.co.uk
Website: www.kpf.com

Principals
A. Eugene Kohn, FAIA RIBA JIA
William Pedersen, FAIA FAAR
Robert L. Cioppa, FAIA
William C. Louie, FAIA
Lee A. Polisano, FAIA RIBA
David M. Leventhal, AIA

Gregory Clement, AIA
Michael Greene, AIA
Paul Katz, AIA
Paul Kevin Kennon, AIA
Peter Schubert, AIA
James von Klemperer, AIA

Project Types
Commercial
Educational
Entertainment
Government
Hotel/Resort
Institutional

Interior Design
Master Planning
Renovation
Residential
Retail
Transportation

Additional Projects
Baruch College New Academic Complex, New York, New York
Bloomingdale's, Aventura, Florida
Children's Hospital of Philadelphia, Pennsylvania
Espirito Santo Plaza, Miami, Florida
Federal Reserve Bank of Dallas, Texas
Goldman Sachs European Headquarters, London, UK
Lincoln Square, New York, New York
Mohegan Sun Phase II, Uncasville, Connecticut
Philadelphia International Airport, International Terminal One, Philadelphia, Pennsylvania
Procter & Gamble World Headquarters, Cincinnati, Ohio
The Rothemere Institute for American Studies, Oxford University, Oxford, UK
Telecom Headquarters, Buenos Aires, Argentina
Jon M. Huntsman Hall, The Wharton School of the University of Pennsylvania, Philadelphia, Pennsylvania

Selected Clients
AT&T
Boston Properties
Capital Cities/ABC Inc.
Central Japan Railway
CGI
CUNY/Baruch College
First Union National Bank
Four Seasons Hotels Ltd
Gannett Co. Inc.
General Services Admin.

Goldman Sachs & Co.
Hines Interests Ltd
Hong Kong Land Ltd
ING Real Estate Group
Markborough Properties Ltd
MOMA
PGGM
Tishman Speyer Properties
Trimp & Van Tartwijk Property
US Airways

Design Philosophy and History
Kohn Pedersen Fox was founded on an insistence upon design excellence, partner commitment, and client service. KPF believes that the best solution emerges from an intensive dialogue with the client, the site, and the program. The firm works from the 'inside out' and the 'outside in' to achieve a degree of craft and detail that elevates the firm's projects to the highest level of both beauty and practicality.

KPF recognizes the civic responsibility of buildings, as well as the importance of engineering technology and sustainability, in shaping our built environment. The firm examines the physical and historical context of each project to ensure that each relates to its environment in a sensitive and invigorating fashion. By considering the growing influences of environmental concern and workplace standards, as well as the changing ways of conducting business, KPF brings an informed perspective to the effective fulfilment of the unique functional, aesthetic, and social goals of each project.

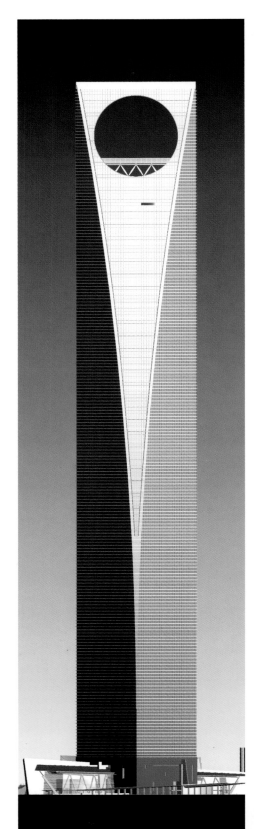

Shanghai World Financial Center, Shanghai, China
Computer Rendering: Edge Media

IBM World Headquarters, Armonk, New York, USA
Photo credit: Peter Aaron/ESTO

The World Bank Headquarters, Washington, DC, USA
Photo credit: Timothy Hursley

Thames Court, London, UK
Photo credit: H.G. Esch

Greater Buffalo International Airport, New York, USA
Photo credit: Timothy Hursely

Provinciehuis, The Hague, the Netherlands
Photo credit: Christian Richters

Westend Str. 1/DG Bank Headquarters, Frankfurt am Main, Germany
Photo credit: Dennis Gilbert

333 Wacker Drive, Chicago, Illinois, USA
Photo credit: Barbara Karant

Rodin Museum at Samsung Plaza, Seoul, Korea
Photo credit: Kim YongKwan Photography

First Hawaiian Center, Honolulu, Hawaii
Photo credit: Timothy Hursley

Mark O. Hatfield US Courthouse, Portland, Oregon
Photo credit: Timothy Hursley

Kuwabara Payne McKenna Blumberg
Architects

Bruce Kuwabara, Shirley Blumberg, Marianne
McKenna and Thomas Payne
Photo credit: Ron Baxter Smith

Canada
322 King Street West
Toronto, Ontario M5V 1J2
Tel: +(1 416) 977 5104
Fax: +(1 416) 598 9840
E-mail: kpmb@kpmbarchitects.com

Partners
Bruce Kuwabara
Thomas C. Payne
Marianne McKenna
Shirley Blumberg

Senior Associates
Christopher Couse
Luigi Larocca

Associates
John Allan
Andrew Dyke
Victoria Gregory
Mitchell Hall
David Jesson
Goran Milosevic
Robert Sims
Judith Taylor

Person to Contact
Heidi McKenzie, Marketing Coordinator

Number of Employees
50

Date of Establishment
1987

Project Types
Civic
Commercial
Cultural
Educational
Government/Public Sector
Hospitality
Institutional
Residential
Retail

Disciplines
Architecture
Interior Design
Urban Design

Current and Recent Projects
Canadian Embassy, Berlin, Germany
Goodman Theatre, Chicago, Illinois
Trinity College Library & Computing Centre,
  Hartford, Connecticut
Art Gallery of Hamilton, Hamilton, Ontario
Stratford Festival Theatre, Stratford, Ontario
Japanese Canadian Cultural Centre, Toronto
Ammirati Puris Lintas Headquarters, New York
Munk Centre for International Studies, Toronto

Selected Clients
Department of Foreign Affairs & International
  Trade
Stratford Festival Theatre
Hilton International
City of Toronto
Disney Development Corp.
Alias/wavefront
Chicago Theatre Group, Inc.
University of Toronto

Design Philosophy and History
Founded in 1987, Kuwabara Payne McKenna
Blumberg has developed an international
reputation for excellence in architecture, urban
design and interior design. The work of the firm
has been recognized for its responsiveness to
the urban context as acts and interventions of
city building, as well as for its careful, rigorous
attention to detailing and technical execution.
The firm has received both national and
international recognition for its achievements
including seven Governor General's Awards for
Architecture (the highest award for architecture
offered in Canada) and has seen their work
published in 10 different countries.

The members of the firm are committed to the
value of working on interdisciplinary teams with
the client and with proficient and talented
consultants. The studio atmosphere of the office
is conducive to a stimulating and creative
environment which fosters complementarity and
collaboration.

1

1 View of courtyard at Chinese Cultural Centre,
  Toronto, Ontario
  Photo credit: Kerun Ip

2 View of the restored Mazzoleni Concert Hall, Royal
  Conservatory of Music, Toronto
  Photo credit: Volker Seding

3 View at night of main entrance to Stauffer Library,
  Queen's University, Kingston, Ontario
  Photo credit: Steven Evans

4 View of Trading Floor, Design Exchange, Toronto,
  Ontario
  Photo credit: Steven Evans

5 View of civic plaza at Kitchener City Hall, Kitchener,
  Ontario
  Photo credit: Steven Evans

2

3

4

5

Legorreta Arquitectos
Architects and Planners

Ricardo Legorreta Vilchis, Victor Legorreta Hernandez

Mexico
285-A, Palacio De Versalles
D.F. 11020
Tel: +(525) 251 9698
Fax: +(525) 596 6162
E-mail: legorret@data.net.mx

USA
2nd Floor, 3440 Motor Avenue
Los Angeles, California 90034
Tel: +(1 310) 391 9976
Fax: +(1 310) 391 0976

Directors
Ricardo Legorreta Vilchis, Principal
Victor Legorreta Hernandez, Lead Designer

Associate
Noe Castro Castro

Persons to Contact
Miguel Almaraz Scanlin, Mexico City
Rosario Lemos Velasco, Mexico City
Bill Berenstein, Los Angeles, California

Number of Employees
42

Date of Establishment
1963

Project Types
Cathedrals	Plazas
Factories	Public Buildings
Hotels	Residential Complexes
Houses	Restorations
Laboratories	Schools
Libraries	Stores
Museums	Universities
Offices	

Disciplines
Architectural Design
Interior Design
Urban Planning

Current and Recent Projects
Chiron Life & Science Laboratories, Emeryville
  City, California, USA
Tech Museum of Innovation, San Jose,
  California, USA
College of Santa Fe Visual Arts Center, New
  Mexico, USA
ITESM Campus Santa Fe, Mexico City, Mexico
ITESM Graduate School of Business, Monterrey,
  Nuevo Leon, Mexico
University of Chicago Residence Halls, Chicago,
  Illinois, USA
Public Building University of San Francisco,
  California, USA
Art Museum, Mouggins, France
Mexican Pavilion for the World Fair, Hannover,
  Germany

Selected Clients
Chiron Life & Science
UCLA
Tech Museum of Innovation
Marco
ITESM
Tom Monaham
College of Santa Fe
City of San Antonio
City of Los Angeles
University of Chicago
University of San Francisco
City of Mexico
Televisa
Stanford University

Design Philosophy and History
As a Mexican firm, Legorreta Arquitectos has been exposed and influenced by Mexican vernacular architecture. This has taught the firm to resolve problems in a fresh and spontaneous way, responding to programmatic and budget issues with creative solutions. They have also learned the important role that human values play in architecture.

Legorreta Arquitectos seeks to create an architecture that will serve society, and contribute to build better cities. By achieving functionality, efficiency and cost, the firm can design an environment that is humane and friendly, and has an atmosphere of intimacy, peace and optimism. The use of colour, light, water, mystery and humour, is more of an emotional response to architecture than an intellectual one.

The firm believes that good architecture needs to be carried through as a whole, and for this reason, the firm likes to be involved in every aspect of the design, including the landscaping, interiors, graphics and lighting. In order to achieve a successful project, the firm encourages the close and active interaction with the client.

The firm selects projects not by reason of size, type or economic revenue, but rather for the possibilities of creating good architecture.

1

1 Camino Real Hotel, Ixtapa, Mexico
  Photo credit: Lourdes Legorreta

2 Solana Complex, Dallas, Texas, USA
  Photo credit: Lourdes Legorreta

3 College of Santa Fe Visual Arts Center, New Mexico,
  USA
  Photo credit: Lourdes Legorreta

4 The Tech Museum of Innovation, San Jose,
  California, USA
  Photo credit: Lourdes Legorreta

5 Greenberg House, Los Angeles, California, USA
  Photo credit: Lourdes Legorreta

6 Chiron Life & Science Laboratories, Emeryville City,
  California, USA
  Photo credit: Lourdes Legorreta

2

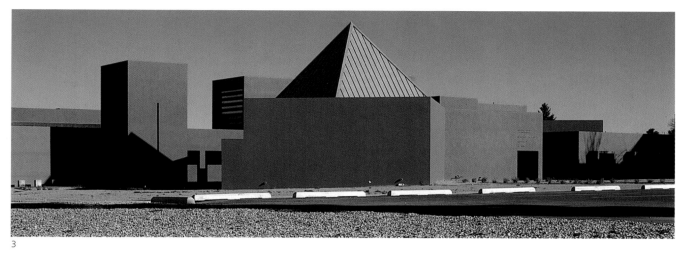

3

4

5

6

Levin and Associates
Architect

Brenda Levin, FAIA

USA
Suite 900, 811 West Seventh Street
Los Angeles, California 90017
Tel: +(1 213) 623 8141
Fax: +(1 213) 623 9207
E-mail: blevin@levinarch.com

Directors
Brenda Levin, FAIA, President

Associates
Bob Knight
Kaitlin Drisko
Robert Stone

Person to Contact
Brenda Levin, FAIA, Los Angeles

Number of Employees
12

Date of Establishment
1980

Project Types
Academic
Adaptive Reuse
Art Galleries
Historic Restoration
Master Planning
Multi-family Housing
Museums
Parks
Retail/Restaurants
Sports Facilities
Urban Design

Disciplines
Architecture
Interior Architecture
Master Planning
Urban Design

Current and Recent Projects
Occidental College Johnson Student Center, Los Angeles
Scripps College Campus Commons, Claremont
The Huntington Gallery, San Marino
University Art Museum, Santa Barbara
Oakwood School Music Dance Athletic Center, Los Angeles
Los Angeles City Hall
Barnsdall Park Master Plan, Los Angeles
Echo Park Senior Housing, Los Angeles

Selected Clients
St. James School
Occidental College
Scripps College
City of Los Angeles Recreation and Parks
Oakwood School
State of California
University of California
The Huntington Library, Art Collection and Botanical Gardens

Design Philosophy and History
In two decades of practice in Los Angeles, Brenda Levin's achievements cover a wide variety of projects. These include: historic renovations and restorations; a range of academic and arts-related buildings; multi-family housing and civic projects; and urban design master plans.

This broad spectrum reflects Levin & Associates' deep concern for the texture and character of the urban environment at every scale, from broad strokes to fine detail. In projects such as the Grand Central Market in downtown Los Angeles' historic core, they manifest their grasp of the interaction between the social and the visual qualities of public architecture, weaving both strands into the vital renovation of a popular facility. The same subtle union of function and flair is evident in their academic and educational buildings, including the renovation and expansion of the Johnson Student Center at Occidental College, originally designed by Myron Hunt in the 1920s, the Scripps College Campus Commons, and the Math/Science Building and Music/Dance Athletic Center at Oakwood School. Levin & Associates' method of collaboration with the users of the buildings the firm designs, a process described as 'visioning charrettes', encourages participants to consider each project's architectural tradition, character, and the quality of its spaces.

Levin & Associates' portfolio also displays a fine sensitivity to detail and nuance in their restoration and renovation of some of Los Angeles' most valued historic structures. These include, among others: the famed Bradbury Building, designed by George H. Wyman in 1893; Wilshire Boulevard's landmark 1931 Art Deco Wiltern Theater; and the Los Angeles City Hall. It is largely due to the firm's many successful projects in this field, coupled with Levin's skillful civic advocacy and ability to coax local regulatory agencies into a flexible interpretation of building codes and bylaws, that historic preservation now has an established methodology and vocal constituency in Los Angeles.

Levin & Associates has won numerous awards in recognition of its nationally known record in historic preservation, including the 1989 Distinguished Achievement Award in Historic Preservation. In 1990, Brenda Levin received the State of California Legislature Woman of the Year Award for her achievements, and in 1997 was elected to the American Institute of Architects College of Fellows.

1 Oakwood School, Math Science Building
   Photo credit: Michael Gustad
2 Oakwood School, Math Science building atrium
   Photo credit: Michael Gustad
3 Wiltern Theater
   Photo credit: Bob Ware
4 The Bradbury Building
   Photo credit: Julius Shulman
5 Johnson Student Center, Occidental College
   Photo credit: Alex Verticoff
6 Johnson Student Center Servery
   Photo credit: Alex Verticoff

1

2

3

4

5

6

LPT
Architects Ltd.

Hong Kong
4/F China Overseas Building
139 Hennessy Road
Wanchai, Hong Kong
Tel: +(852) 2861 1728
Fax: +(852) 2529 6419
E-mail: lpt@lpt-architects.com

Managing Director
Keith Griffiths

Directors
Agnes Ng
David Roberts
Kyran Sze
John Fitzgerald
Stephen Coates

Number of Employees
130

Date of Establishment
1982

Project Types
Civil & Community
Hotel
Industrial and Infrastructure
Office Building
Residential
Retail

Firm Profile
Since LPT's establishment in Hong Kong over 17 years ago, it has evolved as a prominent architectural practice with significant involvement and influence across a broad range of diverse market sectors including industrial, infrastructure, commercial, hotel, residential and retail in Hong Kong and throughout South East Asia. LPT's experience covers all forms of projects from both government and private sector. LPT has the resources and expertise to carry out a full range of consultancy services including project management, planning, design and documentation.

LPT focuses on efficient, cost-effective and well designed solutions for its clients and follows these through with sophisticated specification, careful attention to detail and fast track programmes which are planned for the firm's best value for clients. LPT obtained the HKIA Certificate of Merit in 1996 and the Quality Management Award from Mass Transit Railway Corporation in 1997 and 1998.

LPT's Quality Assurance System accredited by HKQAA has been in operation since 1993 and has been continuously improved.

Current and Recent Projects
Civil & Community
ASD Indoor Recreation Centre and Library, Ma On Shan, Hong Kong (2000)
ASD Castle Peak Beach, Tuen Mun, Hong Kong (1999)
ASD Stanley Market & Playground, Hong Kong (1998)
Hotel
Sheraton Hotel Refurbishment, Hong Kong, (1998)
Renaissance Hotel Refurbishment, Kowloon, (1998)

1

3

2

Industrial and Infrastructure
KCRC East Rail Ma On Shan Line TD-400,
 Tai Wai Station, (2004)
KCRC East Rail Ma On Shan Line TD-500,
 Tai Wai Depot, (2004)
KCRC DD-400 West Rail Yen Chow Street &
 Mei Foo Stations, (2002)
MTRC Contracts 602 & 603 Tseung Kwan O &
 Tiu Keng Leng Stations & Ancillary Buildings,
 (2002)
Kuala Lumpur Sentral Station, Kuala Lumpur,
 Malaysia, (2001)
MTRC Airport Railway Depot, Siu Ho Wan,
 Lantau, Hong Kong, (2000)
Tung Chung Wan Telephone Exchange, Lantau,
 Hong Kong, (1999)
River Trade Terminal, Tuen Mun, N.T., (1998)
AAT Asia Air Cargo Terminal, Chek Lap Kok,
 Hong Kong, (1998)

Office Building
11 Chater Road, Central, Hong Kong, (2002)
63 Ly Thai To, Hanoi, Vietnam, 1998
Saigon Tower, HCMC, Vietnam, (1996)
The Landmark, HCMC, Vietnam, Hong Kong,
 (1994)
John Hancock Tower, Singapore, (1993)

Residential
Zhong Shan Beijing, Beijing, PRC, (2000)
Ellery Court, Homantin, Hong Kong, (2000)
Villa Camellia & Royal Camellia Yuen Long,
 Hong Kong, (1997 & 1998)

Retail
No. 1 Raffle's Link, Singapore, (2001)
Prince's Building Retail Podium, Hong Kong,
 (1999)
Rainbow at Sheraton, Hong Kong, (1999)
Whampoa Garden, Site 1,2,3,5,6,7,9,11,12 and
 Street Scape, (1994-1998)
New World Shopping Arcade and Department
 Store Fitout, Beijing, (1998)
Festival Market Rasuna Park, Jakarta, (1996)
Gaysorn Plaza, Bangkok, (1994)

1 Saigon Tower, Ho Chin Mihn City, Vietnam,
 (1994)
 Photo credit: courtesy LPT Architects Ltd.
2 River Trade Terminal, Tuen Mun, N.T., Hong
 Kong, (1999)
 Photo credit: courtesy LPT Architects Ltd.
3 AAT Asia Air Cargo Terminal, Chek Lap Kok,
 Hong Kong, (1998)
 Photo credit: courtesy LPT Architects Ltd.
4 East Central Plaza, Hong Kong, (1995)
 Photo credit: courtesy LPT Architects Ltd.
5 Terminal 8 West, Hong Kong, (1995)
 Photo credit: courtesy LPT Architects Ltd.

Mackey Mitchell Associates
Architecture, Planning, Interiors

E.J. Mackey, FAIA; D.S. Mitchell, FAIA; J.C. Guenther, AIA; R.B. Kirschner, AIA; P. Wuennenberg, AIA; and, T.F. Moore, AIA

USA
Suite 200, 800 St. Louis Union Station
St. Louis, Missouri 63103-2257
Tel: +(1 314) 421 1815
Fax: +(1 314) 421 5206
E-mail: mma@mackeymitchell.com
Website: www@mackeymitchell.com

Persons to Contact
Gene Mackey, FAIA
Dan Mitchell, FAIA

Project Types
Commercial	Recreational
Educational	Renovation
Healthcare	Residential
Master Planning	Urban Planning

Current and Recent Projects
Washington University
 Student Housing
 Master Plan
WU School of Medicine
 Department of Psychiatry Labs
 McDonnell Paediatric Research Lab
 InVitro Fertilization Clinic and Lab
 Olin Residence Hall Addition
University of Missouri
 Science & Technology Building, Kansas City
 Center for Molecular Electronics, St. Louis
Webster University, Master Plan
 Loretto Hilton Addition, Theater
Saint Louis University
 Verhaegen Hall Renovation
Principia College, Elsah, Illinois
Central Institute for the Deaf
Stix Early Childhood Center
St. Mary's Health Center, renovations and
 additions
Christian Brothers College High School
West Pine Townhouses
Far Oaks Golf Course Club and Pavilion
Edward Jones Family YMCA
Chesterfield Ridge Office Building
East Central College
Corporate Woods Office Building
Trinity Lutheran Church
Pineview Pointe Office Building
Commerce Bank Renovation

Selected Clients
Balke Brown Associates
Sachs Properties
Clayco Construction Co.
Barry-Wehmiller Group
Commerce Bank
Washington University
WU School of Medicine
Saint Louis University
Webster University
Principia College
Central Institute for the Deaf
BJC Health System
St. Mary's Health Center
YMCA of Greater St. Louis
St. Louis Symphony
Missouri Botanical Garden
Missouri Athletic Club

Design Philosophy and History
Founded in 1968, Mackey Mitchell Associates is a professional service firm of architects, planners, and interior designers who bring a balance of quality service and fresh ideas to each commission. The firm successfully integrates its experience with its diverse clientele, all to the client's advantage.

The firm's goal is to design work that has a strong sense of place, is in harmony with the environment, and that shows concern for its users.

Mackey Mitchell Associates' success and reputation can be measured by the many awards they've received, and more importantly, by the increasing number of repeat clients.

1

2

1 Herman Stemme Building, St. Louis, Missouri, USA
 Photo credit: Sam Fentress
2 Shapleigh Fountain, Missouri Botanical Garden
 St. Louis, Missouri, USA
 Photo credit: Jack Jennings
3 Spencer T. Olin Hall, Washington University School
 of Medicine, St. Louis, Missouri, USA
 Photo credit: Alise O'Brien
4 Center for Plant Conservation, Missouri Botanical
 Garden, Missouri, USA
 Photo credit: Sam Fentress
5 Emergency Room, St. Mary's Health Center,
 St. Louis, Missouri, USA
 Photo credit: Alise O'Brien
6 Center for Molecular Electronics, University
 of Missouri, St. Louis, USA
 Photo credit: Sam Fentress
7 Clayco Construction Co Headquarters, St. Louis,
 Missouri, USA
 Photo credit: Alise O'Brien

3

4

5

6

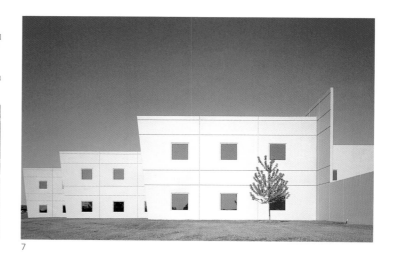

7

Mario Bellini Associati
Architecture, Master Planning, Interiors

Italy
Piazza Arcole, 4
Milano 20143
Tel: +(39 2) 5810 3877
Fax: +(39 2) 5811 3466
E-mail: mba@bellini.it

Design Philosophy and History

Mario Bellini was born in 1935 and graduated in 1959 from the Architecture School in Milan, where he lives and works. His activities range from architecture and urban design to furniture and industrial design.

His fame as a designer dates from 1963 when he became design consultant and department head at Olivetti. He has since worked with a variety of firms in and outside Italy, including B&B Italia, Cassina, Yamaha, Renault, Vitra and Rosenthal. He has won several Compasso d'Oro awards and many other international awards. Many of his designs are now in the permanent collection of the Museum of Modern Art in New York, which honoured him with a one-man show in 1987.

Since the 1980s he has worked chiefly as an architect in Europe, Japan, the US and the Arab Emirates. His best known achievements in Italy include the Portello extension to the Milan Trade Fair, and the exhibition and congress centre in the ground of Villa Erba (Cernobbio). His competition-winning extension to the National Gallery of Victoria in Melbourne is now under construction.

From 1986 to 1991 he was editor of *Domus*, the prestigious art, architecture and design monthly.

Himself an avid art lover and collector, he is also well-known as an art exhibition designer. Milestones in this field include 'The Treasure of St Mark's in Venice' at the Grand Palais in Paris and other museums around the world (1984-87), 'Italian Art in the 20th Century' at the Royal Academy of Arts in London (1989), 'The Renaissance from Brunelleschi to Michelangelo' at Palazzo Grassi in Venice and then in Paris and Berlin (1994-95), and 'The Triumphs of Baroque Architecture in Europe 1600-1750' at the Stupinigi Hunting Lodge in Turin (1999).

1 Risonare-Vivre Club, Kobuchizawa, Japan, 1991/92
  Photo credit: courtesy Mario Bellini Associati

2 Arsoa Headquarters, Yamanashi-Ken, Japan, 1996/98
  Photo credit: courtesy Mario Bellini Associati

3 Natuzzi Americas Headquarters, High Point, USA, 1996/98
  Photo credit: courtesy Mario Bellini Associati

4 Villa Erba exhibition and congress centre, Cernobbio, Italy, 1987/1990
  Photo credit: courtesy Mario Bellini Associati

5 Tokio Design Centre, Tokyo, Japan, 1989/92
  Photo credit: courtesy Mario Bellini Associati

6 Exhibition 'The Renaissance from Brunelleschi to Michelangelo', Palazzo Grassi, Venice, Paris and Berlin, 1994–95
  Photo credit: courtesy Mario Bellini Associati

5

6

Michael Graves & Associates

Michael Graves
Photo credit: Bill Phelps

1

USA
Michael Graves & Associates, Inc.
341 Nassau Street
Princeton, New Jersey 08540
Tel: +(1 609) 924 6409
Fax: +(1 609) 924 1795
E-mail: chancock@michaelgraves.com

Michael E. Graves, Architect, P.C.
Suite 401, 560 Broadway
New York, New York 10012
Tel: +(1 212) 941 5890
Fax: +(1 212) 941 5893

Directors
Michael Graves, FAIA   Gary Lapera, AIA
Patrick Burke, AIA   Karen Nichols, AIA
John Diebboll, AIA   Thomas Rowe, AIA
Susan Howard, Esquire

Persons to Contact
Karen Nichols, AIA, Managing Principal,
   Princeton, New Jersey
Caroline Hancock, Director of Communications,
   Princeton, New Jersey

Number of Employees
75

Date of Establishment
1964

Project Types
The firm's diverse international practice includes multi-use urban developments, corporate headquarters and speculative office buildings, hotels and conference centres, sports and recreation centres, facilities for educational and cultural institutions, multiple-family housing and private residences.

Disciplines
Architectural Design   Furniture Design
Consumer Product   Graphic Design
  Design   Interior Design
Exhibition Design   Master Planning

Selected Clients
The Crown American Corporation; Denver Public Library; Detroit Institute of the Arts; Drexel University; Emory University; The Walt Disney Company; Fortis/AG 1824; The Humana Corporation; International Finance Corporation of the World Bank Group; Lenox China; National Collegiate Athletic Association; The Newark Museum; New Jersey Institute of Technology; Pittsburgh Cultural Trust; United States General Services Administration; Target Stores; Thomson Consumer Electronics; University of Cincinnati; and the University of Virginia.

2

3

4

5

Current and Recent Projects

United States Federal Courthouse, Washington, DC, USA
International Finance Corporation Headquarters, Washington, DC, USA
The Impala Building, New York, New York, USA
The Denver Central Library, Denver, Colorado, USA
The Clark County Library and Theater, Las Vegas, Nevada, USA
Alexandria Central Library, Alexandria, Virginia, USA
French Institute/Alliance Française Library, New York, New York, USA
The O'Reilly Theater, Pittsburgh, Pennsylvania
Miele Appliances US Headquarters, Princeton, New Jersey, USA
1500 Ocean Drive Condominiums, Miami, Florida, USA
Bergen Residence, Cincinnati, Ohio, USA
St. Martin's College Library, Lacey, Washington, USA
Ministry of Health, Welfare and Sport, the Hague, the Netherlands
Fujian Xingye Banking Tower, Shanghai, China
The Miramar Resort Hotel, El Gouna, Egypt
Acacia Hotel, Health Spa and Golf Club, Taba, Egypt
Inter-Continental Hotel, Taba, Egypt
Ortigas Tycoon Twin Towers, Manila, the Philippines
World Trade Exchange Center, Manila, the Philippines
National Museum of Pre-History, Taitung, Taiwan
Fukuoka Hyatt Hotel and Office Building, Fukuoka, Japan
L'Hospitalet Master Plan and Alba Office Building, Barcelona, Spain
Rice University Martel College, Houston, Texas, USA
National Collegiate Athletic Association Headquarters and Hall of Champions, Indianapolis, Indiana, USA
Scaffolding Embellishment for the restoration of the Washington Monument, Washington, DC, USA
Ortigas Tycoon Twin Towers, Manila, the Philippines
World Trade Exchange Center, Manila, the Philippines

Design Philosophy and History

Michael Graves has been at the forefront of architectural and interior design since he began his practice 35 years ago in Princeton, New Jersey, USA, where he has been the Robert Schirmer Professor of Architecture at Princeton University. His firm's distinctive work is fresh and contemporary, yet also draws on a knowledge of history and local context. Throughout the world, Graves has created original, award-winning designs that are functional, efficient, site-specific and sensitive to their cultural milieu.

1 International Finance Corporation Headquarters, Washington, DC, USA
  Photo credit: Andrew Lautman

2 Miramar Resort Hotel, El Gouna, Egypt
  Photo credit: Daniel Aubry

3 Denver Central Library, Denver, Colorado, USA
  Photo credit: Timothy Hursley

4 Humana Building, Louisville, Kentucky, USA
  Photo credit: Paschall/Taylor

5 Washington Monument Restoration Scaffolding, Washington, DC, USA
  Photo credit: Target Stores

6 Fukuoka Hyatt Hotel and Office Building, Fukuoka, Japan
  Photo credit: Toyota Photo Studio, Maeda Corporation

Michael Wilford and Partners Limited
(Incorporating James Stirling Michael Wilford and Associates)

UK
8 Fitzroy Square
London W1P 5AH
Tel: +(44) 20 7388 6188
Fax: +(44) 20 7388 8776
E-mail: mailbox@mwp-architects.demon.co.uk

Directors
Michael Wilford
Laurence Bain
Russell Bevington

Project Types
Museums and Galleries
Universities and Music Academies
Theatres and Performing Arts Centres
Prestigious Office Buildings
Industrial Buildings
Stations

Current and Recent Projects
Lowry Centre, Salford, UK, 1992–
Abando Passenger Interchange and Bus Station, Bilbao, Spain, 1992–
National Performing Arts Centre, Singapore, 1992–
Sto AG Factory Headquarters and Production Plant, Weizen, Germany, 1993–
Ty Llen National Centre for Literature, Swansea, UK, 1993
Royal Library Copenhagen, Demark, 1993
Tate Gallery, Albert Dock, Liverpool, Phase 2, UK, 1993–98
Clore Gallery (Turner Collection), Tate Gallery Refurbishment, UK, 1993–94
Museum of Victoria, Melbourne, Australia, 1994
British Museum, Courtyard Redevelopment, UK, 1994
Sto Ag New Office Building, Weizen, Germany, 1994–97
Technical University, Dresden, Germany, 1994
Sto Regional Depot, Hamburg, Germany, 1994–95
National Museums and Galleries on Merseyside, Liverpool, UK, 1994
British Embassy, Berlin, Germany, 1994–
Music School and CinemaxX, Mannheim, Germany, 1995–
Hanover/Laatzen Trade Fair Station, Hanover, Germany, 1995
National Centre for Industrial Virtual Reality, Salford, UK, 1996–
National Youth Performing Arts Centre, Gloucester, UK, 1997–
Music School, Rostock, Germany, 1997
Hotel, Salford, UK, 1997–
Hamilton Ahead Arts Centre, Hamilton, Scotland, UK, 1997–
National Centre for Virtual Environments, Salford, UK, 1997–
Cultural Quarter, Arts Centre, Shoreham-by-Sea, UK, 1997–
Scottish Parliament, Edinburgh, UK, 1998
Perth 2000, Arts Centre, Perth, UK, 1998
Jubilee Arts, Arts and Multi-Media Centre, West Bromwich, UK, 1998

Design Philosophy and History
The office has an international reputation for producing buildings of the highest architectural quality which satisfy the requirements of the client's brief and respond to the opportunities of site and context. The practice is eminent for its 'design' architecture, which fully involves all phases and aspects of the work. Excellence requires integrity and control of the design process from concept through detailing and construction.

1

2

3

4

The work includes the design of buildings for many clients: institutions such as museums, universities, central and local government, new town corporations, the United Nations and corporate clients such as Olivetti, Siemens, Bayer, B Braun Melsungen, City Acre Property Investment Trust, Chelsfield, and Olympia and York. Work has also been completed for individual patrons of international renown including Lord Palumbo, Baron Thyssen and Rina Brion.

Michael Wilford and Partners' buildings and projects have been illustrated extensively in publications and included in exhibitions throughout the world. James Stirling was the recipient of many awards and honourary fellowships, for instance, the RIBA Gold Medal in 1980, the Pritzker Prize in 1981 and the Praemium Imperiale Award in 1990. In 1997, the practice was awarded the prestigious Sunday Times/RIBA Stirling Prize. The work of the practice has also been the subject of television and film documentaries.

1 Adaptable Theatre and Gallery, The Lowry, Salford, UK
   Photo credit: Richard Davies
2 Night-time view of Building 'K', Sto AG, Marketing and Training Building, Weizen, Germany
   Photo credit: Richard Bryant/Arcaid
3 Concert Hall, Music Academy, Stuttgart, Germany
   Photo credit: Richard Bryant/Arcaid
4 Abando Passenger Interchange, Bilbao, Spain
   Photo credit: Chris Edgcombe
5 Model, Music School and CinemaxX, Mannheim, Germany
   Photo credit: Chris Edgcombe
6 Front elevation, British Embassy, Berlin, Germany
   Photo credit: Richard Davies

5

6

Mitchell/Giurgola Architects

Steven Goldberg; Mark Markiewicz; Paul Broches; Jan Keane; John Kurtz

1

2

USA
170 West 97th Street
New York, New York 10025-6492
Tel: +(1 212) 663 4000
Fax: +(1 212) 866 5006
E-mail: mga@bway.net

Persons to Contact
Steven Goldberg or Paul Broches

Number of Employees
40

Date of Establishment
1986

Disciplines
Adaptive Reuse
Civic
Commercial
Educational
Healthcare
Laboratories
Planning
Renovation

Current and Recent Projects
Columbia University, Chemistry Building, New
  York, USA
Cornell University Medical College, Research
  Laboratories, New York, USA
Department of Defense Dependents Schools,
  New K-12 School Complex, Aviano, Italy
Department of Defense Dependents Schools,
  New K-12 School Complex, Rota, Spain
New York University Medical Center, Research
  Laboratories, New York, USA
Virginia Polytechnic Institute, Chemistry/Biology
  Building, Blacksburg, Virginia, USA
Salisbury State University, Undergraduate
  Teaching Laboratory, Salisbury, Maryland, USA

3

Design Philosophy and History

The studio setting at Mitchell/Giurgola has been an excellent training ground for the current partners and has provided a similar foundation for its associates and staff. A tightly knit working method and design philosophy has been maintained by limiting the size of the office and by assuring substantial and consistent participation in all projects by the principals.

The motivating force for setting a design direction draws upon the characteristics that make each client unique. The diversity of design solutions reflects this approach. The common threads in the work derive from the highly complex programs given to the architects. The synthesis of potentially conflicting demands is a familiar process for the partners as they view buildings in the same way as the fabric of the city. The Mitchell/Giurgola portfolio is replete with projects which are complex in their programs and site conditions, varied in their materials and appearance, yet simple, dignified and clear in their execution.

The partners do not favour the imposition of any particular style on their work. The form of a given project evolves in direct response to the program and specific site characteristics. Ultimately, each building emerges from its context to take on a presence and definition that is unique. It is the tension between these seemingly contradictory qualities that defines the Mitchell/Giurgola signature. The firm's designs are the result of a personal architectural expression informed by history, culture, and human behaviour.

Architecture is fundamentally about the translation of social enterprise into an expressive and dignified built form. The measure of its success is, in the first instance, the way in which it is appropriated by its inhabitants, and secondly, the degree to which it is imbued with a specific identity and a timeless and memorable presence.

4

5

1 Ciba Pharmaceuticals, Life Sciences Building, Summit, New Jersey, USA
   Photo credit: Jeff Goldberg/ESTO
2 New York University Medical Center Laboratories, New York, USA
   Photo credit: Jeff Goldberg/ESTO
3 The Belvedere Park at Battery Park City, New York, USA
   Photo credit: Jeff Goldberg/ESTO
4 Public School 56, Staten Island, New York, USA
   Photo credit: Jeff Goldberg/ESTO
5 Lighthouse International, New York, USA
   Photo credit: Jeff Goldberg/ESTO

Montois Partners S.A.

Belgium
Avenue Maurice 1
B-1050 Brussels
Tel: +(32 2) 647 9893
Fax: +(32 2) 647 9993
E-mail: montois@montois.com
Website: www.montois.com

Persons to Contact
Henri Montois
Ludwig Konior

Date of Establishment
1949

Project Types
Civic
Commercial
Corporate
Educational
Laboratories
Renovation
Research Centres
Residential
Sport Centres
Town Planning
Transportation

Current and Recent Projects
Belgium
Banque Indosuez, Brussels
Brussels International Airport
Central Plaza, Brussels
CFE Headquarters, Brussels
Citibank Belgium HQ, Brussels
European Union Ministry Council, Brussels
European Union, Le Charlemagne, Brussels
Grand-Duchy of Luxembourg Embassy, Brussels
North Galaxy Towers, Brussels
Swiss Life, Brussels
International
I.E.K. Espace Kirchberg, Grand-Duchy of
    Luxembourg
Deutsche Bank, Budapest, Hungary
Kalman-Kozma, Budapest, Hungary
Distribution Center Bokserska, Warsaw, Poland
Business Center Bitwa Warszawska, Warsaw,
    Poland
Matosinhos Hospital, Porto, Portugal
Dr. Ersek Hospital, Istanbul, Turkey
Memling Hotel, Kinshasa, Congo

Selected Clients
Atenor Group
Banco di Roma
Banque Indosuez Belgique
Belgian State
Bernheim-Outremer
Brussels International Airport Company
Catella Belgium
CFE
City of Brussels
Cofinimmo
Fortis AG
Herpain
Hilton International
Immobel
PetroFina
Sabena/Sabena Hotels
Solvay & Cie
Swiss Life (Belgium)
UCL - Université Catholique de Louvain
ULB - Université Libre de Bruxelles

Design Philosophy and History

Since its inception the firm brought to Belgium a sense of international style not seen before in the country on such a scale. Since the mid 1980s, to comply with a moving environment, Montois Partners, which remains faithful to the modernistic vision, has designed a more contextual architecture with a revival to the modern movement today.

Over the years, the firm has completed more than two million square metres of new and renovated buildings. Experience has been gained in virtually all areas: new and renovated office buildings; hotels and mixed-use complexes; hospitals and laboratories; civic and educational buildings; sport centres; and, transportation buildings as well as housing, from single family units to large-scale projects.

Projects such as the Hilton Brussels and the research centres of Texaco Europe and Solvay & Cie, launched the firm as one of the largest in Belgium. The firm has designed many headquarters' office buildings for companies such as Banque Indosuez, CFE, Citibank Belgium, PetroFina, and Swiss Life to name a few, as well as embassies which include countries such as the Grand-Duchy of Luxembourg, Italy and the Netherlands.

Montois Partners is probably the most experienced Belgian firm in university and hospital design: UCL and ULB universities have entrusted the firm on many occasions for more than 30 years. The firm has signed the master plan of the UCL, Université Catholique de Louvain campus, one of the largest in Belgium, as well as most of its building components. Montois Partners has been designing hospitals in Belgium, Africa and other European countries and is presently active in eastern Europe and Turkey.

While Montois Partners has proven, with many repeat clients, to be able to successfully design a timeless architecture for large-scale projects which respond to the occupants' needs and clients' budget and schedule, the firm has also been working over the years in association with many Belgian and foreign architects and consultants on several occasions.

1 Citibank, Brussels, Belgium
    Photo credit: Fabien de Cugnac

2 European Union, Le Charlemagne, rear facade with glass conference hall rotunda, Brussels, Belgium
    General Concept: Murphy/Jahn
    Architect: Arias (Montois, Arc, Noël)
    Photo credit: Marc Detiffe

3 Sheikh Nasser Al-Sabbah Mosque, Kuwait, U.A.E.
    Photo credit: courtesy Montois Partners S.A.

4 Brussels International Airport, pier A under construction, Belgium
    Rendering: courtesy Groep 2000
    Architect: Groep 2000 (D. Bontinck, M. Jaspers, H. Montois, W. Van Campenhout, L.Willox)

5 Matosinhos Hospital, 460 beds, Porto, Portugal
    Photo credit: courtesy Montois Partners S.A.

6 Banque Indosuez, Brussels, Belgium
    Photo credit: Charles Jottard

7 Hilton Brussels, 450 rooms, Belgium
    Photo credit: Bauters s.p.r.l.

1

2

3

4

5

6

7

Moore Ruble Yudell
Architects & Planners

USA
933 Pico Blvd
Santa Monica, California 90405
Tel: +(1 310) 450 1400
Fax: +(1 310) 450 1403
E-mail: mry@pacificnet.net

Principals
John Ruble, FAIA
Buzz Yudell, FAIA

Associates
Jeanne Chen   Michael de Villiers
Virginia Marshall   Neal Matsuno
James Mary O'Connor Mario Violich

Persons to Contact
John Ruble or Buzz Yudell

Employees
40

Date of Establishment
1977

Project Types
Academic   Multi-unit Housing
Cultural/Civic   Performing Arts Centres
Institutional   Residential
Mixed-use   Urban Design/Planning

Disciplines
Architecture and Planning

Current and Recent Projects
Karow Nord Town Master Plan, Berlin, Germany
Regatta Wharf, Pyrmont, Sydney, Australia
Potatisåkern Housing, Malmö, Sweden
Fairmont Towers Hotel, San Jose, California, USA
Hugh & Hazel Darling Law Library, University
  of California, Los Angeles, USA
Tacoma Campus Master Plan, University
  of Washington, USA
Physical Sciences Building, University of
  California, Santa Cruz, USA
Maryland Center for Performing Arts, University
  of Maryland, College Park, USA
Walter A. Haas School of Business
  Administration, University of California,
  Berkeley, USA
Federal Courthouse, Fresno, California, USA
United States Embassy, Berlin, Germany

Selected Clients
U.S. Department of State Foreign Building
  Operations
General Services Administration
Maguire Partners
University of California
University of Washington
Walt Disney Imagineering
Groth + Graalfs

Design Philosophy and History
Since the founding of Moore Ruble Yudell with
Charles Moore in 1977, principals John Ruble
and Buzz Yudell have built a varied body of work
ranging from private residences to multi-million-
dollar institutional, civic and mixed-use
developments. The initial goal of Moore Ruble
Yudell was to have an intensive collaboration
among the principals, and as the firm has
grown this idea has remained its highest priority,
with the collaborative spirit extending to include
project staff and clients. The principals pioneered
the use of client and community workshops in
the design process. Their work on a wide range
of building types has given them extensive

1

experience working with complex client groups
as well as regulatory and governmental
agencies.

An overall concern in the firm's work is the
belief that every good piece of architecture
or planning grows out of an understanding
of the qualities of a specific site, climate,
historical context and client. The firm believes
that perhaps because of this their work has
been as varied as their clients and the places
in which they have built.

From early work in California, through current
planning and building design across the US
and abroad, the firm has drawn on the strength
of familiar regional architecture and the special
character of each site. The firm has developed in
the process an equally keen interest in the goals
and visions of their clients, seeking to bring their
ideas into design at every stage.

Moore Ruble Yudell's responsiveness to
community concerns has led to successful
planning approvals for major mixed-use
projects from Plaza Las Fuentes in Pasadena,
California to Tegel Harbor in Berlin. This
experience has fostered a design approach that
places value on richness and diversity, in which
they have been able to resolve conflicts without
compromise.

The firm has received numerous major awards
for design excellence, and in 1992 was
honoured by the California Council of the
American Institute of Architects as Firm of the
Year. Publications on the firm include: *Moore
Ruble Yudell Building in Berlin* (Images, 1999);
*Campus and Community: Moore Ruble Yudell
Architecture & Planning* (Rockport, 1997); a
special edition of *A+U* (August 1992); *Moore
Ruble Yudell Houses and Housing* (Rockport,
1994); and, *Moore Ruble Yudell* (Academy
Editions, 1993).

2

1 Tegel Harbor Housing, Berlin, Germany
  Photo credit: Timothy Hursley

2 Tacoma Campus University of Washington,
  Washington, USA
  Photo credit: Timothy Hursley

3 Nishiokamoto Housing, Kobe, Japan
  Photo credit: Timothy Hursley

4 Potatisåkern Housing, Malmö, Sweden
  Photo credit: Lars Finnström

5 Hugh & Hazel Darling Law Library, University of
  California, Los Angeles, USA
  Photo credit: Timothy Hursley

6 Church of the Nativity, Rancho Santa Fe, California,
  USA
  Photo credit: Timothy Hursley

7 Peek & Cloppenburg, Leipzig, Germany
  Photo credit: Werner Huthmacher

3

4

5

6

7

NBBJ
Architecture, Design, Planning

1

2

3

USA
111 S. Jackson Street
Seattle, Washington 98104
Tel: +(1 206) 223 5555
Fax: +(1 206) 621 2300
E-mail: website@nbbj.com

1555 Lake Shore Drive
Columbus, Ohio 43204
Tel: +(1 614) 224 7145
Fax: +(1 614) 232 3293
E-mail: website@nbbj.com

Other Offices
Los Angeles, California, USA
San Francisco, California, USA
New York, New York, USA
Research Triangle Park, North Carolina, USA
Oslo, Norway
Taipei, Taiwan
Tokyo, Japan

For more information please visit
website: www.nbbj.com

Partners
Neil Anderson
William Bain
Freidl Bohm
Richard Buckley
Dennis Forsyth
Lawrence Helman
James Jonassen
Susan Jones
John Pangrazio
Scott Wyatt
David Zimmerman

Persons to Contact
Scott Wyatt, CEO Seattle
Neil Anderson, CEO Columbus

Number of Employees
800

Date of Establishment
1943

Project Types
Airports
Commercial Architecture
Corporate Design
Healthcare
Higher Education
Justice
Research and Advanced Technology
Retail Concepts
Sports and Entertainment
Urban Design and Planning

Disciplines
Architecture
Economics and Financial Feasibility
Graphic and Environmental Design
Interior Design
Planning
Urban Design

Current and Recent Projects
Telenor World Headquarters, Oslo, Norway
Reebok World Headquarters, Canton,
  Massachusetts, USA
Adobe Systems Regional Headquarters, Seattle,
  Washington, USA
Staples Center, Los Angeles, California, USA
Starbucks Corporate Headquarters, Seattle,
  Washington, USA
Tzu Chi Taichung Tantzu Medical Center, Tai
  Chung, Republic of China
City of Hope Medical Center Replacement
  Hospital, Los Angeles, California, USA
Huntington Bank Processing Center, Columbus,
  Ohio, USA
Koo Foundation Sun Yat-Sen Cancer Center,
  Taipei, Taiwan
Novartis Agricultural Discovery Institute, San
  Diego, California, USA
Novartis Institute of Functional Genomics, Inc.,
  San Diego, California, USA
Paul Brown Stadium, Cincinnati, Ohio, USA

Selected Clients
Adobe Systems Inc.
City of Hope Medical Center
Huntington Bank
LG Group
Microsoft
Novartis
Ralph Lauren Polo
Reebok International Ltd
Starbucks Coffee Company
Swedish Medical Center
Teledesic
Telenor
Vulcan Northwest

Design Philosophy and History
Founded in 1943, NBBJ has grown to become
an international practice committed to achieving
design excellence. Today it is the world's fifth
largest architectural firm with a staff of 800 and
projects located throughout North America,
South America, Asia, and Europe. Rigorously
design-focused, the firm practices in 21 studios
spread among six US offices. Each studio is
strongly committed to serving its clients and
society through a balance of design, technology,
process, and communication. No building or
interior designed by the firm reflects a single
firm-defining style, but all are informed by the
same set of complex deeply held principles.
NBBJ is recognized for its innovative design
solutions in healthcare, sports and
entertainment, corporate office buildings and a
wide range of other building types.

4

5

1&2 Rendering, Hall of Still Thought
   3 Staples Center, Los Angeles, California, USA
      Photo credit: courtesy NBBJ
4&5 Adobe Systems Regional Headquarters, Quadrant
      Lake Union Center, Seattle, Washington, USA
      Photo credit: Assassi Productions
   6 505 Union Station, Seattle, Washington, USA
      Photo credit: courtesy NBBJ

NBBJ

6

Nicholas Grimshaw & Partners Limited
Architects, Planners & Industrial Designers

Chairman: Nick Grimshaw CBE
RAHon DLitt AADip(Hons)
FCSD Hon. FAIA RIBA
Photo credit: Hanya Chlala

David Harriss AADip RIBA

Christopher Nash BA(Hons)
DipArch RIBA

Neven Sidor BA(Hons) BArch
RIBA

Andrew Whalley BArch AADip
RIBA

UK
1 Conway Street
Fitzroy Square
London W1P 6LR
Tel: +(44 20) 7291 4141
Fax: +(44 20) 7291 4194/4195
E-mail: media@ngrimshaw.co.uk

Project Directors
Florian Eames BA(Hons) DipArch
Michael Pross Dipl Ing Architekt

Senior Associates
Ingrid Bille Dipl Ing Arch RIBA
Keith Brewis BArch(Hons) DipArch RIBA

Associates
Garry Colligan BSc(Hons) BArch RIBA
David Kirkland BSc(Hons) MA(RCA)
Christian Male BA(Hons) DipArch RIBA
David Portman BA(Hons) DipArch RIBA

Person to Contact
Florian Eames

Number of Employees
110

Date of Establishment
1980

Project Types
Arts Buildings
Bridges
Education
Exhibitions
Housing
Industrial
Offices
Public Buildings
Sport and Leisure
Transport

Disciplines
Architecture
Planning
Industrial Design

Current and Recent Projects
Nicholas Grimshaw & Partners (NGP) has recently completed a Grand Stand for Lord's Cricket Ground in London, the redevelopment of airport terminals at Manchester and Heathrow and a call centre for Hutchison Telecom in Darlington. In Germany Ludwig Erhard Haus in Berlin (the Stock Exchange and Communications Centre) and a landmark office building for MABEG at Soest were also completed in 1999.

The practice is working on the master planning and redevelopment of Paddington Station in London and the design of four Millennium Commission funded projects in the UK; the Eden Project in Cornwall, the National Space Science Centre in Leicester, Millennium Point at Digbeth near Birmingham and a modern spa facility in historic Bath Spa.

Internationally NGP is designing the redevelopment of Zurich Airport, an art gallery in A Coruña in Spain, the Donald Danforth Plant Science Center in St. Louis, USA, a transport station in Bijlmer and a bridge project in Ijberg, both in the Netherlands.

Design Philosophy and History
Nicholas Grimshaw & Partners was founded in 1980 and has steadily gained a reputation for design excellence through its emphasis on quality, innovation and a vigorous approach to detail. The practice is equally committed to building on time and within budget. The results are legible, economic and beautiful buildings, designed with confidence.

NGP believes that buildings should be understandable both spatially and organizationally, that they should reflect the activities within them, and that they should be flexible enough to respond to changing needs. The practice uses environmentally-responsible materials where possible and incorporates energy saving features into each project.

Selected Clients
BAA
BMW (UK) Ltd
British Railways Board
Citroën (UK) Ltd
Department of Trade & Industry
Eurotunnel Developments
Financial Times Ltd
Greater London Enterprise Board
Heathrow Airport Ltd
Herman Miller Ltd
Homebase Ltd
IBM (UK) Ltd
Igus GmbH
Liverpool City Council
London Docklands Development Corporation
Marylebone Cricket Club
Oxford City Council
Parque Expo '98 Lisbon
RAC Motoring Services Ltd
Railtrack
Rush & Tompkins Leisure
J Sainsbury plc
Scottish Development Agency
The Sports Council
Standard Life Assurance Company
Tambrands France
Thames Water & Utilities Ltd
Trafalgar House (Investments) Ltd
University College, London
Vitra GmbH
The Western Morning News Co Ltd
Westminster City Council
Wiltshire Radio Ltd
Xerox Research (UK) Ltd
Yorkshire Television

Nicholas Grimshaw & Partners Limited
ARCHITECTS PLANNERS INDUSTRIAL DESIGNERS

1

2

3

4

6

1 Ludwig Erhard Haus, Berlin, Germany
Photo credit: W. Huthmacher

2 Lord's Grand Stand, London, UK
Photo credit: Peter Cook/VIEW

3 Eden Project, Cornwall, UK
Photo credit: Imagination

4 Ijburg Bridge, Amsterdam, the Netherlands
Photo credit: Nicholas Grimshaw & Partners CGI Department

5 Fundación Caixa Galicia, A Coruña, Spain
Photo credit: Nicholas Grimshaw & Partners CGI Department

6 Bath Spa Project, Bath, UK
Photo credit: Nicholas Grimshaw & Partners CGI Department

NIKKEN SEKKEI LTD
Planners, Architects, Engineers

Director
Eiji MAKI, Dr. Eng., JIA
President

Japan
Head Office
Nikken Sekkei, Osaka
4-6-2 Koraibashi
Chuo-ku Osaka 541-8528
Tel: +(81 6) 6203 2361
Fax: +(81 6) 6204 1570
E-mail: webmaster@nikken.co.jp

Nikken Sekkei, Tokyo
2-1-3 Koraku
Bunkyo-ku Tokyo 112-8565
Tel: +(81 3) 3813 3361
Fax: +(81 3) 3811 9391
E-mail: webmaster@nikken.co.jp

Nikken Sekkei, Nagoya
4-15-32 Sakae
Naka-ku Nagoya 460-0008
Tel: +(81 52) 261 6131
Fax: +(81 52) 263 9840
E-mail: webmaster@nikken.co.jp

Person to Contact
Akio Takenaka, General Manager,
Corporate Communications Office

Number of Employees
Total 2,022

Date of Establishment
1950

Project Types
Airports	Media
Auditoria	Medical
Commercial	Monuments
Convention centres	Museums
Corporate Complexes	Public Facilities
Educational	Recreational facilities
Exhibition facilities	Residential
Financial	Sport facilities
Hospitality	Towers
Laboratories	Transportation facilities
Libraries	Training Facilities

Disciplines
Architectural
Engineering
Planning

Current and Recent Projects
Osaka World Trade Center Building
 'Cosmo Tower'
Japan Tabacco Inc. Headquarters Building
 'JT Building'
Tokyo Gas Earth Port
Lake Biwa Museum
Osaka Municipal Central Gymnasium
TIMES SQUARE BUILDING
Osaka Dome
Meiji University Surugadai Campus
 'Liberty Tower'
Iwate Prefectural University
The Museum of Art, Ehime

NIKKEN SEKKEI LTD
planners | architects | engineers

Firm Profile
Nikken Sekkei is a comprehensive consulting firm providing architectural, building engineering, civil engineering, urban design, urban planning, interior design, and, consulting and management services. Since its inception in 1900, Nikken Sekkei has maintained an uncompromising commitment to fiscal independence, a design company's most important attribute. While growing to its present high standing, this company has constantly focused on the development of new methods and technologies that redefine design for current needs and priorities.

Nikken Sekkei has completed more than 14,000 projects in over 40 countries, and its resources amount to over 2,000 specialists, including those in subsidiaries. This adds up to one of the largest networks in the world. Moreover, its contacts extend beyond national borders. Nikken Sekkei is closely affiliated with many noted design offices and consultants around the world.

History
Inaugurated in 1900, and reorganized in 1950. Nikken Sekkei's inauguration dates back to the year 1900 when one of the old Japanese conglomerates, 'Sumitomo Head Office', established its building design/construction supervision section. It was staffed with over 150 personnel during its busiest periods. In 1933, this section was separately incorporated, and named 'Hasebe, Takekoshi and Associates, Inc.' which continued through some changes during and after World War II. To keep up with the professional modernization of Japan, the firm was reorganized in 1950 into the present form of the corporation, independent of any parent organization. That year there were 92 employees. Its distinguished reputation and achievements grew rapidly as did the staff which increased to 400 in just a few years. During the last five decades, Nikken Sekkei's constant achievements has made it grow into one of the largest planning-architecture-engineering firms in the world.

Philosophy
The basic operating principles of Nikken Sekkei are:

To serve their clients in assuring a competitive advantage by providing high quality services of incomparable value;

To create sound and progressive designs that firmly take root in the community and achieve harmony with the environment;

To keep a high standard of professional ethics and maintain an independent and neutral position both as a consultant and as a business entity;

To take a multi-disciplinary design approach not only to fully meet the needs of any commission and to assure the best quality services.

The spiritual attitude as the firm's basic code of behaviour is to serve their clients and society with sincerity, to always look inward and strive for the best, and to be appreciative of all kindness extended to them, and;

To encourage all individuals in the firm to better themselves as professionals, with pride and confidence, so that the firm always has the capacity to provide ever better services to their clients.

Kakegawa City Hall
Photo credit: Mitsumasa Fujitsuka

Nagano All Sports Arena White Ring (The Nagano Winter Olympic Games Figure Skating Arena)
Photo credit: Hajime Kitamura

Museum of Ehime History and Culture
Photo credit: Mamoru Ishiguro

Pacific Convention Plaza Yokohama (PACIFICO Yokohama)+QUEEN'S SQUARE YOKOHAMA (in association with Mitsubishi Estate Co., Ltd.)
Photo credit: Hiroshi Shinozawa

Paatela & Paatela, Architects

Mikael Paatela, M.Sc. Arch

Finland
Ahertajantie 3
Espoo, 02100
Tel: +(358 9) 4520 510
Fax: +(358 9) 4520 5151
E-mail: archimed@paatela-arch.fi

Directors
Mikael Paatela, M.Sc.Arch

Person to Contact
Mikael Paatela

Number of Employees
12

Date of Establishment
1919

Project Types
Health Centres
Hospitals
Industrial and Commercial Buildings
Old Peoples' Facilities
Public Buildings
Research and Educational Buildings

Disciplines
Architectural Design
Functional Design
Interior Design and Equipping
Master Planning
Programming
Project Management

Current and Recent Projects
Turku University Central Hospital/New Hospital
Hainan Provincial People's Hospital, Haikou, PRC
National Pet-centre of Finland, Turku
AVA-Clinic, private hospital reconstruction,
 St. Petersburg, Russia
Spitak Health Centre, Armenia
Vaasa Central Hospital, Vaasa
Several hospital renovation and modernization
 projects

Selected Clients
Helsinki University Central Hospital
Turku University Central Hospital
Vaasa Healthcare District
Several cities and municipalities
Provincial Health Bureau of Hainan, PRC
Finnish Red Cross
A. Palmberg Oy Construction Company
Ministry of Foreign Affairs, Finnish International
 Development Agency

Design Philosophy and History
The architectural practice of Paatela & Paatela, Architects was founded by Professor Jussi Paatela and his brother Tolvo 1919. The practice has remained in the same family ever since, and is now run by the third generation of Paatela architects. This makes it one of the oldest architectural firms in Finland.

In the course of its 80 years of operations, Paatela & Paatela, Architects has enhanced its expertise and experience, notably in the design of hospitals and other healthcare facilities and in the development of related functions. The firm has made a marked contribution to the construction of Finland's hospital network in the 1900s, having been involved in the design and development of a number of university hospitals, central hospitals and health centres.

Activities going back many years have given Paatela & Paatela, Architects a sound basis for continuous development in healthcare sector projects and active participation in international co-operation. The new building for Turku University Central Hospital, one of the firm's most recent assignments, expresses the functional requirements, philosophy of care and construction solutions of a 'high-tech high-touch' hospital of the future in a manner appropriate to the new millennium.

In addition to healthcare projects, the firm has acquired experience and proficiency in the design, planning and implementation of research institutions, educational facilities, commercial and industrial premises and public buildings.

The architectural quality of each project together with understanding of the client's needs and objectives and the functional requirements of the project, form the design basis of the office's work. The firm has succeeded in its aims by demonstrating its ability to retain long-standing clients and forge new contacts.

Due to the knowledge and experience gained by Paatela & Paatela, Architects in the healthcare sector, it has increasingly broadened its scope to include international projects. Among these are feasibility studies, preliminary sketch designs and full-scale architectural and functional design services for the construction of a whole range of facilities, from local health centres to major hospital complexes.

In addition to governmental, municipal and private clients, Paatela & Paatela, Architects has served as a consultant for Finnish construction companies, the Finnish International Development Agency FINNIDA, Finland's Ministry for Foreign Affairs and various international healthcare organizations.

The most recent international projects undertaken by the firm are located in Russia and China. Finland's proximity to Russia and the Baltic countries gives the firm added value when offering healthcare design services to planners and investors in these countries. Paatela & Paatela, Architects also has design experience in a number of countries in Africa and the Middle East.

In addition to planning and design assignments, members of the practice have acted as consultants and lecturers for a range of prestigious clients including the Ministry of Public Health. PRC, and the World Health Organization (WHO).

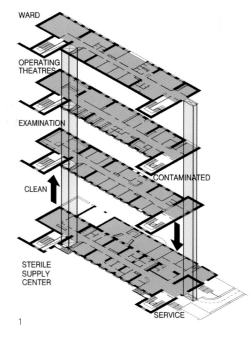

WARD

OPERATING THEATRES

EXAMINATION

CLEAN

CONTAMINATED

STERILE SUPPLY CENTER

SERVICE

1

2

3

4

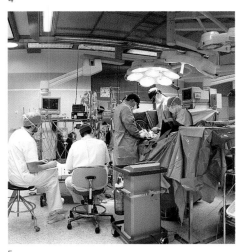

5

6

1 AVA Clinic, private hospital reconstruction,
  St. Petersburg, Russia

2 Turku University Central Hospital
  Photo credit: Timo Kauppi

3 Helsinki University Central Hospital, Hospital for
  Dermatological and Allergic Diseases, Helsinki,
  Finland
  Photo credit: Gero Mylius

4 Oulunkylä Rehabilitation Hospital, Helsinki
  Photo credit: Gero Mylius

5 Operating Theatre, Vaasa Central Hospital
  Photo credit: courtesy Vaasa Central Hospital

6 Hainan Provincial People's Hospital, Haikou, P.R.
  China
  Photo credit: Tomas Westerholm

Perkins & Will

USA
330 North Wabash
Chicago, Illinois 60611
Tel: +(1 312) 755 0770
Fax: +(1 312) 755 0775
E-mail: info@perkinswill.com

Offices
1382 Peachtree Street, N.E.
Atlanta, Georgia

1130 East Third Street
Charlotte, North Carolina

801 Brickell Avenue
Miami, Florida 33131

701 Fourth Avenue South
Minneapolis, Minnesota

One Park Avenue
New York, New York

234 East Colorado Boulevard
Pasadena, California

2700 Colorado Avenue
Santa Monica, California

Board of Directors
Gaylaird Christopher	Henry Mann
G. William Doerge	I. Lewis Nix
Michael Fejes	Carl Ordemann
Phil Harrison	Robert Peterson
Ralph Johnson	Gary Wheeler
Jean Mah	

Persons to Contact
Gary Wheeler, Chicago
Bill Viehman, Atlanta
Philip Shive, Charlotte
Jose Gelabert-Navia, Miami
Dave Paeper, Minneapolis
Carl Ordemann, New York
Gaylaird Christopher, Pasadena
Michael Fejes, Santa Monica

Number of Employees
450

Date of Establishment
1935

Project Types
Commercial	Interiors
Corporate	K-12 Education
Healthcare	Laboratories and
Higher Education	Research Development
Hospitality	Residential

Disciplines
Architecture
Interiors
Planning

Current and Recent Projects
McDonnell Paediatrics Research Building, Washington University, St. Louis, Missouri
Kimmel Cancer Center, Thomas Jefferson University, Philadelphia, Pennsylvania
American Hospital Association, Chicago, Illinois
Deloitte & Touche, Phase II, Chicago, Illinois
Arrowhead Regional Medical Center, San Bernardino, California
CORE Center, Chicago, Illinois
W.W. Grainger Headquarters, Lake Forest, Illinois
Sogutozu Business Center, Ankara, Turkey
Trinity Valley School, Fort Worth, Texas
New Albany Learning Community, New Albany, Ohio
Temple Hoyne Buell Hall, University of Illinois, Urbana, Illinois
Classroom Building, George Mason University, Prince William County, Virginia

Design Philosophy and History
Perkins & Will, founded in 1935, is a professional service firm staffed with architects, interior designers, and planners. The firm, with offices in Chicago, Atlanta, Charlotte, Los Angeles, Miami, Minneapolis, New York, and Paris, practices on a international basis and has completed projects in 49 states and 37 foreign countries.

1 Grainger Headquarters, Lake Forest, Illinois
  Photo credit: Hedrich-Blessing

2 Peggy Notebaert Nature Museum, Chicago Academy of Sciences, Chicago, Illinois
  Photo credit: Steinkamp/Ballogg

3 Skybridge at One North Halsted Street, Chicago, Illinois
  amd Rendering

4 Kimmel Cancer Center, Thomas Jefferson University, Philadelphia, Pennsylvania
  amd Rendering

Opposite:
  Deloitte & Touche, Chicago, Illinois
  Photo credit: Hedrich-Blessing

3

1

4

Pete Bossley Architects Ltd
Architects, Interior Designers

New Zealand
2/55 Mackelvie Street
Auckland
Tel: +(64 9) 361 2201
Fax: +(64 9) 361 2202
E-mail: peteboz@ihug.co.nz

Director and Contact Person
Pete Bossley

Number of Employees
5

Project Types
Commercial   Residential
Museums/Galleries   Restaurants

Disciplines
Architecture

Current Projects
Jarvis complex, Bay of Islands, New Zealand
Honore-Morris house, Hamilton (Cavalier
  Bremworth Award), New Zealand
Scanlan apartments, Auckland, New Zealand
James house, Clevedon, New Zealand
Plaw house, Auckland, New Zealand
Mace complex, Bay of Islands, New Zealand
Shaw house, Auckland, New Zealand
Lockwood houses, series of eight, New Zealand
Manson house, Auckland, New Zealand
Wright house, Coromandel, New Zealand

Recent Projects
Heatley complex, Bay of Islands, New Zealand
  (Two NZIA Awards 1999, House of the Year
  1998)
Foodtrain Restaurant, Te Papa Museum of New
  Zealand, Wellington, New Zealand
Treaty of Waitangi Exhibit, Te Papa, Wellington,
  New Zealand
Aotea Art Gallery, Auckland, New Zealand
The Oval restaurant/bar, Auckland, New Zealand
Mosso restaurant, Auckland, New Zealand
Parnell Post Office (while at Jasmax), Auckland,
  New Zealand
TePapa Museum of New Zealand (while at
  Jasmax, co-designer), Wellington, New Zealand
  (NZIA Award)
Brunswick Apartments, Queenstown, New
  Zealand (NZIA Award)
Flagstaff Gallery, Devonport, Auckland, New
  Zealand
Kelland Nelson house, Auckland, New Zealand
  (NZIA Award)

1

2

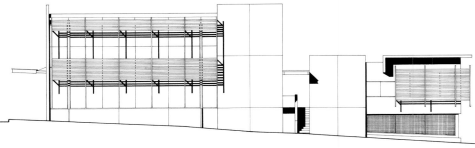

3

4

5

6

7

Design Philosophy and History

Pete Bossley Architects is an architectural and interior design practice established to provide intense input into a deliberately limited number of projects, in order to devote more experience and attention to each commission.

Each project is believed to be a journey with an unpredictable outcome, a journey which client and architect traverse together. Projects vary significantly from each other; in this way the practice refrains from establishing an 'in-house style', preferring instead that projects are linked by a common approach to ideas and theory.

Articulation of the spirit of the context, be it landscape or urban, is an integral approach to any project, combined with exploration of essential issues such as openness and delicacy contrasted with enclosure and density.

Pete Bossley has been practising architecture for 20 years, and for 18 of those has been the Director of three successful practices: Bossley Cheshire Architects, Jasmax Architects, and Pete Bossley Architects. An extensive list of built projects has attracted many architectural awards.

As a Director at Jasmax Architects, Pete was the design principal jointly in charge of the design and documentation of the Te Papa Museum of New Zealand in Wellington. This project was the winner of an international competition, and has subsequently become a highly acclaimed addition to the Wellington foreshore, attracting international attention as one of the world's largest and most challenging new museums.

In 1996, Pete Bossley Architects designed the Treaty of Waitangi exhibit, a significant exhibit located in the heart of the museum, with a budget of $1.5 million.

Because visitor numbers at the museum greatly exceeded all predictions, attracting over two million in its first year, Pete Bossley Architects was commissioned to replace an existing cafe with a restaurant double the size of the original.

Pete believes the need to engage theory and practice is crucial for successful architecture, and is committed to teaching as an aid to exploring and achieving this. He is Adjunct Professor at Unitec School of Architecture, Auckland.

He has been the recipient of 10 New Zealand Institute of Architects Awards, the New Zealand Home of the Year Award, the Cavalier Bremworth Award and Carter Holt Harvey Environmental Award.

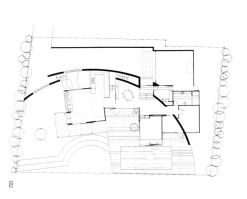

8

9

1,2,6,7
  Heatley House, Bay of Islands, New Zealand
  Photo credit: Patrick Reynolds
3&4
  Parnell Post Office, Auckland, New Zealand
  Photo credit: courtesy Pete Bossley Architects
5
  Te Papa from Cable Street, Museum of New Zealand
  Te Papa Tongarewa, Wellington, New Zealand
  Photo credit: Michall Hall
8&9
  Private House, Remuera, Auckland, New Zealand
  Photo credit: Patrick Reynolds
10&11
  Jarvis House, Bay of Islands, New Zealand
  Photo credit: James Downey

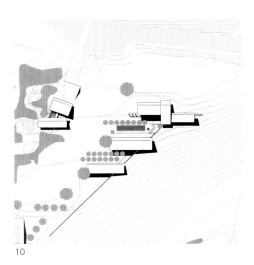

10

11

Ray Kappe, FAIA
Kappe Architects/Planners

Ray Kappe
Photo credit: courtesy Kappe Architects Planners

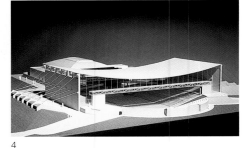

4

USA
715 Brooktree Road
Pacific Palisades, California 90272
Tel: +(1 310) 459 7791
Fax: +(1 310) 459 2643
E-mail: rkappe@sciarc.edu

Ray Kappe, FAIA is an internationally recognized architect/planner/educator who has practiced architecture in Los Angeles since 1953. Besides design, his career has included social and community advocacy, urban design and planning, and education. He has authored publications on environmental planning and urban design, as well as completed energy and advanced technology research. His involvement with education has produced one of the nation's most innovative and progressive schools, the Southern California Institute of Architecture (SCI-ARC). He was the founding director in 1972, and in 1976 was awarded the AIACC Excellence in Education Award. He was the first chairman of Architecture at California State Polytechnic University, Pomona in 1969.

Ray Kappe's much awarded and published work is considered to be an extension of the early Southern California master architects: Wright, Schindler, Neutra and Harwell Hamilton Harris. He is well-known for his work in the 1960s and 1970s which was published in *GA Houses 1* and the monograph on his work in Toshi Jutaku 8203. His work of the 1980s and 1990s has been featured in subsequent *GA Houses* books, as well as many other national and international journals and books. The Images Publishing Group recently published a monograph on some of his residential work entitled *Ray Kappe: House Design, Variations on a Theme*.

He is the recipient of numerous design awards and is the only architect to receive all of the following major awards:

The Neutra Award for excellence in architecture.

AIA/ACSA Topaz Medal, the highest award for architectural education in the United States.

The Maybeck Award from the American Institute of Architects/California Council, the highest state award recognizing life-long individual achievement in architectural design.

The LA/AIA Gold Medal for 'Lifetime achievements as an innovative designer, enlightened planner and inspired educator who

1 Kappe Residence
  Photo credit: courtesy Kappe Architects Planners
2 Sultan/Price Residence
  Photo credit: courtesy Kappe Architects Planners
3&5 Santa Monica Bus Administration Building
  Photo credit: Marvin Rand
4 Loyola Marymount Gymnasium
  Photo credit: courtesy Kappe Architects Planners
6 Timeline of office work over five decades
  Photo credit: courtesy Kappe Architects Planners

5

has influenced generations of students and practitioners'.

At the 1996 Pacific Design Center Westweek, he was honoured by being named a *Star of Design* for Lifetime Achievement for Architectural Design.

In 1997 his own residence received the 25-year Award from the American Institute of Architects/California Council.

In 1998 he received the first ever Distinguished Alumnus Medal in Architecture from the College of Environmental Design and CED Alumni Association.

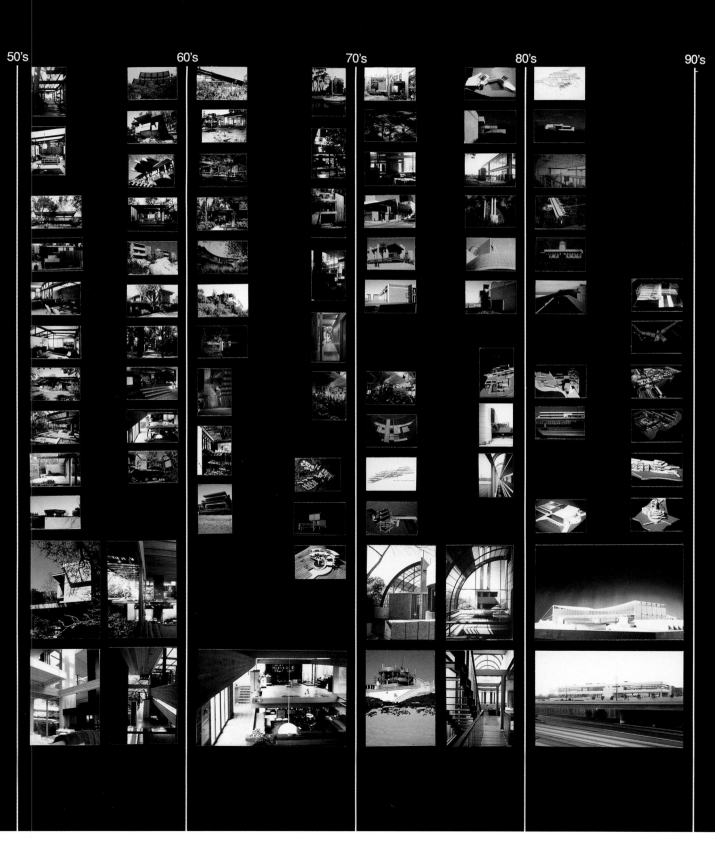

6

Regina Pizzinini, Leon Luxemburg, Tryggvi Thorsteinsson
Architects

Leon Luxemburg, Regina Pizzinini, Tryggvi
Thorsteinsson
Photo credit: Torfi Agnarsson

USA
2828 Donald Douglas Loop North #27
Los Angeles, California 90405
Tel: +(1 310) 452 9667
Fax: +(1 310) 452 9697
E-mail: pizzilux@ni.net

Austria
Steindlglasse 2/14
Vienna 1010
Tel: (43 1) 532 0928
Fax: (43 1) 532 0929
E-mail: pizzilux@netway.at

Luxembourg
Grand Rue, 24
Luxembourg L-1660
Tel: +(352) 22 7644
Fax: +(352) 22 7517
E-mail: pizzilux@vo.lux

Directors
Regina Pizzinini
Leon Luxemburg
Tryggvi Thorsteinsson

Number of Employees
16

Date of Establishment
1989

Project Types
Housing
Entertainment Centres
Shopping Complexes
Corporate Offices and Studios

Disciplines
Architecture
Urban Design
Environment

Current and Recent Projects
Don Wallace Radio Museum, Rancho Palos
  Verdes, California, USA
Gould House, Malibu, California, USA
House on Linden Drive, Beverly Hills, California,
  USA
Western Museum of Flight, Los Angeles,
  California, USA
Fashion outlet centres, Tuscon, California, USA
California health & rejuvenation centres,
  California
Student Housing, Vienna, Austria
Residential redevelopment, Vienna, Austria
Social housing, Cents, Luxembourg
Hentzig residence, Luxembourg
Urban redevelopment project, Luxembourg
Monastery Marienthal, ecological center,
  Luxembourg
'Sauermillen' Housing for the Physically
  Disabled, Luxembourg
Urban Design, Martinsplatz, Bonn, Germany

Design Philosophy and History
International architectural practices are common, but the 10 year partnership of Regina Pizzinini and Leon Luxemburg differs from most in the regularity with which these two young mavericks shuttle back and forth between their offices in California and Europe. In their mobility, as in the joyous exuberance of their residential projects, they are true heirs of the late Charles Moore, who inspired them to move from Austria to Los Angeles in 1983, and invited them to study and work with him.

Together, Pizzinini, Luxemburg and Thorsteinsson have designed residences of growing scale and complexity, playing variations on recurring themes: simple geometric forms, interlocking volumes, and primary colours. Like most young architects, they started small, with a guest house and remodels, graduating to residences, and competing for the design of public buildings.

1

1 Rockenwagner House, Venice, California, USA
  Photo credit: Jeremy Samuelson

2 Villa Petite, Bridal, Luxembourg
  Photo credit: Gert von Bassewitz

3 Corman Guest House, Santa Monica, California, USA
  Photo credit: Dominique Vorillon

4 House, Schoenfels, Luxembourg
  Photo credit: Yvan Klein

5 Kieffer Photo Studio, City of Luxembourg,
  Luxembourg
  Photo credit: Jean-Paul Kieffer

6 House, Niederthai, Austria
  Photo credit: Gert von Bassewitz

2

3

4

5

6

Renzo Piano Building Workshop

Renzo Piano
Photo credit: Stefano Goldberg

Italy
Via P.P. Rubens 2P
16158 Genova
Tel: +(390 10) 61711
Fax: +(390 10) 617 1350

Current and Recent Projects
Auditorium Parma, ex-area Eridania, Parma, Italy
PTT Telecom office tower, Rotterdam, the
  Netherlands
Completion open spaces, Old Harbour, Genova,
  Italy
High-rise office block, Sydney, Australia
Mercedes Benz Design Center, Stuttgart,
  Germany
Cultural Center Jean Marie Tjibaou, Nouméa,
  New Caledonia
Wind tunnel for Ferrari, Maranello, Modena,
  Italy
Reconstruction of Potsdamer Platz, Debis Tower,
  Theatre,Casino, Imax Cinema, Residential
  Building and Retail Offices, Berlin, Germany
Ushibuka Bridge, Kumamoto, Japan
Museum of the Beyeler Foundation, Riehen,
  Basel, Switzerland
Museum of Science and Technology,
  Amsterdam, the Netherlands
Reconstruction of the Atelier Brancusi, Paris,
  France

Recent Awards
The Pritzker Architecture Prize, The White
  House, Washington, DC, USA, 1998
Telecom Prize, Napoli, Italy, 1996
Erasmus Prize, Amsterdam, the Netherlands,
  1995
Praemium Imperiale, Tokyo, Japan, 1995
Art Prize of the Akademie de Künste, Berlin,
  Germany, 1995
Officier dans l'Ordre National de Mérite in Paris,
  France, 1994
Goodwill Ambassador of Unesco for
  Architecture, 1994
American Academy of Arts and Letters Honorary
  Fellowship, USA, 1994
Honorary Doctorship, Delft University, the
  Netherlands, 1992
Kyoto Prize, Inamori Foundation, Kyoto, Japan,
  1990
Cavaliere di Gran Croce award by the Italian
  Government, Roma, Italy, 1989
RIBA Royal Gold Medal for Architecture,
  England, 1989

1

History
Renzo Piano was born in Genoa in 1937, and
brought up in a builder's family. He graduated
from the school of architecture at Milan
Polytechnic in 1964, and during his studies he
worked under the design guidance of Franco
Albini and, in his spare time, worked at his
father's building sites.

From 1965 to 1970 he worked with Louis I.
Kahn in Philadelphia and Z.S. Makowsky in
London. During this period he met Jean Prouvé,
a friendship which had a profound influence on
his work. His collaboration with Richard Rogers
dates from 1971 (Piano and Rogers) and from
1977 with Peter Rice (Atelier Piano & Rice). He
now has offices in Genoa, Paris and Berlin under
his current business name Renzo Piano Building
Workshop.

2

3

4

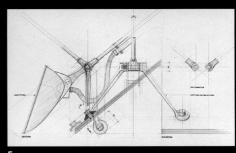

5

6

1 Glass facade, Debis Tower, Potsdamer Platz, Berlin
Photo credit: M Denance

2 External glass stairway, Debis Tower, Potsdamer Platz, Berlin
Photo credit: G. Berengo Gandin

3 Atrium, Debis Tower, Potsdamer Platz, Berlin
Photo credit: G. Berengo Gandin

4 Debis Tower, Potsdamer Platz, Berlin
Photo credit: M. Denance

5 Atrium roof suspended glass assembly, Debis Tower, Potsdamer Platz, Berlin

6 View of construction site, Debis Tower, Potsdamer Platz, Berlin
Photo credit: M. Denance

Architects: Renzo Piano Building Workshop, Bernard Plattner, assistant architect, Christoph Kohlbecker

Richard Rogers Partnership
Architects

UK
Thames Wharf, Rainville Road
London W6 9HA
Tel: +(44 171) 385 1235
Fax: +(44 171) 385 8409
E-mail: enquiries@richardrogers.co.uk

Directors
Richard Rogers
John Young
Marco Goldschmied
Michael Davies
Lawrence Abbott
Graham Stirk
Ivan Harbour
Lennart Grut
Amarjit Kalsi
Andrew Morris

Associates
Stig Larsen
Marcus Lee
Avtar Lotay
Richard Paul
Simon Smithson

Person to Contact
Robert Torday, Head of Communications

Number of Employees
120

Date of Establishment
1977

Project Types
Airports
Banks
Business Parks
Hotels
Laboratories
Law Courts
Master Plans
Museums
Residential
Stations

Current and Recent Projects
Law Courts, Bordeaux, France
Millennium Dome, Greenwich, UK
Law Courts, Strasbourg, Germany
Headquarters, Channel 4, London, UK
Daimler–Benz site, Potsdamer Platz, Berlin,
  Germany
Lloyds Register and Shipping, London, UK
European Court of Human Rights, Strasbourg,
  Germany

Selected Clients
Centre Culturel d'Art Georges Pompidou
Lloyd's of London
Reuters Ltd
Channel 4
Daimler-Benz
Marseille Airport
European Court of Human Rights, Strasbourg
New Millennium Experience Co.
Ministère des Affaires Culturelles/Ministère de
  l'Education Nationale. Chairman: Robert
  Bordaz
Jean Luc Bianardi (Head of Administration)
  Conseil de l'Europe

Practice Profile
Richard Rogers formed Team 4 with Norman Foster, Wendy Foster and Su Rogers in 1963. In 1971 Richard Rogers went into partnership with Renzo Piano, and together they won the international competition for the Centre Pompidou in Paris, coming first out of 681 entries.

The Richard Rogers Partnership was founded in 1977 by Richard Rogers, John Young, Marco Goldschmied and Mike Davies, all of whom have worked together for over thirty years. The formation of the practice coincided with its winning entry in the limited competition for the Lloyd's of London Headquarters.

This was completed in 1986, and since that time the practice has continued to grow with important commissions both in the UK and abroad. As much as 50% of commissions are for projects abroad in Germany, France, Spain, Italy, the Far East and the US and almost half of the work is for commercial developers.

1

2

3

4

5

1 Court rooms from public passerelle, Le Palais De Justice, Bordeaux, France
  Photo credit: Christian Richters courtesy Richard Rogers Partnership
2 Night view, Le Palais De Justice, Bordeaux, France
  Photo credit: Christian Richters courtesy Richard Rogers Partnership
3 Interior view of criminal court, Le Palais De Justice, Bordeaux, France
  Photo credit: Christian Richters courtesy Richard Rogers Partnership
4 Profile of ancient and modern, Le Palais De Justice, Bordeaux, France
  Photo credit: Christian Richters courtesy Richard Rogers Partnership
5 Interior view of atrium showing the 'Liberty Bell' by artist Pascal Convert, Le Palais De Justice, Bordeaux, France
  Photo credit: Christian Richters courtesy Richard Rogers Partnership

Rijavec Architects
Architects + Urban Designers

Australia
4 Wood Street
Fitzroy, Melbourne 3065
Tel: +(613) 9417 6942
Fax: +(613) 9416 0319
E-mail: rijavec@internex.net.au

Director
Ivan Rijavec

Number of Employees
10

Date of Establishment
1979

Project Types
Commercial
Institutional
Residential

Disciplines
Architecture
Interior Design
Urban Design

Current and Recent Projects
Fire Stations: Lillydale, Kerang
Commercial Development

Selected Clients
CFA
Joske Consulting Pty Ltd
City of Yarra
City of Stonnington

Design Philosophy and History

Rijavec Architects was established in January 1979 and since then has worked in most conventional areas of architectural practice.

The practice has been recognized by the architectural profession, architectural media and by academic institutions in Victoria and interstate as a high profile design office. Recognition has been expressed in the form of RAIA Merit Awards, invitations to participate in forums and architect in residency programmes, and requests to deliver lectures to Professional & Academic Institutions throughout Australia. The practice is known for innovative contemporary work which expresses relevant cultural idioms.

Since 1984 the practice has been awarded eight merit awards for outstanding architecture, one commendation and has been short-listed for nine other awards, including a national RAIA Merit Award for interior design.

The firm's projects have been featured in excess of 40 publications, including periodicals, design journals and hardback editions. Five books coinciding with the end of the millennium will feature Rijavec Architects' work including one devoted to the work of the practice.

This is an innovative practice which has been recognized for its contribution to contemporary Australian architecture.

1 Penthouse, Central Melbourne
  Photo credit: Tim Griffith
2 Chen Residence, Kew, Melbourne
  Photo credit: John Gollings
3 St. Thomas Walk condominium towers, Singapore
4 Low-rise condominium units, Singapore
5 Liberty Steel Construction Option
6 Boutique Cinemas on uppermost level designed to accommodate a variety of box office capacities
7 Chen Residence, interior, Kew, Melbourne
  Photo credit: John Gollings
Computer renderings: courtesy Rijavec Architects; Da Code; Pixel Junkie

1

2

3

5

6

4

7

RTKL Associates Inc.

Architects – Planning & Urban Design – Engineering
Interior Architecture – Landscape Architecture – Graphic Design

USA

Head Office
One South Street
Baltimore, Maryland 21202
Tel: +(1 410) 528 8600
Fax: +(1 410) 385 2455
E-mail: info@bal.rtkl.com

2828 Routh Street
Dallas, Texas 75201
Tel: +(1 214) 781 8877
Fax: +(1 214) 871 7023
E-mail: info@dal.rtkl.com

1250 Connecticut Avenue, NW
Washington, DC 20036
Tel: +(1 202) 833 4400
Fax: +(1 202) 887 5168
E-mail: info@dc.rtkl.com

333 South Hope Street
Los Angeles, California 90071
Tel: +(1 213) 627 7373
Fax: +(1 213) 627 9815
E-mail: info@la.rtkl.com

140 South Dearborn
Chicago, Illinois 60603
Tel: +(1 312) 704 9900
Fax: +(1 312) 704 9910
E-mail: info@chi.rtkl.com

UK

22 Torrington Place
London, WC1E 7HP
Tel: +(44) 171 306 0404
Fax: +(44) 171 306 0405
E-mail: info@lon.rtkl.com

Japan

5-17-6 Roppongi
Minato-ku, Tokyo 106-0032
Tel: +(81 3) 3583 3401
Fax: +(81 3) 3583 3402

Senior Staff

Harold L. Adams, FAIA, RIBA, JIA, Chairman and CEO
David C. Hudson, AIA, President and COO
David J. Brotman, FAIA, Vice Chairman
Paul G. Hanegraaf, AIA, Senior Vice President
D. Rodman Henderer, AIA, Vice President
Paul F. Jacob, AIA, Senior Vice President
Lance K. Josal, AIA, Senior Vice President
Kenneth V. Moreland, CPA, Senior Vice President and CFO

Persons to Contact

Diane Blair Black, AIA, Managing Director, Baltimore
Lance K. Josal, AIA, Managing Director, Dallas
Kurt Haglund, AIA, Managing Director, Washington, DC
David J. Brotman, FAIA, Managing Director, Los Angeles
James C. Allen, AIA, Managing Director, Chicago
Candace Sheeley, AIA, Managing Director, London
Ron LaVoie, Managing Director, Tokyo
Jeffrey J. Gunning, AIA, Retail/Entertainment, Dallas
Todd C. Lundgren, Hospitality, Dallas
John R. Gosling RIBA, AICP, Residential, Washington, DC
Jerry L. Quebe FAIA, Health, Chicago
Kurt A. Haglund AIA, Corporate, Washington, DC
David V. Thompson, Government, Baltimore

Number of Employees

700

Project Types

Corporate
Government
Health
Hospitality
Office
Mixed-Use
Retail/Entertainment
Residential
Transportation

Disciplines

Architecture
Electrical Engineering
Graphic Design
Historic Preservation
Interior Architecture
Landscape Architecture
Mechanical Engineering
Planning/Urban Design
Structural Engineering

Current and Recent Projects

Al Ghurair Center, Mixed-Use Development, Dubai, UAE
Ariel Rios Federal Building Renovation, Washington, DC, USA
Calderdale NHS Trust Replacement Hospital, Halifax, UK
Centro Comercial Colombo, Lisbon, Portugal
Citrus Park Town Center, Tampa, FL, USA
Desert Passage at Aladdin Retail/Entertainment Center, Las Vegas, USA
Embassy of Ethiopia, Washington, DC, USA
Gateway-Uhmlanga Town Centre, Durban, South Africa
Lucayan Beach Resort, Grand Bahama Isle
Mandarin Oriental Hotel, Miami, USA
Mark•E Retail/Entertainment Center, Houston, USA
Shanghai Scienceland Museum Center, China
St. Louis Gateway Renaissance Hotel, St. Louis, USA
T. Rowe Price Corporate Campus, Baltimore, USA
US Customs-ICC Modernization for the EPA Headquarters, Washington, DC, USA
Worcester Royal Infirmary, Replacement Hospital, Worcester, UK

Selected Clients

The Coca-Cola Companies
Computer Sciences Corporation
Corporate Property Investors
Daewoo Corporation
Disney Development Company
Forest City
Hyatt Development Corporation
IBM Corporation
Johns Hopkins Medical Center
Legg Mason
Mandarin Oriental Hotel Group
Marriott International
MCI Telecommunications Company
Northwestern Memorial Hospital
Post Properties
The Rouse Company
Simon Property Group
The Architect of the Capital
Trizec/Hahn
Urban Retail Properties
USA Department of State, Office of Foreign Buildings Operations
USA Environmental Protection Agency
USA General Services Administration

Design Philosophy and History

Founded as a two-man office in 1946, RTKL has evolved into one of the world's largest multi-disciplinary design firms, with an international portfolio of retail/entertainment, hotel and resort, office, mixed-use, health, government, and residential projects. Today, more than 650 architects, engineers, planners and urban designers, interior and landscape architects, and graphic designers work in its Baltimore headquarters and in Dallas, Washington, DC, Los Angeles, Chicago, London, Tokyo, and Hong Kong offices.

Guided by a design philosophy that emphasizes cooperative client relations, respect for excellence, and dedication to enhancing the human environment, RTKL has played a leading role in the shaping of skylines around the world. Characterized by a sensitivity to scale and context, the firm's early award-winning work set the tone for RTKL's growing portfolio of architectural projects, while its involvement with the famed revitalization of Baltimore's Inner Harbor led to planning and urban design commissions for dozens of cities around the world. Today, RTKL is at work on projects in Asia, Europe, North and South America, Australia, and the Middle East.

1

2

3

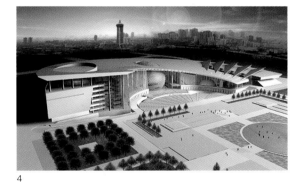

4

1 Digital World Centre, Salford Quays, Manchester, UK
   Client: National Landmark Millennium Lowry Project
   The Digital World Centre, a part of the National Landmark
   Millennium Lowry Project at Salford Quays, Manchester, will be
   an exciting showcase for innovation in digital technology, virtual
   environments and the next generation internet.

2 Gateway, Umhlanga Town Centre, Durban, South Africa
   Client: Old Mutual Properties
   RTKL's entertainment design division, ID•8, is providing the
   architecture, imaging, landscaping and graphics for this
   150,000 square metre retail centre located on 28.3 hectares in
   Durban, South Africa.

3 The Mandarin Oriental Hotel, Miami, Florida, USA
   Client: Mandarin Oriental
   Mandarin Oriental, one of Asia's premier hotel chains, selected
   the city of Miami as the location for its first US hotel, and RTKL
   as its architect.

4 Shanghai Scienceland, Shanghai, China
   Client: Shanghai Scienceland Development Co. Ltd
   RTKL is designing the Shanghai Scienceland museum/centre, a
   new millennium project intended to serve as an educational
   institute to promote advances in science and technology. RTKL
   was awarded the Shanghai Scienceland project following an
   international design competition.

Shim•Sutcliffe Architects

Canada
441 Queen Street East
Toronto, Ontario, M5A 1T5
Tel: +(1 416) 368 3892
Fax: +(1 416) 368 9468
E-mail: shimsut@ibm.net

Directors
Brigitte Shim
Howard Sutcliffe

Person to Contact
Brigitte Shim

Number of Employees
4

Date of Establishment
1994

Project Types
Institutional
Recreational
Residential
Landscape

Disciplines
Architecture
Furniture
Landscape

Current and Recent Projects
Alterations to Massey College, University of
  Toronto, Toronto
Moorelands Camp Dining Hall, Lake Kawagama
Point William Boathouse, Muskoka, Ontario
Ledbury Park, Toronto
Rundles Restaurant and adjacent residence,
  Stratford, Ontario
Craven Road House, Toronto

Selected Clients
Massey College, University of Toronto
City of Toronto, Parks and Recreation
  Department
Moorelands Camp

Design Philosophy
Brigitte Shim and Howard Sutcliffe together
form an architectural practice that emphasizes
the complete interrelationship of furniture,
landscape and architecture—a practice in which
aspects of landscape, or the urban context, find
expression not only in the built work, but in
every aspect of design detail. This approach, in
which inside and outside fully permeate and
articulate each other, in which nature and
architecture combine, has been the key
ingredient in a series of projects that involve, at
one extreme, the periphery of the northern
wilderness, and at the other, the dense city
centre: projects which include not only garden
pavilions and public parks, but also
commissioned furniture pieces.

1

2

1 Orchard House
   Photo credit: James Dow

2 Ledbury Park, view of plaza from canal
   Photo credit: James Dow

3 Laneway House
   Photo credit: James Dow

4&5 Garden Pavilion
     Photo credit: James Dow

3

4

5

Skidmore, Owings & Merrill LLP

PARTNERS

Mustafa K. Abadan
Stephen A. Apking
William F. Baker
Leigh Stanton Breslau
David M. Childs
Raymond J. Clark
Roger F. Duffy
George J. Efstathiou
Peter G. Ellis
Philip J. Enquist
Carl E. Galioto
T.J. Gottesdiener
Gary P. Haney

Craig W. Hartman
John L. Kriken
Brian D. Lee
Peter J. Magill
Jeffrey J. McCarthy
Larry K. Oltmanns
Gene J. Schnair
Adrian D. Smith
Marilyn J. Taylor
Richard F. Tomlinson
Anthony T. Vacchione
Robert L. Wesley
Carolina Y.C. Woo

DIRECTORS

Nicholas A. Jacobs
Roger G. Kallman
Roger Whiteman

CHICAGO

224 South Michigan
Avenue, Suite 1000
Chicago, IL 60604
Tel: +(1 312) 554 9090
Fax: +(1 312) 360 4545

NEW YORK

14 Wall Street
New York, NY 10005
Tel: +(1 212) 298 9300
Fax: +(1 212) 298 9500

SAN FRANCISCO

One Front Street,
Suite 2400
San Francisco, CA 94111
Tel: +(1 415) 981 1555
Fax: +(1 415) 398 3214

LONDON

30 Millbank, 3rd Flr.
London SW1P 4SD,
United Kingdom
Tel: +(44 171) 798 1000
Fax: +(44 171) 798 1100

Other Offices:
Washington, D.C.;
Los Angeles; Hong Kong;
Sao Paulo

Employees: 850
Established: 1936

Info@som.com

DISCIPLINES

Architecture
Engineering–Structural, Civil,
Mechanical, Electrical, Plumbing
Interior Design
Urban Planning
Graphics

RECENT PROJECTS

Jin Mao Tower, Shanghai, China
Hong Kong Convention Center
San Francisco International Airport
Symphony Center, Chicago
New York Mercantile Exchange
Atlantico Pavilion, Lisbon

CLIENTS

Bloomberg LLP
General Motors
Stanford University
United Airlines
University of Texas Medical Center

Skidmore, Owings & Merrill LLP (SOM) is an international architectural, planning and interior design firm, founded in 1936. The firm's worldwide reputation is based on a commitment to respond fully and creatively to our clients' needs, a commitment that has produced over six decades of exceptional work.

SOM's sophisticated technology innovations, combined with consistent design quality, have produced a portfolio that features some of the most important architectural achievements of this century.

From its beginning, SOM has been continually involved in major projects that have influenced urban, suburban, and community development throughout the United States, as well as abroad. The firm's long-standing integration of urban design and master planning, architecture, engineering, and interior design has resulted in more than 10,000 projects located in over 50 countries.

In 1996, SOM celebrated its 60th anniversary and received for the second time the American Institute of Architects' Architecture Firm Award, the highest honour given to a collaborative practice for design excellence. SOM was the winner of the award when it was inaugurated, in 1961.

SOM's work ranges in scope from interior design to the master planning of entire communities. Projects include civic and commercial office buildings, airports, museums and cultural complexes, recreational and sports facilities, educational institutions, governmental and judicial buildings, residential developments, and hospitals. Significantly, the practice has gained the trust and respect of many leading client organizations, working in partnership to create projects of immediate and lasting value.

Skidmore, Owings & Merrill LLP

Architecture and Urbanism at the Millennium

1995–2000

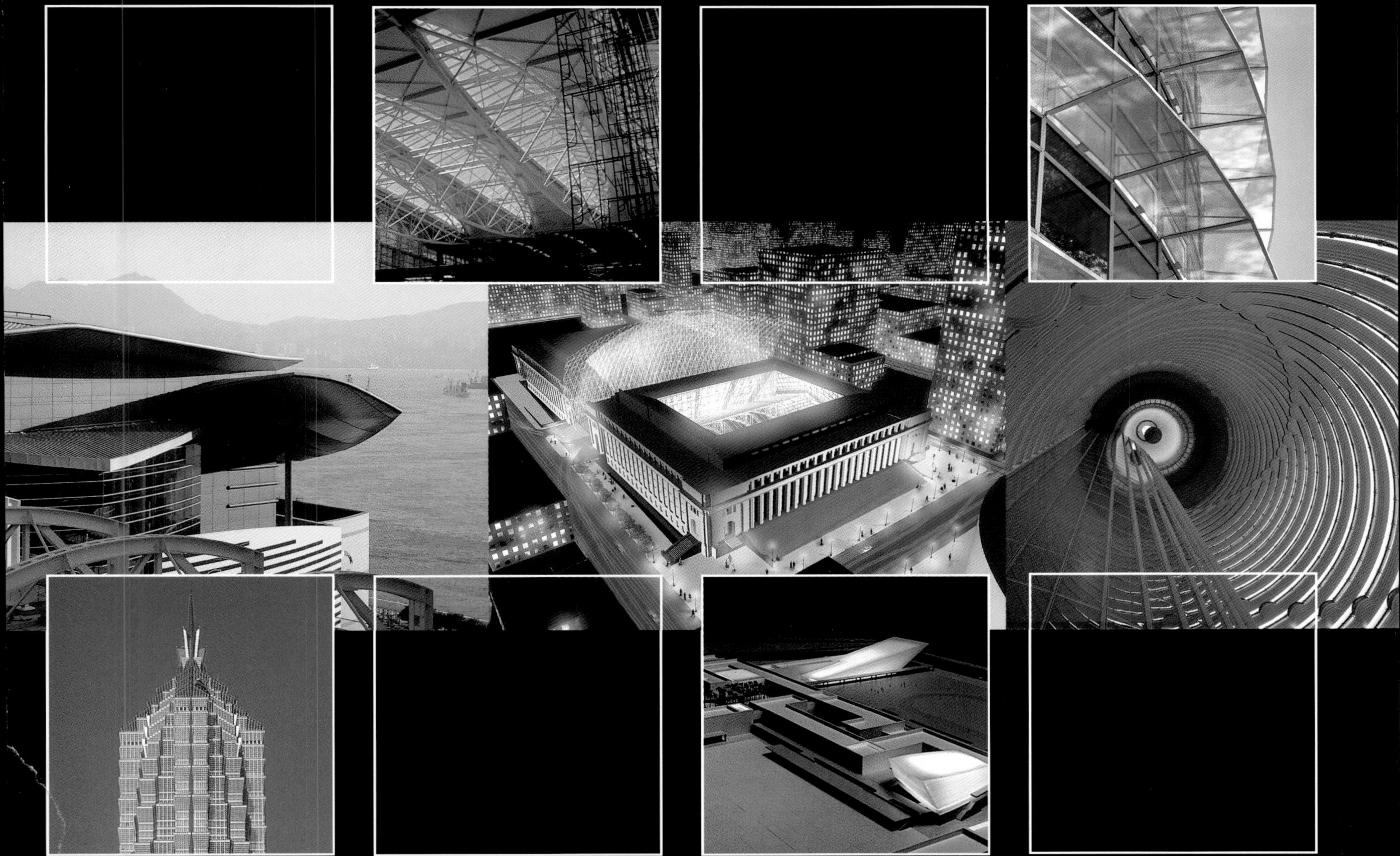

Spatium Associated Studio of Architecture

Rocco Magnoli, architect and Lorenzo Carmellini, designer
Photo credit: Tanya Levoni, Milan

Italy
Via Vincenzo Monti, 25
Milan 20123
Tel: +(39 02) 439 0267
Fax: +(39 02) 4800 8498
E-mail: segr.dept@spatium.it

Directors
Rocco Magnoli, architect
Lorenzo Carmellini, designer

Associates
Annamaria Magnoli, architect

Persons to Contact
Lorenzo Carmellini
Rocco Magnoli
Annamaria Magnoli

Number of Employees
30

Date of Establishment
1978

Project Types
Commercial
Landscaping
Residential
Town Planning

Disciplines
Architecture
Interior Design
Refurbishment

Current and Recent Projects
Halkin Hotel, London, UK
Villa in Al Wajbah, Doha, Qatar
Gianni Versace Boutique, Fifth Avenue, New
  York, USA
Versace Jeans Couture, New Bond Street,
  London, UK
Londra Palace Hotel, Venice, Italy
Hotel du Lac et du Parc, Riva del Garda, Italy
Hotel Cristallo, Cortina d'Ampezzo, Italy
Porto Letizia, resort village, Porlezza, Italy
Palazzo Versace, Gold Coast, Australia

Selected Clients
Gianni Versace S.p.a., Italy
Canali S.p.a., Italy
Cesare Paciotti S.p.a., Italy
Verri, Italy
De Waal International B.V., The Netherlands
Emir of Qatar
Sunland Group Limited, Australia
Comojo Limited, Great Britain

1

1 Versace, Fifth Avenue, New York
  Photo credit: Peter Aaron/ESTO, New York
2 Versace, Fifth Floor, Fifth Avenue, New York
  Photo credit: Peter Aaron/ESTO, New York
3 Versace, Sixth Floor, Fifth Avenue, New York
  Photo credit: Peter Aaron/ESTO, New York
4 Sillo, Legnago
  Photo credit: Studio Azzurro, Milan
5 Halkin Hotel, London
  Photo credit: Ezio Prandini, Lomazzo (I)
6 Sillo, view towards top
  Photo credit: Studio Azzurro, Milan
7 Halkin Hotel, suite on fifth floor
  Photo credit: Ezio Prandini, Lomazzo (I)

Design Philosophy and History
Lorenzo Carmellini and Rocco Magnoli established their architectural studio in 1978. At that time, the growth and explosion of Milan as the fashion capital of Italy was one of the reasons that led them to an initial interest in interior architecture, specifically in the field of fashion retail interiors.

After the opening of the first Gianni Versace boutique in Milan in 1979, they have designed more than 300 boutiques placed in the centres of the most important fashion cities in the world, and they arrived up to the meaningful restoration of the Vanderbilt residence in Fifth Avenue, New York.

The interiors of the fashion palaces have been like a 'spring-board' for other important challenges in architecture, in the form of structural volumes and of exteriors.

The theme that links the interventions of Carmellini and Magnoli is the design of the space. Whether the project is refurbishment and interior decoration of historic buildings in New York, Paris, London, or a new building designed completely from the shell to the furniture (Halkin Hotel, London), the true objectives are always the geometric proportions and the invention of an image that has to be fixed in memory.

In the last few years the studio enhanced its presence in the field of planning first category hotels and resort villages. Carmellini and Magnoli have worked all over the world, from the Bahamas to Australia, always starting from the surroundings so the hotel or village is perfectly included in its future context.

The studio counts on 30 collaborators who use all kinds of design techniques, from computers to artistic drawings.

2

3

4

5

6

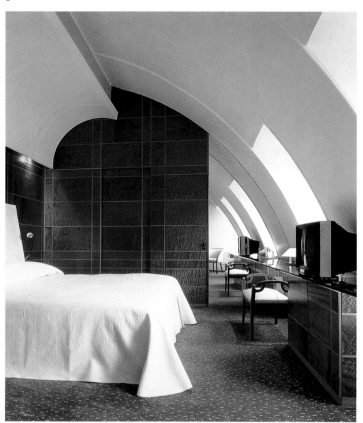

7

Steven Holl Architects

USA

Suite 402, 435 Hudson Street
New York, New York 10014
Tel: +(1 212) 989 0918
Fax: +(1 212) 463 9718
E-mail: mail@stevenholl.com
Website: www.stevenholl.com

Recent Awards

Chrysler Design Award, 1998
Alvar Aalto Medal, 1998
National AIA Design Award Chapel of
 St. Ignatius, Seattle University, 1998
Japanese Building Society Award, 1997
National AIA Religious Architecture Award
 Chapel of St. Ignatius, Seattle University, 1997
New York AIA Medal of Honour Award, 1997
Progressive Architecture Awards, 1996
 Knut Hamsun Museum, Bødo, Norway
 Museum of the City, Cassino, Italy
NYC AIA Design Awards, 1995
 Cranbrook Institute of Science, Michigan
 Chapel of St. Ignatius, Seattle University
NYC AIA Architecture Project Award, 1993
 Makuhari Housing, Makuhari, Japan
AIA National Honour Award, 1993
 Texas Stretto House, Dallas, Texas
AIA National Honour Award, 1992
 D.E. Shaw & Co. Offices, New York
NYC Art Commission Excellence in Design
 Award, 1991, The Strand Theater renovation,
 Brooklyn

Design Philosophy and History

Steven Holl Architects (SHA) was founded in
New York by principal Steven Holl in 1976. SHA
is a design oriented office, with a current staff
of 16, including four registered architects. The
firm has been recognized internationally with
numerous awards, publications and exhibitions
for quality and excellence in design. In 1993
Steven Holl Architects was awarded the winning
design among 516 entries in the competition for
the new Museum of Contemporary Art,
Helsinki. This project opened to the public in
May 1998. Other current projects include the
Cranbrook Institute of Science in Bloomfield
Hills, Michigan, the Bellevue Art Museum, in
Bellevue, Washington, the College of
Architecture and Landscape Architecture at the
University of Minnesota, and the Knut Hamsun
Museum in Hanarøy, Norway.

Steven Holl Architects has extensive experience
working both nationally and overseas on a
variety of public and private works. Projects
experience include museums, galleries,
exhibition design, housing, residential,
educational facilities, religious institutions, retail
design, office design, public utilities, and master
planning.

1   Exterior 'Kiasma' Moca, Helsinki
    Photo credit: Jussi Tainen

2–4   Exterior 'Kiasma' Moca, Helsinki
      Photo credit: Voitto Niemula

5   Ramp to second floor gallery, 'Kiasma' Moca,
    Helsinki
    Photo credit: Voitto Niemula

6–10   Interior, 'Kiasma' Moca, Helsinki
       Photo credit: Voitto Niemula

4

5

6

7

8

9

10

The Stubbins Associates, Inc.
Architecture, Planning, Interior Design

1

USA
1033 Massachusetts Avenue
Cambridge, Massachusetts 02138-5387
Tel: +(1 617) 491 6450
Fax: +(1 617) 491 7104
Website: www.tsa-arch.com

Person to Contact
Richard Green, FAIA, Chairman
E-mail: rgreen@tsa-arch.com

Number of Employees
90

Principals
Richard Green, FAIA
W. Easley Hamner, FAIA
Scott Simpson, FAIA
C. Ronald Ostberg, AIA
James E. Beyer, AIA
William A. McGee, AIA
Philip T. Seibert, IIDA

Disciplines
Architecture
Interior Design
Landscape Design
Planning

Project Types
Corporate/Commercial
Educational
Healthcare
Hospitality
Institutional

Current and Recent Projects
Amgen Center, Cambridge, Massachusetts, USA
Biosquare, Boston, Massachusetts, USA
Emily Fisher Landau Center for the Visual Arts,
 Cushing Academy, Ashburnham,
 Massachusetts, USA
Hulings Hall Biological Sciences Building,
 Carleton College, Northfield, Minnesota, USA
Indiana Historical Society, Indianapolis, Indiana,
 USA
New and Renovated Math and Science Facilities,
 University of Minnesota, Morris, Minnesota,
 USA
MBNA Hall, School of Business and Economics,
 University of Delaware, Newark, Delaware,
 USA
Motorola ISG Online Network Operations Center
 Renovation, Mansfield, Massachusetts, USA
Glenn T. Seaborg Science Center, Northern
 Michigan University, Marquette, Michigan, USA
Learning Technology Center, Vanderbilt
 University, Nashville, Tennessee, USA
North Carolina State University Alumni Center,
 Raleigh, North Carolina, USA
North Carolina State University Undergraduate
 Science Teaching Laboratory, Raleigh, North
 Carolina, USA
US Embassy, Singapore
Venetian Casino Resort, Las Vegas, Nevada, USA

Recent Clients
Amgen
Bally's Park Place Casino Hotel
Boston Design Center
Boston University
Bristol-Myers Squibb Company
Carleton College
Citibank
Commission of Foreign Trade, Anhui Province
Coopers & Lybrand
Cornell University
The Cousteau Society
Development Bank of Singapore
Doubletree Hotels Corporation
Duke University
Federal Reserve Bank of Boston
Fidelity Capital Corporation
Harcourt General, Inc.
Harrah's Marina Hotel Casino
Harvard University
Houghton Mifflin Company
Indiana Historical Society
JMB/Urban Development Company
Kuwait Ministry of Planning & Public Works
Lotus Development Corporation
Maersk Inc.
Marriott Corporation
Massachusetts General Hospital
The MITRE Corporation
Mitsubishi Estate Co., Ltd
Motorola
North Carolina State University
The Prudential Insurance Co. of America
Ronald Reagan Presidential Library Foundation
The University of Chicago
US Department of State
US General Services Administration
University of Massachusetts
Vanderbilt University
Venetian Casino Resort
Westinghouse Furniture Systems

Design Philosophy and History
Established in 1949, The Stubbins Associates
(TSA) has successfully completed an unusually
broad range of projects both nationally and
internationally. Professional services include
feasibility studies; programming and master
planning; architectural, interior and landscape
design; and technical services including
construction documentation and construction
administration. The firm utilizes the most
advanced CAD technology, including 3-D
modeling, on all projects.

Directed by seven principals, the firm's highly
qualified and experienced professional staff take
pride in their teamwork with client, consultants,
and contractors. The size and structure of the
firm is designed for active, hands-on
participation by a principal-in-charge, who is
assisted by a project manager and project
designer to ensure a high degree of
communication, coordination, and continuity for
each and every project.

TSA is one of the few firms to have been
awarded the prestigious 'Architectural Firm
Award' by the American Institute of Architects,
placing it at the highest echelon of the
profession. In addition, TSA's projects have won
more than 160 awards for design excellence,
both nationally and internationally. Some of its
better known projects include Citicorp Center in
New York, the Federal Reserve Bank of Boston,
the Ronald Reagan Presidential Library in
California, Congress Hall in Berlin, and the
Landmark Tower in Yokohama - the tallest
building in Japan.

1 Citicorp Center, New York, NY, USA
 Photo credit: courtesy The Stubbins Associates, Inc.

2 Biological Sciences Learning Center and Jules F.
 Knapp Medical Research Complex, The University
 of Chicago, Chicago, Illinois, USA
 Photo credit: Hedrich-Blessing

3 Landmark Tower, Yokohama, Japan
 Photo credit: courtesy Nikko Hotels

4 Harcourt General Executive Offices, Chestnut Hill,
 Massachusetts, USA
 Photo credit: Warren Jagger

5 Bristol-Myers Squibb Pharmaceutical Research
 Center, Wallingford, Connecticut, USA
 Photo credit: Nick Wheeler/Wheeler Photographics

6 Carnegie Center Master Plan, Princeton,
 New Jersey, USA
 Photo credit: courtesy The Stubbins Associates, Inc.

7 Federal Reserve Bank, Boston, Massachusetts, USA
 Photo credit: Nick Wheeler/Wheeler Photographics

8 Chancery Building, United States Embassy, Singapore
 Photo credit: Hans Schlupp

9 Psychology Building, Vanderbilt University, USA
 Photo credit: Timothy Hursley

2

3

4

8

5

7

9

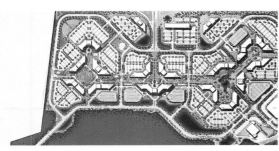

6

Studio Downie Architects

1

2

3

UK
146 New Cavendish Street
London W1M 7FG
Tel: +(44 20) 7255 1599
Fax: +(44 20) 7636 7883

Director
Craig Downie

Associate
Andrew Jackson

Number of Employees
8

Date of Establishment
1993

Project Types
Apartments
Archives
Art Galleries
Business Centres
Commercial Offices
Exhibitions
Industrial
Laboratories
Libraries
Private Residences
Public Spaces
Reading Rooms
Swimming Pools
Visitors' Centres

Disciplines
Feasibility Studies
Furniture Design
Historical Sites and Landscapes
Interior Design
New Buildings
Planning Applications
Refurbishment

Current and Recent Projects
Archives, reading room and exhibition space,
 Kensington Gore, London, UK
Gallery upgrade, The Mall, London, UK
Rare book archives, visitors' centre and reading
 room, Cambridge, UK
Film viewing suite and library, Fitzroy Square,
 London, UK
Pool and pool house, Chichester, UK
Private residence, Fulmer, UK
Technology Cafe, Twickenham, UK
IT Training Centre, Hounslow, UK
Headquarters Building, St James' Square,
 London, UK
Private residence and pool, Halesworth,
 Suffolk, UK
Apartments, Belgravia, London, UK
Business Centre, Hounslow, UK

Selected Clients
The Royal Geographical Society (with IBG)
Corpus Christi College, Cambridge
The Image Bank
The Institute of Contemporary Arts (ICA)
BAA Lynton
Microsoft/KPMG
Sculpture at Goodwood
West London Training and Enterprise Council
Caisse Des Depots (CDC - IML)
Concord Lighting
BBC Resources
BAA Heathrow Airport Ltd

Design Philosophy and History
Craig Downie studied architecture within the
layered environment of fine art, sculpture,
graphics and textiles at Duncan of Jordanstone
College of Art, Dundee. First influences were
Schumacher's 'Small is Beautiful', Jane Jacobs
'Life and Death of American Cities', and the
building plans of James Stirling. There were
periods in the offices of Terry Farrell and Lord
Norman Foster and in Australia and California,
and travels to the work of Aalto, Asplund, Siza,
Scarpa and Ando, and in California Neutra and
Ellwood.

Craig Downie formed the practice in 1993, with
Andrew Jackson joining in 1994. The 1950s
Californian School in particular set the first clear
program for the practice from which a philosophy
is continuously evolving and is seen as only truly
accountable through the realizations of the built
form: simplicity, elegance and pragmatism. Many
interior projects have involved altering ingrained
perceptions of corporate imagery with
challenging installations. Influences have included
the work of artists Ben Nicholson and Donald
Judd, with sculptured, layered forms, objects and
colours.

In 1994 Craig Downie was one of six chosen for
the RIBA exhibition and seminar series, 'Emerging
UK Architects', chaired in Tokyo by Dr Kisho
Kurokawa and Professor Dennis Sharp. In 1995
the practice won a National Design Business
Award for the commercial effectiveness of design
for their Acton Next Step Centre and in 1996
they were appointed Interior Design Advisors by
BAA-Heathrow Airport Ltd for Terminal 2. In
1996 Studio Downie's Hat Hill Sculpture Gallery
was the subject of a solo exhibition at the RIBA
London. Within their first five years, they have
won several prestigious and demanding projects,

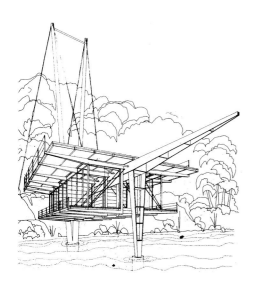

4

5

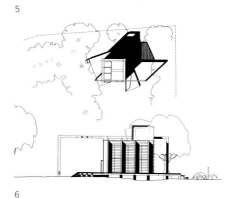

6

7

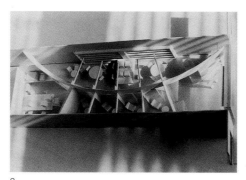

8

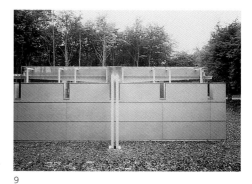

9

10

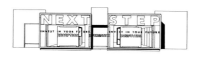

11

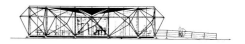

12

including the Royal Geographical Society (with IBG), Corpus Christi College, Cambridge and the ICA. In 1997 they were chosen for inclusion in the Architecture Foundation's 'Best New UK Practices'. The practice work has been published in Japan, France, Spain, Australia, Switzerland,

Canada and the US and Craig Downie has taught at the Architectural Association in London. He has been a design advisor on several urban regeneration projects, and was recently appointed an RIBA competition assessor.

Tadao Ando Architects & Associates

Tadao Ando
Photo credit: Tadao Ando Architects & Associates

Japan
5-23 Toyosaki
2 Chome Kita-Ku, Osaka 531-0072

Date of Establishment
1969

List of Some Works
Row House, Sumiyoshi, Osaka
Koshino House, Kobe, Hyogo
Time's, Kyoto
Church of the Light, Osaka
Museum of Literature, Himeji, Hyogo
Water Temple, Awaji Island, Hyogo
Japan Pavilion Expo '92, Sevilla, Spain
Naoshima Contemporary Art Museum & Annex,
   Okayama
FABRICA (Benetton Research Centre), Treviso,
   Italy
Rokko Housing II, Kobe
Chikatsu-Asuka Historical Museum, Osaka
Suntory Museum, Osaka
Meditation Space, UNESCO, Paris
Daylight Museum (Hiroki Oda Museum), Gamo-
   Gun, Shiga

Church of the Light
This church is located in a quiet residential
suburb of Osaka. It consists of a rectangular
volume sliced through at a fifteen-degree angle
by a completely free standing wall that
separates the entrance from the chapel. Light
penetrates the profound darkness of this box
through a cross which is cut out of the altar
wall. The floor and pews are made of rough
scaffolding planks, which are low cost and also
ultimately suited to the character of the space.
Tadao Ando has always used natural materials
for parts of a building that come into contact
with people's hands or feet, as he is convinced
that materials having substance, such as wood
or concrete, are invaluable for building, and that
it is essentially through people's senses that we
become aware of architecture.

Openings have been limited in this space, for
light shows its brilliance only against a backdrop
of darkness. Nature's presence is also limited to
the element of light and is rendered exceedingly
abstract. In responding to such abstractions, the
architecture grows continually purer. The linear
pattern formed on the floor by rays from the
sun and a migrating cross of light expresses with
purity man's relationships with nature.

Rokko Housing I, II, III
Near Kobe the central mountains of Japan come
in closest proximity to the ocean. This building is
located in a residential district at the foot of
Kobe's Rokko Mountains, and its site is a south
facing slope. From the site, there is a panoramic
view extending form Osaka Bay to the port of
Kobe. Havoc has been wrought on Japan's
natural areas by cutting out stepped building
lots, so at this site Tadao Ando was determined
to take a fresh approach to the way a building
relates with nature. In order to merge the
structure into its verdant surroundings it was
necessary to sink it into the ground along the
slope and restrain its height. The building is
composed of a group of units, each measuring
5.4 metres by 4.8 metres. In section, it follows
the slope, and in plan, it is symmetrical. In
stepping up the slope, gaps are intentionally
created. The gaps relate to each other and serve
to unite the entire building at the same time
they serve as a plaza. The dry areas at the edges
of the building serve as mechanical spaces and
promote ventilation and insulation. The twenty
units piled up on the face of the slope are all
different in type and size. Each unit has a
terrace, and there are many different views
available.

Koshino House
Two inorganic concrete boxes, arranged in
parallel so as to avoid scattered trees, are half-
buried in the verdant slope of a national park.
The building, though autonomous, obeys the
logic of nature. The two boxes of different sizes
are linked by an underground corridor and also
flank a courtyard.

1 Rokko Housing I, II, III
   Photo credit: Mitsuo Matsuoka
2 Church of the Light
   Photo credit: Mitsuo Matsuoka
3 Rokko Housing II
   Photo credit: Hiroshi Ueda
Opposite:
   Koshino House
   Photo credit: Tomio Ohashi

1

2

3

Tai Soo Kim Partners
Architects & Planners

T.W. Iglehart, D. Hwang, R. Szczypek and T.S. Kim
Photo credit: courtesy Tai Soo Kim Partners

USA
285 Farmington Avenue
Hartford, Connecticut 06105
Tel: +(1 860) 547 1970
Fax: +(1 860) 249 0695
E-mail: TSKP@tskp.com

Korea
Seocho-3-Dong
Seocho-Gu, Seoul 1506-64
Tel: +(822) 588 2703
Fax: +(822) 588 2706
E-mail: TSKP@chollian.dacom.co.kr

Directors (Partners)
Tai Soo Kim, FAIA
Ryszard Szczypek, AIA
T. Whitcomb Iglehart, AIA

Persons to Contact
Ryszard Szczypek, AIA
T. Whitcomb Iglehart, AIA

Design Philosophy

For the firm, design is about bringing passion and training into a built realization. It is a careful balance of client and site requirements, creative initiative, and an understanding of over 5,000 years of theory and practice. The firm's process involves melding the specifics of site and program with resonant memories of place and a broader understanding of architectural precedent. This ultimately leads to work that is fresh, uncomplicated and balanced, engaging the built environment and sparking the imagination of its audience.

While the firm's approach to its work is rooted in modern architecture, the work resists stylistic labelling. The objective of each project is to arrive at a site-specific solution that goes beyond the client's requirements and engages and lifts the human spirit.

History

The year 2000 marks the 30th anniversary of Tai Soo Kim Partners. The firm was established in 1970 in Connecticut as the Hartford Design Group. Hard work and determination brought change, recognition and growth to the firm. In its early work, the firm attained national recognition for its civic architecture in a wide range of building types, such as the Groton Senior Center, the Rocky Hill Fire & Ambulance Complex, the Middlebury Elementary School, and the U.S. Naval Submarine Training Facility in New London.

In the 1980s the firm won several large and prominent commissions, further advancing its profile and its experience with larger-scale and more complex projects, such as the 145,000 square foot Gray Cultural Center for the

University of Hartford, the restoration and expansion of Hartford's historic Union Station, and Korea's 300,000 square foot National Museum of Contemporary Art. The success of these projects caught the attention of both national and international press.

During the 1990s, the firm's portfolio continued to diversify with larger planning and design projects such as the 16 acre urban educational campus called The Learning Corridor adjacent to Trinity College in Hartford, the 1.3 million square foot Research & Development Park for the LG Group, and the 4 million square foot Central City entertainment and retail development in downtown Seoul. In the spring of 1999, the firm was selected by the US Department of State to design a new US embassy in Tunisia.

As a comprehensive body of work, the firm's portfolio consists of a wide range of projects for education, cultural institutions, corporations and governments.

1

2

1 National Museum of Contemporary Art, Seoul, Korea
  Photo credit: Paul Warchol
2 LG Research & Development Park, Daeduk, Korea
  Photo credit: Timothy Hursley

3

4

5

6

3 Gray Cultural Center, University of Hartford, West
  Hartford, Connecticut, USA
  Photo credit: Nick Wheeler

4 Helen & Harry Gray Court, Wadsworth Atheneum,
  Hartford, Connecticut, USA
  Photo credit: Robert Benson

5 Gray Conference Center, University of Hartford,
  West Hartford, Connecticut, USA
  Photo credit: Nick Wheeler

6 Middlebury Elementary School, Connecticut, USA
  Photo credit: Steve Rosenthal

TAI
SOO
KIM

Terry Farrell & Partners

UK
7 Hatton Street
London NW8 8PL
Tel: +(44 20) 7258 3433
Fax: +(44 20) 7723 7059
Email: enquiries@terryfarrell.co.uk

14 Torphichen Street
Edinburgh EH3 8JB
Tel: +(44 131) 229 3353
Fax: +(44 131) 229 6106

Hong Kong
Baskerville House
22 Ice House Street
Central Hong Kong
Tel: +(852) 2523 0183
Fax: +(852) 2596 0216

Key Personnel
Terry Farrell, Senior Partner
Toby Bridge, Managing Partner
Doug Streeter, Design Partner
Brian Chantler, Financial Director
Aidan Potter, Design Director
John Campbell, Technical Director
Steve Smith, Director of Urban & Infrastructure
  Design

Project Directors
Paul Bell
Steve Brown
Mark Shirburne-Davies
Dennis Dornan
Mike Stowell
Julian Tollast

Associates
Chris Barber
Tony Davey
Richard Davies
Bobby Desai
Tom Gent
Tom Kimble
Nick Willars
Simon Wing

Person to Contact
Paul Downey

Number of Employees
90, UK
125, Worldwide

Date of Establishment
1980

Project Types
Civic
Commercial
Cultural
Education
Housing
Industrial
Landmark Development
Landscape
Leisure
Recreational
Research
Retail
Transport

Disciplines
Architecture
Interior Design
Master Planning
Urban Design

Current and Recent Projects
Bank One, Cardiff
Barreiro Ferry Terminal, Lisbon
British Consulate & British Council, Hong Kong
Carlton TV Headquarters, London
Crescent Housing, Newcastle
Do Rossio Station, Lisbon
Edinburgh International Conference Centre,
  Edinburgh
Greenwich Pier, London
Inchon Transportation Centre for International
  Airport, Korea
International Centre for Life, Newcastle
Kowloon Station Development, Hong Kong
London Bridge Station, London
Medway Works, Kent
Newcastle Quayside, Newcastle
Port of Lisbon Master Plan, Lisbon
River Hull Corridor Masterplan, Kingston-upon-
  Hull
Royal Institution, London
Sainsbury's, Harlow
Samsung Europe Headquaters, London
South Kensington Station, London
The Deep, Kingston-upon-Hull
The Peak Tower, Hong Kong
Three Quays Hotel, London
Westferry Circus, Canary Wharf, London
West Rail, Hong Kong

Selected Clients
Bank One
Blue Circle
Canary Wharf Ltd
Carlton TV
Centros Miller
Her Majesty's Foreign Office
J. Sainsbury
Mass Transit Railway Corporation, Hong Kong
National Galleries of Scotland
Samsung
Scottish Widows
Stanhope PLC
Whitecliff Properties

Design Philosophy and History
Terry Farrell established the practice in 1965 and has continued it in his own name since 1980. Terry Farrell & Partners (TFP) is an internationally acclaimed architecture practice with experience in master planning and urban design. TFP has an acknowledged reputation for design excellence, based upon construction, use and function, as well as the social context of a place. The company combines forward-looking design with conservation, building rehabilitation and restoration work on historic buildings. TFP's projects have achieved recognition and awards, and have been featured in publications worldwide.

The practice is motivated by innovative technical and conceptual thinking based on an understanding of the client's requirements and aspirations; the history and context of the project; and the needs of those who will enjoy the building.

TFP's recent work continues to elude categorization; it resolutely takes risks; and it persists in recognizing the demand in architecture for a bolder, popular touch. The practice is renowned for its ability to develop a distinctive and appropriate aesthetic for each scheme, rather than an overriding stylistic manner.

1 Newcastle's £60 million **International Centre for Life**, due for completion in 2000, is the flagship millennium project exploring genetic science. The regenerated site comprises an exhibition space with an education facility, a genetics research building and laboratory/office space. This is arranged around the first major urban square in Newcastle for over a century. The site is planned as an embryo motif – a reference to evolution and development. The Life Centre is the largest building on the site (9,100 square metres), striking for the leaf-like pre-patinated copper roof punctuated with a large rooflight. Largely reliant on CAD technology, its structural form bypasses pre-set geometries, twisting like a skeletal leaf along ten arches.
Photo credit: Airfotos Ltd

2&3 **The Dean Centre** in Edinburgh, completed in 1999, transforms Thomas Hamilton's Grade A-listed orphanage into a visionary exhibition space housing an extraordinary collection of surrealist and dadaist artworks. Eschewing the oft-worn 'white box' formula for an intense arrangement of colours and materials, TFP has designed a series of spaces using devices that aim to intrigue: mirrors and *enfilade* doors, wall breaks, surprise portholes, changes of level and a void filled with a 9-metre-high Paolozzi sculpture.
Photo credit: Antonia Reeve

4 **The Deep** is a £37 million millennium project in Hull comprising a visitor attraction/education/ research facility for all aspects of marine science (its main exhibit is a world-class aquarium) and a two-storey business centre. Fissures streak the building's three-tone facade, which is clad in sparkling concrete, steel, titanium and glass. A footbridge and riverside walkway, also designed by TFP, connects the city of Hull to its east side. The project is due for completion in 2001.
Photo credit: Andrew Putler

5 **Inchon International Airport**, at 3 million square metres, is among the world's largest infrastructure projects. The building, developed on reclaimed land, forms the stop-off point for ground transportation to and from Seoul. It comprises four railway links, 5,000 below-ground car parking spaces and a people-mover system. When complete, in time for the 2002 football World Cup, Inchon will serve as the focal point for transatlantic expeditions and inter-Asia travel. The significance of the building as the gateway to Korea and a national symbol of the reunified country is represented in its dramatic design: the Great Hall has 180-metre clear spans, creating a magnificent window to the airport.
Photo credit: Samod/DMJM/Terry Farrell & Partners

6 TFP's **Kowloon Station and Master Plan** scheme is among the world's largest station construction projects, providing a focus for the development of a new city district on the reclaimed land of West Kowloon (due for completion 2008). The 173,500 square metre railway station links Central Hong Kong to Chek Lap Kok Airport, providing podium infrastructure works, a master Plan for an air-rights property development above the station and a ventilation building. An atrium roof signifies the station entrance and becomes the focal point for the development's central square.
Photo credit: courtesy Terry Farrell & Partners

1

2

3

4

5

6

Tomás Taveira

Av. da República, 2 - 1.°
Lisbon 1050-191
Tel: +(351) 21 313 8770
Fax: +(351) 21 313 8794

Fátima Apartments

This building is located in Fátima, and is made up of two sections each facing different streets, and are linked by a basement where there is a small shopping centre. Both sections above ground are made up of small apartments to be rented to the Turistic people.

The idea of designing something against the cultural urban context of Fátima City was what the firm wanted to achieve, however the administrative city rules ensured that the number of floors and the relationship to the street was standard.

Therefore the balconies were designed in an undulating form to give the building character, which also helped emphasise the colour used throughout the project. The colour and the way it was applied helps to 'fragment' the facade design.

The building is made up of 27 apartments, 58 boutiques, one cinema and car parking.

Olaias Metro Station

This metro station is included in the EXPO 98 Metro Line. This line was built to link Lisbon's inner city with EXPO 98 areas, however this station serves and is located in the centre of a residential area which was built by the firm over the last twenty years, which is called Olaias Quarter.

This metro station is basically made of three major areas: the main reception hall which is shaped like a fish tail with two entrances in opposite positions 110 metres apart, the second area is the access to the trains, and the third is an access to a future train station which will be built within two years.

The reception area has its walls totally covered with specially designed ceramic tiles and the floor is covered with high wearing, resistant materials. The staircases are protected with metal grids in order to emphasise the shape of the space. Lighting consists of a large chandelier made of metal. The use of colour throughout the station is abundant from the ceramic tiles in the receptions area, to the ceilings, the chandelier, and the walls of the access areas to the trains.

Noronha's House

This small house is located in Portugal near Oporto, and was designed for a couple of young physicians with a child. The site is a small compound made up of single houses for the middle and upper class sections of the community.

The house has three floors. The basement includes a garage and a special area for 'hedonistic ceremonies'. The entrance floor has several social areas: the living room, dinning area, kitchen, physicians office, and the swimming pool area outside. The third floor is the private area, with sleeping rooms and one 'atelier de peinture' which belongs to the lady owner.

The firm's intention was not to be too offensive to the 'context', however the shape of the building, the colours and the way it is inserted on the site has provoked curiosity.

1

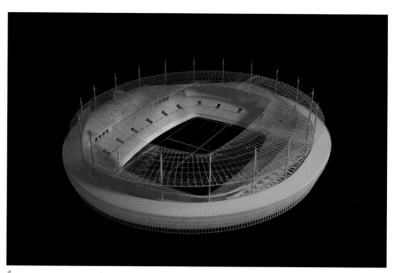

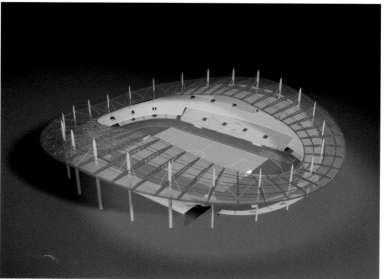

1 Fátima Apartments, internal patio, view from top
   Photo credit: Tomás Taveira sa / ana carvalho

2 Olaias Metro Station, main reception hall, detail of fish sculpture
   Photo credit: Tomás Taveira sa / ana carvalho

3 Noronha's House, view from west
   Photo credit: Tomás Taveira sa / ana carvalho

4 Stadium of Aveiro
   Computer rendering

5 Stadium of Benfica
   Computer rendering

6 Stadium of Leiria
   Computer rendering

TRO/The Ritchie Organization
Architecture, Planning, Engineering and Interior Design

USA
Head Office
80 Bridge Street
Newton, Massachusetts 02458
Tel: +(1 617) 969 9400
Fax: +(1 617) 527 6753
E-mail: Info@troarch.com

3050 Bee Ridge Road
Sarasota, Florida 34239
Tel: +(1 941) 923 4911
Fax: +(1 941) 922 7940

115 21st Street, North
Birmingham, Alabama 35203
Tel: +(1 205) 324 6744
Fax: +(1 205) 521 0591

Principals
Robert W. Hoye, AIA, President and CEO
Wendell R. Morgan, Jr., AIA, Chairman
Joseph L. Bynum, AIA
Wm. Kregg Elsass, AIA
Stephen N. Evers, AIA
Douglas A. Farber, CHC
Robert J. Farrow, AIA
Fred C. Frederick, AIA
Edward P. Hughes, CPA
Mark Jussaume, PE
Dennis L. Kaiser, AIA
Michael Keweshan
Joanne MacIsaac, IIDA, IFMA
Brendan Morrisroe

Persons to Contact
Robert W. Hoye, AIA, President, Massachusetts
Tricia McConville, Director of Marketing,
  Massachusetts
Bill Slocum, Director of Marketing, Florida
Cleo Kathryn Donovan, Director of Marketing,
  Alabama

Number of Employees
180

Date of Establishment
1909

Project Types
Healthcare
Institutional
Senior Living

Current and Recent Projects
Cullman Regional Medical Center, Cullman,
  Alabama
Saint Elizabeth's Medical Center, Brighton,
  Massachusetts
Lowell General Hospital, Lowell, Massachusetts
Saint Francis Hospital and Medical Center,
  Hartford, Connecticut
Milford Hospital, Milford, Connecticut
South Shore Hospital, South Weymouth,
  Massachusetts
Morton Plant Hospital, Clearwater, Florida
Stamford Hospital System, Stamford,
  Connecticut
Newton-Wellesley Hospital, Newton,
  Massachusetts
Phoebe Northwest, Albany, Georgia

1

2

3

4

Design Philosophy and History

For the past 45 years, the firm has specialized exclusively in healthcare-related facilities. Currently, TRO is ranked fourteenth among the top US healthcare facilities' design firms (*Modern Healthcare* magazine, March 22nd, 1999). The firm's award-winning project experience has ranged from renovations of patient care floors, to the design of ambulatory care centres, to the replacement of entire hospitals. TRO's volume has encompassed over 400 clients with construction projects totalling more than three-and-a-half billion dollars.

Outstanding client service, coupled with a fundamental understanding of the ever-evolving demands of the healthcare delivery system, are at the forefront of TRO's business philosophy. Responsiveness, availability, commitment, constant communication, and full team involvement are the cornerstones for the firm's success in project delivery.

TRO works with their clients to define a standard of excellence that responds to their needs with flexibility, imagination and the highest quality design services. The firm's record of repeat business is over 90 percent. Client relationships have spanned decades, some for over 40 years, attesting to their clients' utmost satisfaction with their performance.

1   Saint Francis Hospital and Medical Center, Hartford, Connecticut, USA
    The 358,000 square foot Patient Care Tower is a major component of the overall project in which TRO was engaged to plan and design a $113 million expansion and modernization program for the Hospital.
    Photo credit: Scott McDonald © Hedrich-Blessing

2   Lowell General Hospital, Cancer Center, Lowell, Massachusetts, USA
    A rhythm of repetitive bays is used to establish a contextual fabric appropriate to the historic courtyard.
    Photo credit: Edward Jacoby

3   Saint Francis Hospital and Medical Center, Hartford, Connecticut, USA
    Large atrium windows allow sunlight to pour into entry rotunda and adjacent waiting areas.
    Photo credit: Scott McDonald © Hedrich-Blessing

4   Newton-Wellesley Hospital Ambulatory Surgery Pavilion, Newton, Massachusetts, USA
    To meet the escalating market shift towards ambulatory services, the hospital recently opened its new Ambulatory Surgery Pavilion.
    Photo credit: Edward Jacoby

5   Cullman Baptist Regional Medical Center, Cullman, Alabama, USA
    When designing this replacement hospital, TRO's design team worked carefully with the features of the pristine, 73-acre site in order to capitalize on the natural healing qualities of the landscape.
    Photo credit: Timothy Hursley

TRO
THE RITCHIE ORGANIZATION

5

TSP Architects & Planners Pte Ltd

Goh Chong Chia, Yam Siew Chow, Teh Weng Kuang,
Low Leong Leong

Singapore
Head Office
TSP Architects & Planners Pte Ltd
30 Robinson Road, #08–01
Singapore 048546
Tel: +(65) 225 0606
Fax: +(65) 323 0353
E-mail: tsparch@pacific.net.sg

Malaysia
Akitek Majubina TSP
11A Jalan SS 21/56b
Damansara Utama
Petaling Jaya 47400
Selangor

Directors
Teh Weng Kuang, D. Arch (Singapore) FSIA
   APAM RIBA FSPM MA (Urban Planning) MSIP
Goh Chong Chia, D. Arch (Birmingham) B. Sc
   Hons Arch (Aston) FSIA APAM RIBA FSPM
Yam Siew Chow, D. Arch (Melbourne) MSIA
   APAM RIBA ARAIA

Associate Director
Low Leong Leong, B. Arch (Singapore) BA (A.S.)
   (Singapore) MSIA RIBA

Associate
Siti J Banafie, B. Arch BA (A.S.) (Singapore)

Selected Projects
Indonesian Embassy, Singapore
Comcentre III, Singapore
Institute of Technical Education Headquarters &
   Technical Institute, Singapore
Valley Park Condominiums, Singapore
HDB Design and Build Woodlands N5C1,
   Singapore
Valley Point Local Shopping, Singapore
Causeway Point Commercial, Singapore
Office/Residential, Malaysia
Master Planning Citypark, Malaysia
Commercial/Residential/Golf Course, Indonesia
Pacific Palisades Development, Hong Kong

1

2

3

4

Project Awards
1st Prize
Comcentre III Design Competition
Institute of Technical Education Headquarters &
Technical Institute
HDB Design and Build, Woodlands N5C1
Singapore Polytechnic 5th Phase Expansion

3rd Prize
PWD Competition for the development of
Kandang Kerbau Hospital in association with
Archurban Architect Planners, Chua Ka Seng
and Partners and Gordon Benton & Associates

SIA Honourable Mention
Tong Building
Mediterranean Townhouses
Wollerton Park
Claymore Point
Pasir Ris Telephone Exchange

CIDB Award for Construction Excellence
Sentosa Radio Tower (1994)
Leonie Condotel (1996)

Design Philosophy and History
TSP Architects & Planners Pte Ltd treats each
project as a unique combination of
opportunities. The clients' values, aspirations
and policies are the springboards for
architectural ideas. Discussions with clients
involve frank exchange of views, often leading
to the raising of the 'sights' of both clients and
the architect. Finding the best answer to the
client's needs, providing the best quality of life
for all users and ensuring the greatest
usefulness of the building are the key issues of
architecture. A great deal of effort is put into
the understanding of clients' daily operations
and long-term plans.

For each client, TSP aims to arrive at the
optimum building form and appropriate
architectural language achieved by the careful
selection and adaption of constructional
vocabulary. The aim in each case is to bring
together in a creative way, visual quality and
economy of means.

Teamwork is the essence of TSP's approach
which leads to projects being more than the
sum of the inputs of individual members.

Staff from TSP are constantly involved in
architectural education through part-time
teaching and as examiners which enable them
to be in touch with emergent theoretical ideas
in the field of architecture. In addition,
involvement with the Singapore Institute of
Architects and arbitration and mediation works
enable TSP to be professionally in contact with
all aspects of the practice.

In December 1997, TSP was awarded the ISO
9001 certification for quality management
system in architectural consultancy services.

TSP Architects & Planners Pte Ltd is a long
established regional practice with successful
building, urban design and planning projects in
Singapore, Malaysia, Indonesia, Brunei, Thailand
and Hong Kong. The practice was formed in
1946 under the name of E.J. Seow. In 1970,
after 24 years of steady growth, the name was
changed to SLH Partners. Upon the retirement
of E.J. Seow in 1974, the firm was renamed
Timothy Seow & Partners. In 1988, the practice
name was abbreviated to TSP Architects &
Planners to reflect a more corporate image and
in 1995, it became licensed corporate to
facilitate a multi-disciplinary practice with an
enhanced competitive edge.

Wood Marsh Architecture

Australia
466 William Street
West Melbourne, Victoria 3003
Tel: +(613) 9329 4920
Fax: +(613) 9329 4997
E-mail: wm@woodmarsh.com.au

Directors
Roger Wood
Randal Marsh

Person to Contact
Roger Wood
Randal Marsh

Number of Employees
15

Date of Establishment
1987

Current and Recent Projects
Malthouse Development, Melbourne, Australia
Curtis House, Richmond, Melbourne, Australia
Taylor House, Prahan, Melbourne, Australia
Docklands Infrastructure, Melbourne, Australia
Mansion Hotel, Werribee Park, Australia

Design Philosophy and History
Roger Wood and Randal Marsh have been in private practice since 1983 after extensive experience in architectural offices in Melbourne and graduating from the Royal Melbourne Institute of Technology. From 1983 they were founding directors of Biltmoderne Pty Ltd. In 1987 they formed Wood/Marsh Pty Ltd Architecture.

During this period the company's design work has won 15 RAIA awards for excellence including the 1998 Victorian Architectural Medal and the National Walter Burley Griffin Award. It has also attracted international recognition through publications and lectures, and been shown in numerous exhibitions of architecture and furniture design. Work has been acquired by the National Gallery of Victoria, the Australian National Gallery, RMIT University and private collectors.

Academic contributions have been made nationally and internationally through public lectures and tutoring at universities and institutions, public galleries and publications. Most recent projects include the National Philatelic Centre (Australia Post); sound barriers on the Eastern Freeway; Deakin University (Burwood Campus); and RMIT University (Bundoora Campus).

Wood Marsh Pty Ltd have just been awarded the commission for the Malthouse Development which includes the new Australian Centre for Contemporary Art, Playbox Theatre Set construction building and dance rehearsal spaces for Chunky Move, and were recently appointed as design architects for the Docklands Infrastructure Project.

1

2

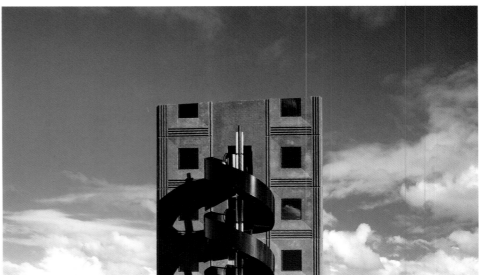

3

4

5

6

Index

Acknowledgments

IMAGES wish to thank all participating firms for their valuable contribution to this publication.